# 100 PLACES THAT CAN CHANGE YOUR CHILD'S LIFE

## From Your Backyard to the Ends of the Earth

### KEITH BELLOWS

AWARD-WINNING WRITER & EDITOR, *NATIONAL GEOGRAPHIC TRAVELER* MAGAZINE

NATIONAL GEOGRAPHIC

WASHINGTON, D.C.

# Contents

# Foreword

..............................................................

I am the person—and journalist—I am today because of what I experienced by seeing the world at a very young age. My father was in the U.S. Air Force, and we lucked out by getting many overseas assignments. I was born in Taiwan and lived in Panama, Brazil, and Spain as well as in the States. Seeing the world so young opened my eyes to the huge diversity of history, culture, and language that makes our planet so fascinating. It was the best education—a global classroom. As a result, I am fluent in both Spanish and Portuguese, essential languages in this day and age. Because travel was so important to me growing up, we take our boys with us every opportunity we get. They were both just months old and couldn't even sit up for their first passport photos. Recently we visited my family in Brazil, and for the first time my children really began to understand the many issues facing today's world. They saw the extremes of wealth and poverty, and experienced a new language (and learned to say a few words in Portuguese). They loved the adventures they experienced in another country. They keep asking where we'll go next—and when.

I know how much travel has changed my life. Now it is doing the same for my kids. For those looking to get started on a lifelong journey with their children, Keith Bellows's book *100 Places That Can Change Your Child's Life* offers ideas and inspiration to help you and your kids explore all that the world has to offer.

— Natalie Morales

# Introduction

........................................

I was conceived in the late 1940s at a lodge near the crest of Victoria Falls, one of the world's greatest cataracts (see page 188). My parents were living in Leopoldville, Belgian Congo, where I'd spend my first four years (a memory: the baby elephant we kept in our yard). In 1954, concerned about impending riots that would forever transform what is now the Democratic Republic of the Congo, we left Leopoldville and flew to Canada to make a new home. You could say that those early years in a distant land—and that adventurous flight—confirmed me as a born traveler. Inspired by the travel path my parents established for me, this book celebrates the pure power of travel.

Fittingly, I'm writing this at 36,000 feet, returning from some of the places in this book—the Taj Mahal, the Serengeti, Petra, Istanbul, London. Places that, like everywhere I go, thrill me because they remind me just how foreign and fascinating the world is beyond the precincts of my home in Washington, D.C. (which also is plenty compelling; it's in the book, too).

I took my firstborn son, Adam, now 23, abroad when he was three months old. Since then he has traveled hundreds of thousands of miles from home—San Francisco and Montreal, the Grand Canyon and Big Sur, Berlin and the Norwegian fjords, Peru's Andes and the Greek Islands. My other kids are six and seven and they're starting to go global, too—and to inspire me to see the world through their eyes.

I wrote this book for them. Because they'll inherit the world. And I want them to understand it. To know it. To experience it.

Like I did.

I'm convinced that any parent willing to give the gift of travel offers the gift that keeps on giving. Children who learn to travel will travel to learn. And they will do it all their lives.

A 2006 National Geographic/Roper poll of young Americans drew a stark, sad picture of our children's cultural literacy: Only 37 percent could find Iraq on the globe, 20 percent thought Sudan is in Asia (it's the largest country in Africa), and half couldn't find New York on a map.

It's clear: The passport is the new diploma. *National Geographic*'s editor emeritus Gil Grosvenor nailed it: "Two weeks in another country is worth a degree in geography." Learning happens between the poles not just between the ears. The world is the greatest classroom we have.

Our kids are our future. And helping them understand and navigate an increasingly globalized world is as important as making sure they know how to drive a car.

I grew up believing that education is all about the proverbial three Rs. We should now make it four Rs: reading, 'riting, 'rithmatic, and roaming.

The places in this book are a Whitman's Sampler of what the world has to offer. And the book itself is as much about parenting as it is about travel. I want you to consider how and why to travel with kids—not just about where. It's not just the place you visit but how you experience it that matters. I've tapped parents and experts who can bring a pint-size eye to an adult-size world. To help see places through a child's eyes.

Now, you might think, as some of my friends have suggested:

"Well, these places are so far away."

Or: "It will cost me too much to visit."

Understood.

You don't have to get on a plane to discover the foreign. If you can't afford to go to China, then visit your nearest Chinatown. Look to your own backyard for ethnic restaurants, intriguing celebrations, little shops that sell authentic goods from afar, street life that expresses the unique rhythms and traditions of another culture.

I'm not a travel snob. Last spring our family flew to Florida to pay homage to the holy grail of Disney. We stayed at Wild Kingdom and ogled the giraffes that loped outside our bedroom window. We visited the parks. Had our pictures taken with a gaggle of princesses. Did the Pirates of the Caribbean and Toy Story rides. The children were ecstatic, the parents reduced to rubble. Such a travel experience is a rite of passage—and it is terrific.

But the world is more than that. I never went to a theme park until I was an adult. The world was my theme park. And that's what I wish for my kids—and yours. I want them to discover the real, not just the faux, and to find it here, not just abroad. I want them to thrill to all the planet has to offer. And see as much of it firsthand and soon.

Tim Cahill, a writer and friend, said it best: "The world is inexhaustible, so it leaves that gate to wonder open." It's all about wonder. That's what we owe our kids. In fact, it's what we owe ourselves. This book is dedicated to exploring the world together. And finding the wonder.

— Keith Bellows

# How to Use This Book

I've put the voice of parents—and folks who know kids—into the main text. But you can find ideas and opportunities to enlighten and have fun with kids in the little boxes we have peppered throughout the book:

**Buy Worthy**
Authentic products that express a sense of place.

**Words of Wisdom**
These are intriguing ways to jump-start conversations with your kids. Words contain the truth of the world.

**Yum!**
Where kids will find food (and atmosphere) they'll actually like. These are places tolerant of loud and messy.

**Objects of Wonder**
Cool culture that fascinates children—and expresses the local zeitgeist.

**Get Involved**
How you and your kids can help change people's lives when you travel. Also check out natgeotakeaction .org, globalcitizens.org, and volunteeramerica.net.

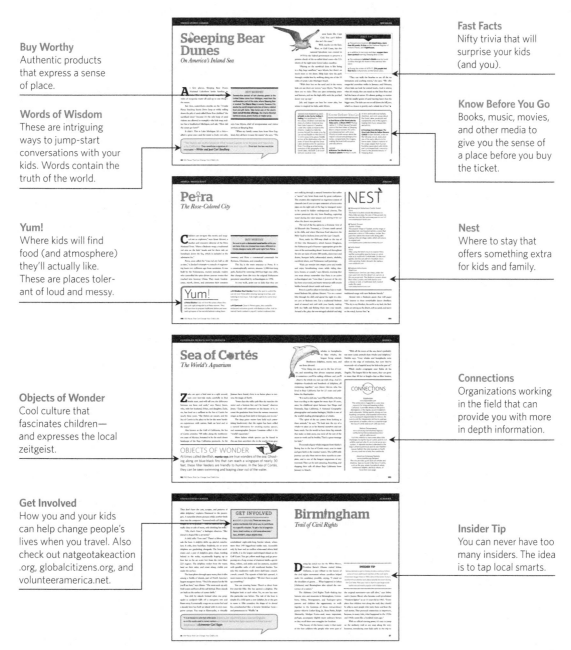

**Fast Facts**
Nifty trivia that will surprise your kids (and you).

**Know Before You Go**
Books, music, movies, and other media to give you the sense of a place before you buy the ticket.

**Nest**
Where to stay that offers something extra for kids and family.

**Connections**
Organizations working in the field that can provide you with more in depth information.

**Insider Tip**
You can never have too many insiders. The idea is to tap local smarts.

You can also read and share more ideas with me on **Facebook** (www.facebook.com/KeithBellowsNatGeo) and **Twitter** (twitter.com/NGSTravelEditor).

Arctic
Ocean

Alaska
(U.S.)
□ *Denali*

*Glacier Bay* □

*Inside
Passage*

CANADA

*Avalon
Peninsula*

NORTH
AMERICA

*Canadian
Rockies* □        *Dinosaur
Provincial
Park* □

*Saguenay Fjord* □

*Boundary Waters* □                    "*Lighthouse Route*"

*Yellowstone
National Park* □                              *Muskoka*
□ *Adirondacks*

□ *Mount Rushmore*        *Sleeping Bear
Dunes* □                *Cape Cod
Nantucket Island*

*Muir Woods* □    "SIERRA NEVADA PARKS"
                  *Yosemite Nat. Park* □
                  *Kings Canyon*          *Arches
                  Nat. Park* □    *Nat. Park* □    *Chicago* □    *Gettysburg*    □ *Manhattan*
*Big Sur* □       *Sequoia Nat. Park* □                UNITED STATES            *District of Columbia* □
                  *Grand*                    *Great Sand Dunes* □                         *Chesapeake Bay*
                  *Canyon* □      *Mesa Verde Nat. Park* □                    *Great Smoky*
                           □ *Petrified Forest*                        *Mountains* □
                             *Nat. Park*

Pacific
Ocean

Mississippi River

□ *Birmingham*

Atlantic
Ocean

*Marco Island* □

**Map Key**

□ Selected point of interest

Hawai'i
(U.S.)

*Hawai'i Volcanoes
Nat. Park* □

0                    800 miles

0                    1,200 kilometers

# United States & Canada

......................

# Cape C⚙d
## *Arms in the Sea*

C ape Cod's flexed, sandy arm reaches about 60 miles into the Atlantic Ocean. Turn left at the elbow to transport kids back to a shoreline little changed from when the *Mayflower* expedition approached nearby First Encounter Beach in 1620.

The gem of the cape is the—at first look—barren, 44,000-acre living classroom called the Cape Cod National Seashore. Bordered on the west by gentle Cape Cod Bay and on the east by the open Atlantic, the area was established by President John F. Kennedy in 1961 to preserve the history, culture, and ecosystems of the Outer Cape (the Atlantic side).

On a visit there, stop first at the Salt Pond Visitor Center in Eastham to get oriented. The kid-centric museum, hands-on exhibits, and "Sands of Time" film help families understand the Outer Cape's location in the Gulf of Maine ecosystem, the indigenous Wampanoag Native American culture, and the physical processes continuously shaping and reshaping the seashore's marine, estuarine, and freshwater ecosystems.

**BOOKS FOR KIDS**
■ *Good Night Cape Cod* by **Adam Gamble; illustrated by John Andert (2005)** Part of the Good Night Our World board book series, this story is geared especially toward young readers and highlights the Cape Cod coast's unique ecological and cultural features like kettle ponds, herring runs, fishing villages, and lighthouses.

■ *Journey Around Cape Cod and the Islands: From A to Z* by **Martha Day Zschock (2001)**

## Know Before You Go

Former elementary school teacher Zschock takes readers to the locations of her students' favorite field trips. Features Zschock's own watercolor illustrations.

**MUSIC**
■ *Cape Cod Soundscapes* **CD Series by Christopher Seufert (2008-2011)** Cape Cod–based independent filmmaker Christopher Seufert has compiled a collection of field recordings from his audio archives, ranging from the chirps of spring peepers at dusk to the crashes of waves on sand dune–flanked beaches.

■ *Life Is Grand . . . On Cape Cod* by **Silvard (2006)** A pianist, composer, and marine biologist, Silvard was born in the Netherlands but has spent his adult life in Massachusetts. This album contains works dedicated to his beloved Cape Cod.

While there, have the kids close their eyes to navigate the adjacent quarter-mile Buttonbush Trail, says local educator and naturalist Dick Hilmer, who leads families on eco-kayak tours through the national seashore and nearby Nauset Marsh. "Walking with your eyes closed along the 'Braille Trail,' as we call it, opens up senses. In science, you have to observe before you can form a hypothesis. The trail challenges the kids to feel, listen, and navigate without sight, which will make them more aware of their surroundings when they kayak through the marsh, wade in the ocean, or dig on the tidal flats."

Check the daily schedule posted in the visitors center for free and family-friendly, ranger-led events like the Great Island Tidal Flats Foray—a 90-minute license to play in the mud searching for clams, quahogs, green crabs, periwinkles, and the other aquatic life revealed when the tide recedes.

As for swimming, be aware that the untamed Atlantic-side beaches feature water with dangerous rip currents and undertow. Stick to the calmer, warmer bayside beaches for wading, swimming, and boogie boarding.

The 100-foot-high undulating sand dunes lining the national seashore are off-limits, which, although frustrating to kids eager to scramble to the top, offers parents the chance to talk about why conservation is important and what could've been there—high-rise hotels, asphalt parking lots, and T-shirt shops—if the dunes hadn't been protected. There are legal paths to the beaches up, over, and through the sand giants.

If your kids really need to do a dune, end your day with dinner of fish-and-chips at the Beachcomber in Wellfleet. The converted 1872 lifesaving service station, tucked between the dunes and surf at Cahoon Hollow Beach, has been a family favorite since the 1950s and is the Cape's only Atlantic-side waterfront restaurant. While the windswept seascape will appeal to adults, kids will remember the pure, primal joy that comes with running barefoot up and down the adjacent dune, the only one they are legally allowed to climb—over and over again. ∎

## FAST FACTS

■ The more northerly portion of Cape Cod, after the bend of the elbow, is called the **Lower Cape,** while the peninsula's southern half, close to land, is called the **Upper Cape.** Seventeenth-century sailors came up with this seemingly counterintuitive terminology. The Massachusetts coast is prone to southwesterly winds, which means that boats headed north usually sail "downwind" to the Lower Cape.

■ **Tropical fish** are sometimes found in the ocean off of the Cape Cod National Seashore because **Gulf Stream** currents transport fish eggs and larva from the Caribbean northward.

■ The word **"cranberry"** originated on Cape Cod. The peninsula's early European settlers called the tiny red fruit that grows along its coast the **"crane berry"** because its flowers reminded them of the **head of a bird—a crane.**

# Nantucket Island

*Where Whales Roam*

According to the history books, Nantucket's tenure as whaling capital of the world ended in the 1840s, when the Great Fire torched the island's wharves and global demand for whale oil tanked. But for natives like Captain Blair Perkins, this idyllic island 30 miles off the coast of Cape Cod remains a whaling hub—only now the focus is on education instead of eradication.

Perkins, who leads small whale-watching tours with his sons from the Nantucket Town Pier, recalls seeing his first beached whale—a dead finback—on the island at age six. The experience was so powerful, he says, it helped shape the course of his life.

"I never forgot how magnificent that animal was, and that's what really inspired me to want to learn more about whales," he recalls. "When kids get the opportunity to see whales up close and learn

how these giant creatures who look so different from us are like us in so many ways, it makes a real impact on them and how they see the world."

Humpback, finback, and minke whales live off the coast of Nantucket year-round, but tours typically run during the island's tourist season, mid-June through mid-October. Because spotting whales in the wild actually requires time—Perkins's tours take six

"Nantucket! Take out your map and look at it. See what a real corner of the world it occupies; how it stands there, away off shore, more lonely than the Eddystone lighthouse."
—*Herman Melville,* Moby-Dick, *1851*

hours round-trip—and patience (this isn't Sea World, where whales appear on schedule), a bit of strategy is required to make a child's first whale watch as monumental as the creatures he or she will encounter.

Spend the day before the tour at the Whaling Museum, where young buccaneers can rummage through sea captains' chests, walk under the 46-foot sperm whale skeleton suspended from the ceiling, and touch the harpoons and other implements people used to hunt whales.

Learning such history helps kids understand Nantucket's whaling past, yet also can evoke some serious questions—and even tears. Perkins recalls: "I remember taking my kids when they were little, and it can be kind of overwhelming when they realize that these incredibly big and beautiful animals can be killed."

Seeing what did—and, in some parts of the world, still does—happen to whales is sobering, but it can amp up enthusiasm for the following day's encounter with actual whales living free in the open Atlantic. "Before we leave the dock, I tell the kids that we are doing a different type of whaling. We are going to visit the whales' home, but we are there to respect them."

When the boat reaches a thriving pod, Perkins cuts off the engines so that the inquisitive whales will approach. Kids line the rail to gaze almost reverently as a mother and calf roll over and look right back—intently and intelligently—at each individual child.

"I love to watch the kids' faces, because they understand immediately that they are seeing an extraordinarily intelligent being," says Perkins. "Looking into a whale's big eye is special—it's an experience that never leaves you." ■

## BOOKS FOR PARENTS

■ *In the Heart of the Sea: The Tragedy of the Whaleship* Essex by Nathaniel Philbrick (2001) This thrilling tale explores the story of *Essex*, a whaling ship sunk in the middle of the Pacific by an 80-foot sperm whale in 1820. Author Philbrick also explains how the whaling industry affected Nantucket society in this gripping story about men lost at sea.

## BOOKS FOR KIDS

■ *Nightbirds on Nantucket* by Joan Aiken (1999) Dido Twite and her journeys aboard Captain Casket's ship are chronicled in this fast-paced story set on Nantucket Island. Dido encounters everything

## Know Before You Go

from mysterious, hidden woods to a pink whale.

■ *Journey Around Nantucket from A to Z (Journeys)* by Martha Day Zschock (2008) For young children this is an alphabet book of color, place, and history. From cranberries to whaling, it will prepare young visitors for their trip.

## BOOKS FOR PARENTS AND KIDS

■ *Nantucket: Island Living* by Leslie Linsley and Terry Pommett (2008) This illustrated book provides an insider's perspective from longtime island residents

Linsley and Pommett. Featured are 200 pages of information and photos of Nantucket's famous historic houses and beachfront cottages.

## BOOKSTORE

■ Nantucket Bookworks When visiting the island, head to Nantucket Bookworks, a store that carries a large selection of children's books, like the island best-seller series *Nat, Nat, Nantucket the Cat* by Susan Arciero, Carol Shaw Barnes, and Peter J. Barnes. Kids can snuggle up on the "Boaris the Babbitt" chair. The store also has a great selection of general-interest books and out-of-print Nantucket titles.

# Ad🌲rondacks

## *America's First Vacationland*

There is no better place to introduce kids to the wilderness than in the six-million-acre Adirondack Park, which ensures that a fifth of New York State will remain forever wild.

The Adirondacks became arguably America's first true vacationland after the 1869 publication of William H. H. Murray's *Adventures in the Wilderness; Or Camp-Life in the Adirondacks.* A tourist avalanche followed and wealthy industrial barons such as the Vanderbilts, Durants, and Rockefellers built the storied Great Camps—grand family summer compounds. Mark Twain loved Lower Saranac Lake.

It was—and is—a *rustic* place that reeks of Americana. Think big stone or cast-iron fireplaces, book-lined libraries, crystal clear water, maple sugar, and tortuously handcrafted Adirondack furniture that kids will love for its often fanciful character. And think true primeval America—it is crisp nights, the loon's cry, the tang of pine, the rough-hewn beauty of place that will captivate kids.

" 'Adirondack' is Native American for 'bark eater,' " says John Graham, father of three and a longtime resident who lives on a pond at the edge of the forest. "It refers to the tough winters when they would eat bark to stay alive."

The Adirondacks are one of the few places on America's East Coast where you can really escape. "You can go five or six days and not see any people," says Ed Palen, president of Adirondack Rock and River Guide Service.

This is a place of 2,000 named mountains (40 exceed 4,000 feet), 3,000 lakes and ponds, and 2,000 miles of hiking trails. Whiteface Mountain boasts the highest vertical drop in the East (3,430 feet). Lake Placid first hosted the Olympic

---

### FAST FACTS

■ The **Adirondack Mountains** were formed about one billion years ago during the Precambrian era.

■ Nowhere in the villages of **Saranac Lake** or **Lake Placid** is there a view of the shorelines of the bodies of water after which the towns are named.

■ The Adirondacks are growing faster than the Himalaya—**one foot higher every 101 years.**

---

## CONNECTIONS

**Visit Adirondacks**
*www.visitadirondacks.com*
Click through lists of top Adirondack attractions and accommodations on the region's official tourism site. It also has pages devoted to local news, regional history, maps, and answers to questions frequently posed by first-time visitors.

**Great Camp Sagamore**
*www.greatcampsagamore.org*
The Vanderbilts vacationed on the Great Camp Sagamore premises from 1901 through 1954. Managed today by a nonprofit educational organization, the estate is one of the region's top historical attractions.

**National Geographic Maps**
**Adirondack Park Explorer 3D**
*www.natgeomaps.com/adirondack_explorer.html*
Build customized maps of the park on your home computer. Enhanced 3D shading means the maps are easier to read, and their imagery more closely mimics reality than those produced by past versions of this software pack. Before printing a map, click on the trails you've decided to include, and you'll get elevation profiles, GPS waypoints, and information about key recreation spots.

**"W Is for the Woods"**
*http://woods.tauny.org*
Bone up on Adirondack folk music's history and contemporary cultural significance on this New York State Music Fund–supported site. After perusing profiles of famous fiddlers, humming along to recordings of some of the genre's most memorable melodies, and flipping through black-and-white photographs of past performances and jam sessions, you'll come to treasure this aspect of the region's artistic repertoire as much as its residents do.

Winter Games in 1932. The second time, in 1980, was when America pulled off its hockey "Miracle on Ice" and speed skater Eric Heiden took five gold medals on an oval that kids can now skate on all winter long. You can also descend the Olympic bobsled run (minimum height 48 inches) and hike or take an elevator to the top of one of only two Olympic ski jumps in the United States.

The nature of the Adirondacks tempts you to spend months here. The best time is mid-June through early October, but Christmas through mid-March is a magic off-tourist time. The reality is you'll probably have but a few days. So make time count. "Walk in the woods," advises Graham. "*Slowly*. Enjoy the sounds. Have the kids check off flowers, trees, rocks, shapes, and bugs they see in a notebook. And equip them well: trail maps, cell phone, whistle, flashlight, water, bug spray, and walking stick.

"This is an opportunity to enjoy what is *real*," he continues. "Kids will be surprised when they see mom and dad leave technology at home and go back to the simple things, like hiking and breathing it all in. The real surprise—how much mom and dad are *capable of doing*." ∎

# Manh🚕ttan

## *Outside Looking In*

**N**ew York is one of those places, like Disney World, that is a child's travel rite of passage.

For a first trip, stick with Manhattan, the classic microcosm of the world. There's no major influence, theme, subject, attraction, or trend that in some way isn't touched or reflected in the work, play, creativity, commerce, ingenuity, and world-class chutzpah that unfolds in the canyons of this great urbanity.

Kids, of course, will be dazzled by its sheer striding-of-the-globe personality (adults are too) and delight in what it offers visitors: all those A-list attractions like the Empire State Building; the emerging new World Trade Center at ground zero; France's gift-to-America, the Statue of Liberty; the often overlooked Children's Museum of Manhattan; and Central Park (don't miss the Alice in Wonderland sculpture and Strawberry Fields, a tribute to John Lennon).

And then there's the "real New York"—Katz's Deli; Wall Street, where New York City began; Grand Central Terminal; the subway that is the city's true artery; and neighborhoods of Little Italy and Chinatown.

First, dispense with the myth that New Yorkers don't care about you. "This

## OBJECTS OF WONDER

Kids of all ages love *Alice in Wonderland,* but New York kids have a special statue located in Central Park. It's an 11-foot-tall bronze of Alice and her friends designed for children's climbing pleasure.

is not an anonymous city," says John Keatts, actor and author of *Tales of New York*. "Someone gets lost, struggles with a map in the subway, and help is there. Every day people tell me how surprised they are that folks are willing to help others. Kids are especially cherished."

The best way a child can understand Manhattan is to leave it—on the Circle Line Cruise. As a New York cabbie would say: "Nothin' better."

"This city is great because of the water, because of the ports," says Keatts, who is also a Circle Line guide. "You see the city differently when you're on the water. Even New Yorkers say that. Kids are astonished at seeing the city's broad strokes. It's like a poor-man's astronaut view of Earth. On the water you see big sections of the city that you miss walking among buildings."

Circle Line cruises run year-round. April to October, when outer decks are comfortable, is prime time—kids can feel the wind and see the water up close. The three-hour cruise (attention-constrained youngsters can take a two-hour semicircle trip) is a 35-mile circle of the island with a little harbor detour: Downriver from 42nd Street on the west side of the Hudson River, past the Empire State Building, Chelsea, Greenwich Village, the rebuilding World Trade Center; into the harbor past Ellis and Liberty Islands; up to the Brooklyn Bridge; then past Wall Street and Midtown (Chrysler and Empire State Buildings); to the mayor's Gracie Mansion; from the East River into and out of the Harlem River to catch Yankee Stadium; and north into the Hudson to Inwood Hill Park and the George Washington Bridge; then back to the beginning.

# NEST

- **Novotel New York**
*Times Square*
This family-friendly hotel allows up to two kids under the age of 16 to stay for free, and also gives them free breakfast at its restaurant Café Nicole. With a terrace overlooking Times Square, it has an ideal location in the theater district.
*www.novotel.com/gb/hotel-0753-novotel-new-york-times-square/index.shtmPlaza*

- **Le Parker Meridien**
*West 57th Street*
Kids can splash in this hotel's rooftop pool after a long day of sightseeing. Just two blocks south of Central Park, it's close to the Museum of Modern Art, Carnegie Hall, and toy store FAO Schwarz.
*www.parkermeridien.com/index1.php*

- **Hotel Edison**
*Midtown Manhattan*
Only a few blocks from Rockefeller Center and Radio City Music Hall, this hotel offers combo suites ideal for families. Featuring the grand art deco style so characteristic of New York's most iconic skyscrapers, it's named for inventor Thomas Edison, who originally turned on the hotel's lights by remote control in 1931.
*www.edisonhotelnyc.com*

This brings home that Manhattan is surrounded by water, but "the biggest comment I get from kids is: 'Why all these bridges?' " says Keatts. "I answer, 'How do you think Manhattan got its food today?' Manhattan is an island. A hundred years ago the Brooklyn Bridge was brand-new. Back then, there was no bridge over the Hudson River. The George Washington Bridge wasn't there until

"Sometimes, from beyond the skyscrapers ... the cry of a tugboat finds you in your insomnia ... and you remember that this desert of iron and cement is an island." —*Albert Camus*

1931 because it had to cross the widest and deepest spot. Now we have 2,027 bridges in all of New York. The point is the water affects almost everything you do every day.

"The Brooklyn Bridge gets the most questions," Keatts continues. "We tell people about John Roebling, who had built a bridge over the Ohio River with a new material called steel, a light, strong metal that was relatively inexpensive. He designed the Brooklyn Bridge with steel—you couldn't build it with iron because it would have been too heavy to support with cables. Today, the bridge seems small, but in 1883 it was almost half again as long as any bridge in the world, the tallest ever in North America. People were terrified because the bridge was so long; they were afraid it would fall down. So Brooklyn and New York hired P. T. Barnum circus elephants to walk across it to prove it wouldn't. It changed architecture around the world. It was called the eighth wonder of the world. The Empire State Building would not be here without steel, which is true of most buildings in town."

Keatts suggests you come to the city armed with questions, which is the great currency between parents and kids. He's used to fielding questions on virtually everything about New York: "What's the Statue of Liberty made of?" "How many bridges are there?" "What are the water tanks on the Upper West Side?"

A Circle Line tour teaches kids geography, creativity, and why things are the way they are. "Being on an island changes how humans do things," says Keatts. "The city is here because of the water. Manhattan is about 11 miles inland from the ocean. It's a perfect natural deepwater port secluded from storms. It's what helped make this city great." ■

# Yum!

■ **All Natural Hot Mini Cakes** This place symbolizes New York's nonstop pace. For a sweet treat on the go, try this beloved tiny stand in Chinatown, where 20 puffy cake morsels costs only a dollar.

■ **EJ's Luncheonette** Located on the Upper East Side, this restaurant is known for its kid-friendly atmosphere. With grilled cheese, milk shakes, and chicken nuggets in the shape of dinosaurs, it will be hard not to find something for even the pickiest eater. It doesn't take credit cards, so be sure to have cash on hand.

■ **Grimaldi's** For a taste of famous New York pizza, check out this spot under the Brooklyn Bridge. Be prepared to wait in line, because the place is known for its coal-fired pizza.

■ **Katz's Delicatessen** Since opening in 1888, this ultimate Lower East Side deli has perfected and expanded its menu with plenty of options, including hot dogs with fries, deli sandwiches, and knishes. The portions are generous, so they can be split between two kids.

# Gettysburg
## *Battle That Shaped America*

"The Civil War was the most important event in American history, the crossroads of our being," says documentary filmmaker Ken Burns, whose 1990 *The Civil War* won 40 major television and film honors. "And it was one hell of a cross-roads. It really forces us to reflect about the meaning of four horrible years in our national life, where, in order to become a nation—we didn't know it at the time—we needed to tear ourselves apart. In the Civil War, we come in contact with the greatest President we've ever had—Lincoln. We come closest to losing our country. If I had to pick the one site of the Civil War for kids to see, it would have to be Gettysburg, the greatest land battle ever fought in America."

Envision the battlefield, ten miles from the Maryland border in Pennsylvania on July 1 to 3, 1863: Little Round Top, the Wheatfield, Devil's Den, Peach Orchard, Culp's Hill, and Cemetery Hill. At Gettysburg, at least 45,000 Americans were killed or injured—more than in any other Civil War conflict.

"Think of that," says Burns. "Almost one percent of our American population lost. A difficult

**INSIDER TIP**

Print out "The Best Field Trip Ever!" planner from the Gettysburg Foundation website and let the kids choose their own adventure as an infantryman, a doctor, President Lincoln, or a civilian. They can also focus on pivotal battle moments. *www.gettysburgfoundation.org/ media/assets/GB_FieldTripPlanner_005.pdf*

thing to communicate to kids. I think children are taught best indirectly."

It is here that the Union crushed Robert E. Lee's Rebels after his win at Chancellorsville two months earlier. Four months after Gettysburg, President Lincoln honored the Union fallen and redefined the war's purpose with his stirring Gettysburg Address. When the South fell, slavery was outlawed in every state.

Just walk the field with your children. Smell the grass. Feel the sun—which often caused oppressive heat—but know that the battle was fought under mostly cloudy skies. Head up the gentle slope of Cemetery Hill, where the Gettysburg Address was delivered, and where Union artillery repelled all Rebel approaches. Barely 40 feet high, the ridge includes the Angle's stone wall and the copse of trees that figure in Pickett's Charge. Take in rugged, boulder-strewn Big and Little Round Top and seek Plum Run Valley between them and Houck's Ridge, a place that became known as the Valley of Death.

Imagine what it must have been like to heft a soldier's load in wool clothing and heavy leather shoes or boots (though many soldiers went barefoot): a ten-pound gun, 80 rounds of ball cartridge, a pound of powder, and five pounds of lead. A soldier—a boy often as young as 16—also carried a foot-square, waterproof canvas haversack with three days' rations; a three-pint canteen (plus apples, blackberries, and other forage); and a knapsack laden with woolen blanket, shelter tent, winter clothing, tin cup and plate, knife, fork, spoon, perhaps some stationery, photographs, a journal, and a Bible, plus tobacco and pipes, and the usual toiletries kit (though the chance of encountering an actual toilet was slim).

"Gettysburg was the turning point of the Civil War," says Burns. "It's this extraordinary three-day battle in a place that has been so well preserved that you can stand on its hills or walk its fields or climb among its boulders and feel as if the ghosts and echoes of our almost inexpressibly wise past are available as teachers—and that's a very special thing.

"The Civil War soldiers accidentally made us a country, made us a nation, not a union or collection of states," Burns continues. Come to the battlefield prepared to tell your children about what happened there. "Read just a little bit," recommends Burns. "Maybe it's just the Gettysburg Address, that beautiful piece of writing. Maybe it's Bruce Catton's or Shelby Foote's extraordinary accounts of the essential Battle of Gettysburg. Come armed with something that gives you a new appreciation of the lay of the land.

"I remember having read the novel *The Killer Angels*," Burns concludes, "having not been to Gettysburg, and then coming here, and suddenly realizing I was in the middle of Pickett's Charge, and then running across the field, sort of reexperiencing the terror and the joy of that terrible, ill-fated attack. *Special. Moving.* Something a child needs to understand." ∎

---

**BOOKS FOR PARENTS**............................
■ *Complete Gettysburg Guide: Walking and Driving Tours of the Battlefield, Town, Cemeteries, Field Hospital Sites, and Other Topics of Historical Interest* by J. David Petruzzi (2009) This guide includes the battleground's hidden gems, army field hospitals, and obscure sites often overlooked. It provides detailed walking and driving tours for the main monuments, such as the National

## Know Before You Go

Cemetery, or for heading off the beaten path to see rock carvings.

■ *Hallowed Ground: A Walk at Gettysburg* by James M. McPherson (2003) Pulitzer Prize winner James McPherson presents the military history of Gettysburg from the point of view of a seasoned Civil War historian. With concise

facts and anecdotes of war generals during battle struggles, this book debunks Civil War myths often thought to be true.

**BOOKS FOR KIDS**............................
■ *Gettysburg* by MacKinlay Kantor (1987) For young readers this book includes the exciting and emotional tales of Civil War generals awaiting battle and recalls the rebels, tyrants, and spies involved in the battle.

# Chesapeake Bay

## *A Place of Discovery*

T here's really no better playground for kids in America than right here," says Tom Hart, an Easton, Maryland, artist who on Saturdays during summer is something of the town's unofficial mayor and a fixture at its farmers market—a place that brims with dogs and kids.

He's talking about the Chesapeake Bay, which is indeed one huge playground. Surrounded by Maryland and Virginia, it's the nation's largest estuary, with 64,000 square miles of bays, marshes, and rivers.

"Heaven and Earth have never agreed better to frame a place for man's habitation," gushed England's John Smith, who mapped the bay between 1607 and 1609.

This vast inland ocean studded with sailboats, skipjacks, and fishing boats hosts more than 300 species of fish and is best known for its Eastern oyster, blue crab, and

## GET INVOLVED

- **TIDAL MARSH RESTORATION EVENTS:** Help restore crabs' natural habitat by going to a tidal marsh restoration event. Volunteer opportunities include grass planting and cleanups. Visit *www.aqua.org/conservation* for information on how you can help.

abundant bird life that constellate around a major eastern flyway—domain of American osprey, great blue heron, bald eagle, and peregrine falcon.

Easton's farmers market—open from May through October—is a cornucopia of dirt-under-the-nails farmers and artisans who produce astonishingly tasty heirloom veggies, handmade soaps, robust flowers, homemade lemonade and tomato pie, Hart's folk art—and, sometimes, live bluegrass.

From there, head to the Oxford Ferry, where you'll find a playground, a small beach, and boat transport for cars, bikes, and walkers to the quaint town of Oxford. Or you can just randomly explore—ask kids to count the cows or llamas while driving down reclusive gravel roads, perhaps dead-ending at a wild, saw grass–fringed shoreline where they'll meet pure nature.

"To me, a tide pool was always much more interesting than an electronic game," recalls former chef Barton Seaver, author of *For Cod and Country* (2011). "I grew up spending summers on the Patux-ent River near Chesapeake Bay. My brother and I would pull large male Jimmy crabs right off the pil-ings of the pier. We'd fish for rockfish from the dock.

"By the time I became a chef, crabs were pro-hibitively expensive," he continues. "There was a moratorium on striped bass. Bluefish had been deci-mated and were just beginning to come back. So I realized the bounty I had as a child had disappeared within 10 or 15 years. It is a real lesson that all kids should understand and appreciate."

But the oyster and blue crab populations have begun to return. One five-year-old now comfortably relies on walking to the end of a friend's Chesa-peake dock and watching wide-eyed as a crab pot is hoisted. Invariably at least three or four scrappy blues seize the tongs as you pull them free of the trap. For a child, it's an arm's-length look at an extraordinary wild creature.

"The Chesapeake offers the joy of discovery and self-discovery," says Seaver, "of understanding a tadpole and a frog and figuring out how they're related. To use cunning and skill, quickness and athleticism to snatch a crab from the water as it snaps back at you, foaming at the mouth, as if to say: *Hands off.* Crabs are magical and mys-terious in their lives, not just in their place of rest on a plate."

James Michener put the Chesapeake on the map with his 1978 eponymous epic book, but

# Yum!

■ **Dolle's Candyland** This is the place to get saltwater taffy, caramel popcorn, chocolate, and many other sweets. Its location on the boardwalk in Ocean City is also where it manufactures most of the candy; tours of the taffy-making process and the chocolate room can be arranged.

■ **Harborside Bar and Grill** A rustic waterfront bar in Ocean City, Maryland, this place was named one of Ocean City's best restaurants. It has fresh seafood as well as burgers and pasta. Be sure to check out the kids' menu.

■ **Harrison's Harbor Watch** For seafood fresh off the boat each morning, up the road in Ocean City, Maryland, check out this spot. It is located at the south end of the boardwalk, overlooking Assateague Island.

■ **Sea Shell Café** The first-place winner in the 2010 Chowder Festival offers a kids' menu that includes grilled cheese and PB&J. The Chincoteague, Virginia, restaurant doesn't stop serving from the luncheon menu until clos-ing. Pooches are welcome too, but only on the porch.

■ **The Soda Fountain at Hills** This small deli is located in a quaint drugstore in Easton, Maryland, and has a family-friendly atmosphere. While the food is known to be amazing, the old-time vibe gives kids a different perspective than the usual restaurants.

the literature kids cherish is Marguerite Henry's *Misty of Chincoteague*. Most people encounter the iconic wild horses that animate her book at Assateague Island National Seashore. The equines are part of two herds of shaggy, pint-size horses that inhabit Assateague Island, a 37-mile-long barrier island. (Warning: Steer clear of and don't feed the horses to better keep them wild.) At the park, you share pony-watching with the boogie board– and surf-obsessed. And you can watch your child watch the ponies who approach, the little clams and horseshoe crabs that wash ashore, or the fellow children who join in a tent of heads over a sand castle.

But if you really want to sense what inspired Marguerite Henry's *Misty* classic, experience the place from remote water, not a crowded beach. Drive past the park signs on MD 113, just off US 50, and go 20 miles to Maryland's Public Landing, just outside Snow Hill, where the 1835 Mansion House sits.

The public landing put-in there is far from the madding crowd. "You can do the beach and umbrella stuff at the ocean," says John Lewis, who grew up here and whose family runs M.R. Ducks, an apparel and travel company out of nearby Ocean City. "Wild horses are the easiest thing to sell a kid on. And out here the horses rarely see humans. They're in their element and truly wild. Going to this part of Assateague is like visiting the Grand Canyon or Yellowstone. It's primal. The shoreline can't be much different than it was a hundred years ago. Bring children here and the cement and asphalt vanish. It's pristine and preserved

# NEST

**■ The Inn at Perry Cabin**
*St. Michaels, Maryland*
This colonial manor house facing the water is set amid lush gardens that have been cultivated for almost 200 years. Kids can learn about the area's nautical history at the Chesapeake Bay Maritime Museum right next door, then go hands-on with sailing lessons through the Offshore Sailing School, whose Chesapeake Bay fleet is stationed at the hotel. *www.perrycabin.com*

**■ Tidewater Inn**
*Easton, Maryland*
Located in the heart of Maryland's Eastern Shore, this hotel's roots trace back to 1712. Take kids sailing or crabbing on the Chesapeake Bay's tributaries, then wander through the antiques shops and farmers markets of Easton's historic downtown. Don't miss the art deco-style Avalon Theater (just across the street from the hotel) or the Academy Art Museum, housed in a nearly 200-year-old building. *www.tidewaterinn.com*

**■ Refuge Inn**
*Chincoteague, Virginia*
This family-owned inn boasts its own herd of Chincoteague ponies, which kids can encounter up close. Explore downtown Chincoteague and Assateague's nature trails with bikes from the hotel's Bike Depot. Kids can try to spot hundreds of different bird species in the Chincoteague National Wildlife Refuge— within walking distance of the hotel—or play along miles of ocean beaches at the Assateague Island National Seashore. *www.refugeinn.com*

—it's stress relief and perfect for a curious child."

Rent a small skippered skiff (Jason Mumford, Ake Marine, Ocean City) and motor out four miles in a diagonal line toward the inland side of Assateague, which is in constant motion—losing sand from the north end and gaining it on the south (a lesson for kids that land is dynamic). Pass Green Run, Bobadell Island (covered in conch shells), Pope's Island Beach, and Mill's Island, where Indian artifacts appear on a shoreline constantly eroded by storm wash.

Boat through water that shallows down to as little as a foot deep, then weave into what watermen call "guts"—narrow water alleys along the shore lined with salty, coarse marsh grass. An occasional abandoned hunting lodge, too dilapidated to welcome children, is mute evidence of the area's annual fall ritual—the hunting of legions of Canada geese, redheads, bluebills, and puddle ducks that use the flyway overhead. Drift through and past flat pans of plegmatis grass as swarms of dragonflies buzz around.

And then you see a stallion and his harem, eight small horses gazing curiously boatward, tails switching, an egret plucking bugs off the back of one. No one really knows how these ponies got here. The most popular theory is that they descended from a hardy breed that survived a Spanish shipwreck.

Drift past the ponies, ground the boat, and walk over the dunes for a wild ocean view, all coal and blue water and ripping surf—traction is best in cool weather when the earth has firmed up.

• • • • • • • • • • • • • • • • • • • • • • • • • • • • • • •

## INSIDER TIP

Using hand lines and dip nets, families can join locals to catch Maryland blue crabs at public piers along the Wye River and in Crab Alley Bay. Crab Alley Marina offers boat rentals for crabbing.

• • • • • • • • • • • • • • • • • • • • • • • • • • • • • • •

Offshore is the surf that befuddled so many who approached these shores in the 1800s. Dozens of ships went down here. Salvagers and wreckers worked the eastern seaboard heavily (down the coast at Nag's Head, North Carolina, they would place a past-its-prime horse, or nag, out in the marsh with a lantern mounted on its saddle; approaching ships saw it as safe mooring, but local scavengers descended when a trusting galleon wrecked on the shallows and stripped it bare).

The barrier islands are supposedly littered with treasure—especially at Pirate Islands. Locals are guarded about details. "But we know that Captain Kidd spent time here," says Lewis. "And Blackbeard made the area his northern port of call because merchant traffic came out of Delaware Bay and New York City. Supposedly Kidd buried a chest of gold in this watery maze of inlets."

"It's at a place called Green Run," says artist Kevin Fitzgerald, who has made a living bringing the stark beauty of this landscape to canvas. "There's a row of trees near a water inlet that marks where a big treasure chest was buried 300 years ago. Of course, the currents and sand shift so much here that it could have moved ten miles away by now."

Lewis adds about treasure hunting: "They do find stuff after a big nor'easter. One fellow who dives around here a lot found a gold bar with a Spanish crown seal on it. Doubloons, tools, old pieces of ships turn up all the time."

But when it comes down to it, nature is Chesapeake's treasure. "The bay has always been this way—down here, on the marsh, watching the sun go up or down," says Lewis. "A storm may reshape things, but the basic place stays the same." ∎

# District of Columbia

## *America's National Treasure*

**T**wo people sprint down the center of the grand reading room in the Library of Congress in Washington, D.C., slip into the librarian's console, and disappear down a stairwell. The FBI, D.C. police, and a SWAT team swarm in.

Cut.

It's a scene from *National Treasure: Book of Secrets,* the sequel to the hit film that furthers the adventures of Ben Gates, who sets out on what the movie's publicists call a "quest to unearth hidden history and treasures"—expressly, something written on the back of the Declaration of Independence. The library plays an essential and breathtaking role in the film—and it can in a child's life.

"It's how you experience a library that makes the difference," says Ford Peatross, the library's curator of architecture, design, and engineering, on the topic of whether libraries are boring for kids. "Children get into this place in a visceral way."

To visit the heart and head of our nation, take your children to the Library of Congress. Start with the "Library of Congress Experience" in its Great Hall, which celebrated Jefferson's 265th birthday in April 2008, by deploying more than ten interactive kiosks to animate a handful of its unique historical and cultural treasures. Three years in the making, the exhibit uses newly digitized materials, and its technology is a big cut above what you've seen elsewhere. Step up to a kiosk touch screen and flip the pages of old

books (from Thomas Jefferson's library volumes to George Washington's annotated copy of the U.S. Constitution to the Gutenberg Bible); zoom in for rich levels of detail; and hover over icons that open notes about the pages.

The exhibit lets you cut to the heart of the library's collections you might want to see—you get a "Passport to Knowledge" that directs you to its greatest hits via self-guided audio tours and carries a barcode allowing your kids (and, importantly, you with them) to play Knowledge Quest and to "bookmark" objects of interest for later exploration on a personalized microsite at *http://myloc.gov/pages/knowledgequest.aspx.*

On the second floor, you can stand in front of a massive "Creating the U.S." interactive video wall that senses your presence and reveals historical information based on where you're standing. The exhibit also allows you to engage with historic

drafts of the Declaration of Independence and a signer's copy of the Bill of Rights, as well as the Articles of Confederation.

Most kids will get a kick out of the library in more ways than viewing its collections. Just the statistics are the stuff of gee-whiz conversation. Arguably the greatest repository of knowledge since the Royal Library of Alexandria, the institution is the controller of all U.S. copyrights (it's cataloged more than 30 million and registers 500,000 new claims a year), with the largest card catalog in the world at 45 million entries. Its website traffic grows by more than a million hits monthly, and it has satellite offices worldwide. ("If we had public space travel," says Peatross, "we'd have an interstellar office.")

Founded in 1800, staffed by 3,500, the Library of Congress is the globe's biggest library: This, America's oldest federal cultural institution—housed in

# Yum!

■ **Cactus Cantina** Near the National Cathedral on Wisconsin Avenue, Cactus Cantina is the place for authentic Tex-Mex in a lively, laid-back environment accustomed to accommodating families and children. Kids are given tortilla dough, coloring books, and crayons to play with while they wait for their meals. Also fun is watching the tortilla-making machine.

■ **Old Ebbitt Grill** Near the White House, this upscale downtown restaurant—and Washington, D.C.'s oldest saloon—caters to locals and out-of-towners alike. They have a great kids' menu with good, no-nonsense American food, hot dogs, mac and cheese, and grilled cheese. Famous for their annual oyster feasts, this place will make your family feel welcome.

■ **Two Amys** A local favorite known for its excellent authentic Neapolitan pizza made with soft-grain flour and cooked in a wood-burning oven. This spot, located between Massachusetts and Wisconsin Avenues, is renowned for being busy and noisy, so parents don't have to worry about telling their kids to sit still. Also noteworthy is its homemade ice cream.

■ **Jimmy T's Place** This is the place to go if you want to feel like you live in the neighborhood. At home in the first floor of an old Capitol Hill row house, this overpacked diner serves breakfast all day; head here for laid-back dining and greasy comfort food.

■ **Café Deluxe** This Cleveland Park restaurant has a local feel and features a tasty menu for adults. Kids can choose from reasonably priced options of pasta and pizza, and the table comes with a huge piece of butcher-block paper and crayons to keep them entertained.

three buildings named after Presidents (Jefferson, Adams, and Madison)—contains, in some 460 languages on 500 miles of shelves, 128 million items—and counting at a rate of 10,000 new items a day. This was the Rock and Roll Hall of Fame of its day, the crown jewel that captured all of America's arts renaissance, when artists, architects, and sculptors from Rome, Paris, and Berlin flooded our shores.

It houses maps, photos, manuscripts, audio and video recordings, digital files, prints and drawings, musical scores, comic books, unpublished books, plays, scripts, films, sheet music, America's largest rare book collection, the world's biggest collection of legal materials—and Thomas Jefferson's personal library, originally purchased for $23,950—and rebuilt with cash from Dallas Cowboys owner Jerry Jones after an 1851 fire destroyed most of the collection.

Whatever your child is into, the likelihood is that he or she can find it covered here.

Then there is the opportunity to have some fun viewing the building itself, which sometimes inspires offbeat reactions from the young. Standing in the Great Hall—the library's main entrance—Peatross, whose infectious love for the place is irresistible, recalls: "I remember two kids about 13 and 8. They look up and gasp. Then one turns to the other and says: 'Dude, look, dude.' And he points to the ceiling and says, 'Homer.' And my heart fluttered. There was the name of the Greek epic poet—which he thought referred to Homer Simpson. They just made their own iconography out of it."

The trick is to alert kids to the icons and symbols that crowd these buildings. At first glance, the

# NEST

■ **L'Enfant Plaza Hotel**
*L'Enfant Plaza, SW*
This hotel's great location (steps from the National Mall, Smithsonian museums, and four Metro lines) makes it a great bet for families looking to hit the city's major attractions. Large rooms, a year-round rooftop pool, and staff accustomed to hosting families with kids are also huge pluses.
*www.lenfantplazahotel.com*

■ **The Willard Intercontinental**
*Pennsylvania Avenue, NW*
This is an upscale option for families with a penchant for the historic. The hotel that has hosted every President since Franklin Pierce is located just two blocks from the White House. The Willard's partnership with the Washington Ballet makes it appealing during the holidays, with a popular Nutcracker brunch.
*www.intercontinental.com*

■ **Embassy Suites**
*Washington Circle, NW*
This all-suite hotel is very popular among families looking for the basics at a good price, and you're likely to run into a lot of kids. In addition to the family-friendly size of the accommodations, the hotel offers free buffet breakfast for kids, an onsite swimming pool, and 5 p.m. movie showings.
*www.embassysuites.com*

■ **Hotel Monticello**
*Georgetown, NW*
Located on a quiet side street of Georgetown in the neighborhood where Thomas Jefferson once lived, this small European hotel offers families a surprising amount of living space. The one-bedroom suites are huge and include large pullout couches, wet bars, microwaves, and continental breakfast. The hotel also offers a two-day Family Package, which puts you in a king-size suite and scores you other useful goods, such as all-day Metro passes.
*www.monticellohotel.com*

library is a treasure trove of luminous paintings, astonishing sculpture, and soaring architecture—but tucked into murals and carved into statues are details that signify much yet often go unnoticed; in a sense, they offer a great scavenger hunt.

"See that woman?" says Peatross. "That's Memory, a widow holding the armor of her fallen warrior husband. At her feet is an urn that holds his ashes. It's a vessel of Memory—and that's what this whole building is." Other symbols abound. "That statue"—Peatross points—"is Imagination. It has wings of genius. Search the building for images of wings. They're everywhere."

And flames. "Look for the flames that fan the imagination. Lamps that light the way. Kids get that. It becomes an adventure that allows history and culture to sneak in. They start looking for these symbols. They can't help themselves."

Don't miss the chance to step into the heart of the library—the Main Reading Room, the most illustrious of 22 here. "It is one of the greatest rooms in Western architecture," says Peatross. The room itself is not some rarefied inner sanctum off-limits to all but doughy researchers. "It has always been,"

says Peatross, "the most publicly available reading room of any major research library in the world."

A picture ID, a letter from a principal, a stop at the desk in the Madison Building—and you're in. But unless you're bent on serious research, it's best to climb the grand staircase to the second level and enter the embayed gallery that surveys the book-bristling floor below; warm-hued walls ribbed with Siena, Tennessee, and Algerian marble; and the great gilded dome that towers 160 feet above.

This is a room of eights—an octagonal structure ringed by eight semicircular stained-glass windows. Eight bronze statues, each more than ten feet tall on marble pedestals, represent foundations of civilized thought and life (religion, commerce, history, art, philosophy, poetry, law, and science), and eight pairs of illustrious men—including Moses, St. Paul, Columbus, Michelangelo, Beethoven, Plato, Homer, Shakespeare, and Newton—signify the pinnacles of human achievement.

Children are awestruck by the scale and majesty of the place. "No wonder Hollywood wanted to shoot *National Treasure* here," says Peatross. "This is one of the finest movie sets in America." ∎

---

**BOOKS FOR PARENTS**..................

■ *Washington, D.C.: A Novel* **by Gore Vidal (2000)** Set in the D.C. of the 1930s, this book is the final saga in Gore Vidal's Narratives of Empire. Vidal's novel is a biting take on Washington politics that opens your eyes to the lives of a powerful conservative senator with presidential aspirations, a young congressional aide, and a greedy newspaper tycoon.

## Know Before You Go

**BOOKS FOR KIDS**..................
■ *Washington Is Burning* **by Marty Rhodes Figley; illustrated by Craig Orback (2006)** Told from the point of view of African-American teenager Paul Jennings, who was a real historical figure and servant to President James Madison, the story takes place during the War of 1812 and is driven by Paul's take

on what it was like to live in the White House during the tumultuous period.

■ *Washington, D.C.: A Scrapbook* **by Laura Lee Benson; illustrated by Iris Van Rynbach (1999)** This is a fictional scrapbook about a class field trip to Washington, D.C. Through the piecemeal collection of brochures, Metro tickets, maps, and museum ticket stubs, kids are introduced to the city.

# Great Smoky Mountains

## *Deep in the Natural World*

**W**e have a *nature deficit* among kids in this country," says Emily Guss, ranger at the Great Smoky Mountains National Park, the most visited in the nation, "but kids will be excited by nature, if we only let them see it and touch it and be in it. Since I was a kid, I played in the woods and learned a lot about life and death by observing nature. The Smokies is a special place for kids because there's beauty everywhere—and there's mystery and exploration. Our kids' world is so shaped by TVs and computers. What they experience here is completely different."

The 500,000-acre national park (a combination international biosphere reserve and World Heritage site) and its fringes—straddling Tennessee

and North Carolina—is one of the richest biodiversity zones in America (more than 13,500 species have been identified in the park, and scientists believe many hundreds more are yet to be discovered). This is a place where children meet nature head-on.

You'll encounter as much biodiversity walking up a mountain in the Smokies as you will hiking 2,000 miles from Georgia to Maine on the Appalachian Trail. There are, for example, 19 kinds of fireflies, 39 reptiles (including turtles, lizards, and snakes), 43 amphibians, 200 birds, and 66 native mammals. Some species, like Rugel's ragwort and Jordan's (red-cheeked) salamander, are found nowhere else.

For ten days in early June, the Smokies host a flash mob of fireflies, insects that are America's only species that can synch their flickering light patterns with each other. To view them, plan ahead and skip the public trolleys. Meet at Elkmont's Little River trailhead, and tour with a naturalist ($10 from the Great Smoky Mountains Association, free for adult-accompanied kids under 12).

This is also the salamander capital of the world; the park harbors 30 species, giving it the planet's most diverse population. "Catching" salamanders in the park is illegal. So the only safe way for kids to hunt for, capture, examine, and then return salamanders to their habitat unharmed is through a ranger- or naturalist-led program—one of the many hands-on junior ranger and Smoky Mountain Field School opportunities available to kids in the park.

Salamanders are bio-indicators—population ebbs and flows can be due to water and air quality or changes in the food chain. "Studying them helps us understand more about the health of the whole park," says Guss, who designed the park's Slimy Salamanders program, "and from there we can start a discussion about climate change. When that spark of discovery goes off, then kids start asking questions about what affects air and water quality, climate change, food chains. We're here to answer those questions and to ask them to think about additional ones." Kids participating in the program collect important data—identifying species and size—that help monitor salamander behavior.

For the program, you gather at the Sugarlands Visitor Center, just inside the park's main Tennessee entrance near Gatlinburg. "Why are you guys here today?" Guss asks.

Kids scream as one: "Salamanders!"

Guss: "Yes, but you're also going to be scientists, though. So let me see your best scientist's pose." She puts her right index finger to pursed lips, tilts her head slightly, gets a quizzical look on her face, and says, "Hmm." The kids mimic her every action.

She takes you to a special secret salamander spot. Salamanders are amphibians and breathe through their skin, Guss explains, so their skin must stay wet, and the oils on human skin can make breathing difficult for a salamander. You must handle them gently because their tails can break off (it takes two years to regrow, sometimes a completely different color).

"A salamander stores fat in his tail, which is his source of energy," continues Guss. "If a salamander loses his tail, he loses his energy. That makes it easier for a raccoon to catch and eat him."

Kids spread out to search for salamanders. They are serious scientists and understand their role as protectors, stepping carefully, looking down, and

"The beauty and charm of the wilderness are his for the asking, for the edges of the wilderness lie close beside the beaten roads of the present travel."—*President Theodore Roosevelt*

helping each other guide squirming salamanders through the water into the bags.

"We have families work as a team," says Guss. "In the past, we had programs that separated parents and kids. The kids did the hands-on and the parents watched. Now some of the parents get into finding and catching the salamanders as much or even more than the kids."

"Whatever creature you are looking for—a salamander, a deer, a butterfly, a black bear—ask your child to *think* like that animal," advises ranger Nola Isobe. "What would they be doing at this time of day and in this weather? If you're looking for a bear in July, he's won't be out because he has a big fur coat and it's hot. And if you are a salamander and your skin must stay damp, you're in the water or under a rock, somewhere dark and damp. Get kids to think like animals."

Smokies scavenger hunt books are available in most park visitors centers. "Work as a family to look for clues and find things on the scavenger hunt list. Animals always leave clues, but people rarely look for them," Isobe explains. "Our hands-on programs like salamander hunts are all about connecting the world to yourself. Kids get to use real scientific tools in a controlled setting—which protects the creatures and the ecosystem—and the ranger is right there to answer their questions and help them understand what they are seeing." She shows a picture. "It's a red-spotted newt. They have three stages—they start out in water, then they go on land, and then they live in water as adults. If you are observant and know what to look for, you'll see all kinds of amazing things in the Smokies." ∎

# NEST

■ **Big Bear Lodging**
*Pigeon Forge, TN*
This family-owned and -operated company offers five-night family value specials for its roomy log cabins. Located conveniently close to the Great Smoky Mountains National Park entrance and other area attractions, the cabins feature fireplaces, deep porches with swings, and secluded mountain views.
*www.pigeonforgemotel.com/index.asp*

■ **Blackberry Farm**
*Walland, TN*
The Great Smoky Mountains form the backdrop for this family-owned resort in the Tennessee foothills. Kids can learn how to fly-fish in Hesse Creek and hike or horseback ride across miles of mountain trails and meadows. The new Junior Adventure Series lets families or older kids explore the surrounding area with one of the hotel's gardening or nature experts.
*www.blackberryfarm.com*

■ **Brookside Resort**
*Gatlinburg, TN*
Family owned and operated, the resort has many kid-friendly amenities, such as two heated pools (one with a slide), Ping-Pong, basketball courts, and a playground. It is also near hiking trails, waterfalls, rafting, and horseback riding attractions.
*www.brooksideresort.com*

■ **Old Smoky Mountain Cabins**
*Townsend, TN*
Old Smoky Mountain Cabins has homes close to the national park, Cades Cove, and Little River. This provides your family more privacy than a hotel and even offers the option of a home-cooked meal.
*www.oldsmokymountaincabins.com*

# Marco Island

## *Playing with Dolphins*

Y ou are outbound from Marco Island, the largest of the 10,000 Islands in the Gulf of Mexico off southwest Florida. At the helm of the *Dolphin Explorer* is Capt. Chris Desmond, leading a three-hour trip (leaving at 9 a.m. and 1 p.m.) with a passel of kids (including a two-year-old in dad's arms).

As founder and director of the 10,000 Islands Dolphins Project, Desmond wants "to extend the eco-experience into science with young co-explorers." Each trip has an onboard master naturalist who translates science jargon into English. This is part tourist jaunt, part serious science.

This trip allows kids—who can become members of the Dolphin Explorers Club—to help identify and catalog the world's largest population of nonmigrating bottlenose dolphins

### FAST FACTS

■ Dolphins are among **the most intelligent animals** on the planet.

■ Like humans, dolphins **navigate using visual clues,** such as shapes on the seafloor.

(25 locally and another 125 in the general area).

"The bottlenoses here have adapted to shallow water," says biologist Kent Morse. "They are smaller than oceangoing dolphins. We're in four feet of water. In the deep sea, food is harder to find.

Here it's spread out and can support smaller groups."

"This is the only known dolphin science project totally supported by tourism," adds Desmond. "The crew knows where the dolphins are and the dolphins know and trust the boat." The crew computer updates dolphin behavior (posted at *dolphin explorerchronicles.typepad.com*).

"Kids carry clipboards with a Master Dolphin Sighting Form that helps us to track the date, time, location, depth, salinity, water temperature, turbidity, tide level—and dolphin activity: mill, feed, travel, play, rest, leap, tail slap, socializing, and tracking the boat, as well as total population and number of calves," says Desmond.

Imagine an aquatic laboratory that allows kids to be players. Children on the cruise match creatures they spot to shots in the "dolphin book." They spot known dolphins—Buttermilk, Trigger, Tattoo, Batman, Sparkle, Hatchet, Notch, Seymour, Patch, Tricia, and El Terrible. Some may see mother Sydney and offspring Jingo—a late-birth calf that was the smallest of its year—who like to follow in the boat's wake, with the steady slap of mom leaping and hitting water and the baby coursing nearby.

The crew summons up dolphin profiles and pictures, with such notes as, "A playful dolphin, Ripple has been playing with leaves, mangrove propagates, and hapless fish, tossing them in the air and retrieving them. Here she is seen with a sea star." They note which dolphins swim together—studying how, say, the arrival of a new calf affects group dynamics.

A typical voyage: You pass an osprey nest atop a pylon with a mom feeding her chicks—mated for life, her partner is nearby. You drift past islands

# NEST

■ **Eagle's Nest at Marco Island**
*410 South Collier Blvd., Marco Island, FL*
This is an oceanfront paradise, with game rooms, pools, poolside bingo, and Monday social events for children to meet other kids staying at the location.
*www.eaglesnestmarco.com*

■ **Hilton Marco Island Beach Resort**
*560 South Collier Blvd., Marco Island, FL*
In addition to a heated pool and tennis courts, this luxury resort on the beach offers parasailing and water scooter rentals right on the beach.
*www.hiltonmarcoisland.com*

■ **Marco Island Florida Marriott Resort & Spa**
*400 South Collier Blvd., Marco Island, FL*
This beachfront island paradise is kid-friendly and has all the perks, including a game room, family bingo, and waterslides. It even offers Tiki Tribe, a day camp filled with outdoor activities and games.
*www.marcoislandmarriott.com*

■ **Olde Marco Island Inn & Suites**
*100 Palm St., Marco Island, FL*
Opened by Captain Bill Collier, this historical inn dates back to 1883. The inn offers the best of both worlds, combining the antique look of the 19th century with modern amenities. Staff provide assistance with planning daily activities, including trips to Big Cypress National Preserve, Fakahatchee Strand Preserve State Park trails, and Collier-Seminole State Park. It accommodates a family's needs, with heated pool, sundeck, museum, and gallery.
*www.oldemarcoinn.com*

populated by white-tailed deer, wild boar, raccoon, bobcat, and Florida panthers.

A dolphin pair arches up from eight-foot-deep water. "The calves are smaller and also smoother.

They don't have the cuts, scrapes, and patterns of older dolphins," explains Desmond to the passengers. A naturalist shoots pictures while another feeds data into the computer: "Seaweed with calf (Star) . . . weighs 80 to 90 pounds . . . first six months calf stays really close to side of mom, only drinking her milk."

"Oh, that's Giza," a biologist observes. "Her dorsal is shaped like a pyramid."

A child yells: "I see one!" There's a blow alongside the boat. A dolphin drifts up, playful, nonchalant. It rolls, does backflips. Suddenly, six or seven dolphins are gamboling alongside. The boat accelerates and a pair of dolphins gives chase, hustling behind in the wake, occasionally leaping up to four feet in the air scant feet from the twin Merc 225 engines. The dolphins rocket from the water, land on their sides, and scoot along, visible just under the surface.

The boat plows through open water, then it idles among a flotilla of islands, part of North America's largest mangrove forest. "You'd be amazed at the life you'll see here," says Morse. "The roots suck up only fresh water and leave all the salt behind. These islands are built on the surface of oyster shells."

You drift by islands formed when one propagule—a seedpod—falls off a mangrove tree and floats away. It eventually snags on an oyster bed and a decade later has built an island with its own mangrove canopy. You stop at Keewaydin, a virtually

---

## GET INVOLVED

■ **ADOPT A DOLPHIN:** There are many programs worldwide that allow you to contribute to a specific mission. To get a list of organizations, check online, or visit *www.ehow.com/ how_4510877_adopt-dolphin.html*.

---

uninhabited eight-mile-long barrier island, where more than 140 loggerhead turtles nest. Accessible only by boat and an endless white-sand debris field of shells, it is the largest undeveloped island on the Gulf Coast. You get yellow mesh bags and go prospecting on a long avenue of shattered shells—gentle blues, whites, and pinks and fan patterns, studded with gemlike nubs of old weathered bottles. You take this meditative walk down shell lane: *crunch, crunch, crunch*. The squeals of kids loft upward. A mom insists to her daughter: "We don't have to pick up *everything*."

You are coasting home. There's a shout from five-year-old Ellie. She has spotted a dolphin. The biologists look at each other. No, no one has seen this particular one before. The rule of the boat is simple: If a child spots a new dolphin, he or she gets to name it. Ellie considers the shape of its dorsal fin—crosshatched like a favorite breakfast food—and pronounces it: "Waffle." ■

---

"It is of interest to note that while some dolphins are reported to have learned English—up to fifty words used in correct context—no human being has been reported to have learned dolphinese."—*Astronomer Carl Sagan*

# Birmingham
## *Trail of Civil Rights*

**D**uring his initial run for the White House, President Barack Obama visited Selma, Alabama, to pay tribute to the heroes of the civil rights movement whose sacrifices helped make his candidacy possible, saying, "I stand on the shoulders of giants . . . What happened in Selma [Alabama] and Birmingham also stirred the conscience of a nation."

The Alabama Civil Rights Trail—linking key historic sites and museums in Birmingham, Greensboro, Selma, Montgomery, and Tuskegee—gives parents and children the opportunity to walk together in the footsteps of those extraordinary giants—Martin Luther King, Jr., Rosa Parks, Ralph Abernathy, Medgar Evers—and, more important, perhaps, accompany slightly more ordinary heroes as they recall their own struggles for freedom.

"The beauty of this history today is that many of the foot soldiers—the people who were part of

the original movement—are still alive," says Selma native Joanne Bland, who became a self-proclaimed "freedom fighter" as an 11-year-old in 1965. "Every place that children visit along the trail, they should be able to meet people who were there and hear the real stories. That personal connection is important, because, to many kids, what happened in the 1950s and 1960s seems like a hundred years ago."

With no official starting point, it's easy to jump on the multicity trail at any stop along the way; however, introducing your kids early in the trip to key concepts such as voting rights, racial equality, segregation, and bus boycotting will prepare them to absorb what lies ahead.

Frances Smiley, Alabama Tourism Department heritage coordinator, recommends beginning that introduction in Montgomery. Her must-sees for children here include the outdoor Civil Rights Memorial, a circular black granite table created by Vietnam Veterans Memorial designer Maya Lin, where kids can reach through the water flowing over the surface to read and touch the time line of key events and the names of 40 civil rights martyrs etched in the polished stone; the Rosa Parks Library and Museum's Children's Wing at Troy University, where a glowing, pulsating "time machine" disguised as a 1955 Montgomery city bus transports passengers back to the Jim Crow era; and the compact, yet compelling Greyhound bus station turned Freedom Riders Museum, honoring the black and

white students who were attacked in 1961 while attempting to integrate interstate bus, train, and air transportation.

Once the kids get a sense of the people and places, walk together along the final steps of the 1965 Selma to Montgomery voting rights march to the state capitol. "You'll pass the little Dexter Avenue King Memorial Baptist Church, where Dr. King started his ministry, the stop where Rosa Parks got on the bus and the one where she was arrested," says Smiley. "You will also see the site where city slave auctions took place, and the spot where the telegram was sent giving the order to fire on Fort Sumter, starting the Civil War. So much symbolism is here in such a short walk. Parents and kids will get chills when they think about all that happened right where they are standing."

From Montgomery, drive either east to Tuskegee and then north to Birmingham, or west to Selma and

---

**BOOKS FOR KIDS**..............................
■ *Child of the Civil Rights Movement* by Paula Young Shelton and Raúl Colon (2009) The daughter of a prominent leader in the civil rights movement shares her memories about growing up in the 1960s Deep South. Rich watercolors capture the emotions brought on by being a youngster in an era of momentous social change.

■ *Marching for Freedom: Walk Together, Children, and Don't You Grow Weary* by Elizabeth Partridge

## Know Before You Go

(2009) This work documents the role young African Americans played in making the voting rights protests a success. Powerful black-and-white photographs accompany stories of staggeringly courageous children.

■ *Through My Eyes* by Ruby Bridges (1999) At six Ruby Bridges became the first African American ever to attend New Orleans's then all-white William Frantz

Public School. In this memoir, she recounts her experience.

**MUSIC**..............................
■ *Voices of the Civil Rights Movement: Black American Freedom Songs 1960-1966*, produced by Smithsonian Folkways This is a collection of songs sung during the Selma to Montgomery voting rights marches and other key junctures in the civil rights movement. An accompanying information booklet describes the history of each song and presents a gallery of historic photographs.

on to Birmingham. If visiting Tuskegee over Memorial Day weekend, bring the story of the first African-American military aviators in the United States armed forces to life by introducing kids to the surviving World War II Tuskegee Airmen at the Tuskegee Airmen Fly-In sponsored by the Negro Airmen International.

In Birmingham—site of the 1963 Children's Crusade, where students were repelled by fire hoses and dogs during their peaceful, antisegregation march to city hall—prepare for some tough questions from kids at the Civil Rights Institute. The collected oral histories, television news footage, stark photographs, and chilling artifacts—including a charred Ku Klux Klan cross—are real, raw, and far removed from most kids' realities, yet they relate directly to concepts and issues they can comprehend, like bullying, hate, and fear.

Once in Selma, help kids understand the significance of the 1965 voting rights march with a visit to the Selma Interpretive Center at the foot of the Edmund Pettus Bridge—start of the Selma to Montgomery National Historic Trail.

Interpretive markers detail what took place on the bridge, but arranging a guided trek across it with a civil rights foot soldier can help empower kids to take what they've learned about freedom and equality on the Alabama Civil Rights Trail and apply it to their lives.

Says Bland, who leads kid-focused tours based on her childhood memories of 1965: "You can't just show kids the bridge. They have to have that background and know why they are walking over. When they come off the bridge they have this whole different perspective. It seems to come together for them."

## INSIDER TIP

For an off-the-beaten-path experience, swing by Gee's Bend, an isolated hamlet on the grounds of a former plantation southwest of Selma. The women there, many of whom are descendants of slaves, have produced artful patchwork quilts since the antebellum era and garnered national attention for their work (Oprah Winfrey featured the community in 2006, and a traveling exhibit of the quilts in the early 2000s made stops at the Smithsonian and the Whitney Museum in New York). The community also houses the church where Martin Luther King, Jr., spoke on the eve of the voting rights march.

Before sending kids across, Bland shares what it was like attempting to cross the same bridge at age 11 with her 14-year-old sister and other marchers.

"The policemen blocked our path by beating people and shooting off tear gas canisters," she recalls. "I was so scared. People were laying everywhere. They were gassed and injured. You couldn't stop to help them for fear you would be beaten."

After Bland shares her story, she challenges kids to become instruments of positive change in their communities.

"I tell the kids: 'Even though you aren't fighting for the same things we were fighting for, it's every generation's responsibility to make sure the next generation has a better world. Walk across this bridge and think about what you are going to do,' " says Bland. "Then I send them across the bridge. They go so proudly. It's amazing to see them then. You know they'll accomplish some amazing things in their lives because they've visited the trail, met the people, and walked on the bridge. They *get it* now." ∎

# Sleeping Bear Dunes

## *On America's Inland Sea*

**A**t first glance, Sleeping Bear Dunes National Lakeshore looks familiar to kids. The drifting sand, seagulls, and miles of turquoise water all add up to one thing—the ocean.

But then, somewhere—maybe on the 7.4-mile Pierce Stocking Scenic Drive loop or while rolling down the pile of sand called Dune Run (dubbed "the sacrificial dune" because it's the sole heap of sand visitors are allowed to trample)—the kids stop, realize this is landlocked Michigan, and ask, "How did the ocean get here?"

It didn't. This is Lake Michigan. It's a lake—albeit a great one—and the water is *fresh,* not salty,

says Lisa Myers, chief of interpretation and visitor services at Sleeping Bear.

"When my family comes here from New England, they all have to *taste* the water," she says. "The

"The Dunes are to the Midwest what Grand Canyon is to Arizona and Yosemite is to California. They constitute a signature of time and eternity. Once lost, the loss would be irrevocable."—*Writer and poet Carl Sandburg*

area looks like Cape Cod. You can't believe this isn't the coast."

Well, maybe not the East, West, or Gulf Coast, but this national lakeshore was created in 1970 by the federal government to preserve a pristine chunk of the so-called third coast—the U.S. shores of the eight-state Great Lakes coastline.

"Playing on the sacrificial dune is like being in a big, huge sandbox," says Myers, but there's so much more to the shore. Help kids view the park through a wider lens by walking along one of the 35 miles of sandy Lake Michigan beach.

"With their feet on the sand and in the water, kids can see there are waves," says Myers, "but that there are *no tides*. They can spot swimming otters and beavers, and see the high cliffs with the perched dunes way up top."

July and August are best for water play, but winter is magical for kids, adds Myers.

> ## FAST FACTS
>
> ■ The park encompasses **26 inland lakes, more than 80 ponds, 8 sites** on the National Register of Historic Places, and **1 lighthouse.**
>
> ■ In addition to raccoons and deer, **cougars have been spotted** roaming Sleeping Bear Dunes.
>
> ■ The endangered **pitcher's thistle** may be found on hikes through the dunes of the national lakeshore.
>
> ■ During the winter of 1870-71, **214 people lost their lives** in shipwrecks on the Great Lakes.

"They can walk the beaches to see all the ice formations and crashing waves," she says. "We offer ranger-led snowshoe walks in January and February, where kids can look for animal tracks. And in winter, when it's windy, they can stand on the Dune Run and feel the forces of nature. It's almost geology in motion with the smaller grains of sand moving faster than the bigger ones. The kids can run or roll down the hill, too, which is a lesson in gravity and a whole lot of fun." ■

---

**BOOKS FOR PARENTS & KIDS** ......
■ *Paddle-to-the-Sea* by Holling C. Holling First published in 1941, this classic children's tale tells the story of a Native American boy from Lake Superior's Canadian coast who wants to travel to the Atlantic. Unable to make the journey himself, he sends a toy figure named Paddle-to-the-Sea in a 12-inch canoe in his place. Paddle arrives at his destination after four years of travel through the Great Lakes and down the St. Lawrence River. Providing an entertaining overview of the geography of the Great Lakes, the book is an excellent pre-vacation read.

## Know Before You Go

■ *Sand Dunes of the Great Lakes* by Edna and C. J. Elfont (1997) Photographer C. J. Elfont has put forward some of his best shots of Sleeping Bear's unique scenery. His wife's accompanying text, with scientifically accurate essays about the region's natural and geological histories, complements the imagery, making the book both evocative and educational.

**MUSIC** .................................
■ *Between Two Worlds* by Lee Murdock (2004) An hour's worth

of new and traditional ballads, chanteys, and work songs about the Great Lakes, produced and compiled by one of the region's leading folk music researchers and artists.

■ *Greetings from Michigan: The Great Lake State* by Sufjan Stevens (2003) Sufjan Stevens, a star on the folk pop circuit, dedicated one of his early albums to his home state. Subject material of his songs ranges from human hardship associated with Michigan's prolonged high unemployment to the pristine beauty of Sleeping Bear.

# Chicago
## *Windy City Walks*

There's a friendly feel to Chicago that helps kids connect to the city of nearly three million (third most populous in the United States) on a personal, pint-size level. That's because the Windy City isn't one big place, but rather 77 distinct neighborhoods, each with its own history, culture, sounds, smells, and tastes.

Local children's book writer Tad Mitchell, who co-authored *Where Is the Sears Tower?* (2011) with his illustrator wife, France, suggests introducing kids to the city's diversity via a walking and tasting tour.

Share bites of signature Chicago food favorites with the kids as you walk through neighborhoods such as Lincoln Park, Chinatown, Grant Park, Pilsen, and Hyde Park.

"Every kid should try the Chicago dog [all beef, no ketchup], Chicago-style pizza [deep dish, stuffed, and thin crust], and Italian beef [sliced round roast dipped in au jus]," says Mitchell. "Deep-dish Chicago-style pizza is the most famous, but kids will like the thin crust. The dough is dry and stiff, almost like a cracker, and it is cut in squares instead of triangles."

---

### BUY WORTHY

Parents, pick up a **blue jellyfish paperweight** from the **Shedd Aquarium.** Each paperweight is hand-crafted with distinct bubble formations.

Kids can explore the ancient Egyptian world with the **Hieroglyphic Alphabet Decoder** from the **Field Museum** store. Use the turn wheel to learn the symbols for eagle, Eye of Horus, and more.

---

Sampling the tastes—even if it's just a bite of each—helps keep kids fueled for a day of foot-powered adventures winding through the Windy City.

To help connect visiting families to the city's neighborhoods, the Chicago Office of Tourism and Culture offers summer Family Adventures, kid-centric guided tours of Chicago neighborhoods on foot and via the "L," Chicago's famous elevated train line. Executive director Dorothy Coyle, who has taken the tours with her kids, says the guided experience gives kids the opportunity to ask lots of questions, meet other children—each tour accommodates up to four families—and participate in hands-on activities.

"Kids coming to Chicago love all the skyscrapers, but it's also important for them to see the ethnic diversity, and where people live and like to play," she observes.

On one tour, Coyle and her kids visited the Garfield Park Conservatory—the city's garden under glass designed by the famous landscape architect Jens Jensen.

"We had quiz sheets to fill out on the walk to the 'L' stop and on the train, so the kids and parents could work together to spot city landmarks," she recalls. "At the conservatory, we did a recycling project where the kids made planters out of old rubber boots and got to take the boots home."

Even if you don't take a guided walking tour, Coyle suggests bringing the kids to the Chicago Cultural Center, where they can look up and count the pieces of glass in the two intricate glass domes, including the world's largest stained-glass Tiffany dome. (There are 30,000 total pieces, so it could take a while.) The landmark building, built in 1897 as Chicago's first central public library, hosts 800 free arts programs each year, includes a visitors center, and is the departure point for city tours.

"Everything in the center relates to Chicago and the essence of the city," adds Coyle.

Even if your kids aren't sports fans, riding the "L" up to Wrigley Field—the ivy-covered brick ballpark of the beloved and much maligned Cubs—will give kids a sense of the city's history, advises Mitchell.

"The 'L' is unique in that it is elevated over the street," he says. "The short trip up to Wrigley Field past all the old brick buildings gives kids a feeling for the city they would not otherwise get, and going

# CONNECTIONS

**Explore Chicago**
*www.explorechicago.org*
Explore Chicago, the city's official tourism site, offers suggestions for budget-worthy trips that don't lack in adventure. Home to many free events, the Chicago Cultural Center hosts live music, film showings, lectures, and art exhibitions throughout the year. Visit one of the Project Onward galleries that supports the creative growth of visual artists with mental and physical disabilities.

**Navy Pier**
*www.navypier.com*
With 50 acres of parks, promenades, and gardens jutting into Lake Michigan, Navy Pier is always thronged with Chicagoans. Its website details the area's many attractions, from amusement park rides to shoreline cruises. Kids can help raise and trim the 11 sails of the tall ship *Windy,* Navy Pier's resident four-masted schooner, and take a turn at the ship's wheel. In the Family Pavilion, the Chicago Children's Museum offers hands-on activities like clambering through a tree house or inventing a flying machine. For stunning views of Lake Michigan and the downtown skyline, ride the 15-story tall Ferris Wheel. It's modeled after the first Ferris wheel, built for Chicago's 1893 World's Columbian Exposition.

**National Geographic Chicago**
*www.travel.nationalgeographic.com/travel/ city-guides/chicago-illinois*
Explore photos of America's "Green City" or plan a family vacation with help from National Geographic's Chicago guide. Suggested activities include letting the kids cool off at Millennium Park's Crown Fountain, hopping on a bike from Bike Chicago and cruising around the city's waterfront, or spotting North American wildlife like polar bears and Mexican gray wolves at the Brookfield Zoo.

into Wrigley Field—either for a Cubs game or on a tour—is magical. It is like stepping into a time machine and going back 100 years."

From Wrigley, head back to the future at Millennium Park, Chicago's downtown summer festival and family events hub. Observes Coyle, "The park has so many great things for families, including the permanent artwork Cloud Gate, unofficially called 'the Bean,' because it looks like a big jelly bean. The 110-ton silver, elliptical sculpture is 33 feet high, 66 feet long, and it brings together the sky and streetscape in a shiny silver surface. Kids can look in it like a mirror, touch it, and lay under it to see multiple images of themselves reflected against the city."

Millennium Park also is home to Crown Fountain—two 50-foot glass-block towers guarding either end of a shallow, granite reflecting pool.

"The towers project video images of Chicagoans on giant LED screens," Coyle explains. "There's water flowing through the towers, creating the illusion that water is shooting out of the mouths of the people on the screens. Kids love it, because it's a significant blast of water cascading over the towers. They can go into the pool, splash around, and watch all the faces."

## FAST FACTS

■ Chicago has the **third largest** Polish population in the world, behind Krakow and Brooklyn.

■ The famous **Route 66** highway starts in front of the Art Institute of Chicago near Grant Park on Adams Street.

■ The **Chicago River** is the only river in the world that flows backward, a result of man-made efforts in 1871, 1885, and 1900 to reverse the direction of the river.

■ **Indiana, Illinois, Michigan,** and **Wisconsin** are visible from the Willis Tower skydeck.

■ Thank Chicago for one of the world's most famous (and oldest) snacks: the **Twinkie.** It was invented here in 1930.

From the park, head up to the Willis (formerly Sears) Tower. At 110 stories, it's the tallest building in the Western Hemisphere, and plucky kids will get a thrill out of standing 1,353 feet above the city in a glass cube projecting 4.3 feet out from the Skydeck observatory. "Looking out from the tower offers a unique perspective on the world, allowing kids to see how the city is laid out firsthand, rather than looking at a map. Go in the afternoon when the sun turns Lake Michigan azure blue." ■

## BOOKS FOR PARENTS

■ *Oldest Chicago* **by David Anthony Witter (2011)** This book depicts the city's oddities and quirky history. Witter spotlights places and faces that have given Chicago its identity, such as some of the city's oldest businesses: jeweler C. D. Peacock, Merz Apothecary, and restaurant Superdawg. The book serves as both a history and a guide to the most notable sites.

## Know Before You Go

### BOOKS FOR KIDS

■ *Imagine Your World: Chicago* **by Grow Books Press (2011)** For the eco-friendly and insightful traveler, this activity lets young kids explore Chicago architecture and landmarks through drawing, writing, and discovery. Suggested projects include collecting signatures,

cultivating a garden, and writing a personal story.

### MOVIE

■ *Haunted History: Chicago* **by History Channel (2009)** This DVD investigates chill-worthy stories such as Bachelor's Grove Cemetery, the ghost of Clarence Darrow, and the Prohibition-era spirits of the St. Valentine's Day massacre.

# Mississippi River

*Paddle-Wheeling Adventure*

"Piloting on the Mississippi River was not work to me," wrote Samuel Clemens, "it was play—delightful play, vigorous play, adventurous play—and I loved it."

Although Clemens's career as a riverboat pilot spanned only four years (two as an apprentice and two as a licensed pilot), his time spent in and on the Mississippi near his boyhood home of Hannibal, Missouri, made an indelible impact on his life, career, and, most notably, his choice of nom de plume—Mark Twain (a riverboat term signifying 12 feet, which was safe water for steamboats in his day).

Reading *Adventures of Huckleberry Finn* and *The Adventures of Tom Sawyer* with your kids can help impart the sense of adventure and freedom young Clemens felt growing up on the river (as well as spark more weighty discussions about slavery, racism, and offensive language; beware of the "N" word). But nothing beats actually visiting Hannibal

and helping to steer a paddle-wheel boat down Huck and Tom's stretch of the Mississippi.

Moline, Illinois–based riverboat captain Scott Schadler, like Twain, grew up on the river (his childhood home was 50 feet from shore). Today, he pilots the *Celebration Belle* paddle wheeler down the Mississippi on sightseeing and educational tours, including overnight trips to Hannibal.

"I've been on the water since I was a little kid, and now my six- and nine-year-olds love coming out on the river with me," says Schadler. "Kids are fascinated by everything that is going on around them on the boat. They see the towboats and want to know what they are carrying, and they all want to go up into the pilothouse because that is where all the action is—all the levers, noises, whistles, and gauges."

For kids used to traveling through the air and on the road, seeing the Mississippi from the deck of a paddle wheeler likely is the first time they realize that a river can be a highway. They also get a front-row view of how locks and dams maintain a minimum nine-foot water depth for safe navigation, allowing vessels to "step" up or down the river from one water level to another.

"The Mississippi is such a vital transportation link for so many goods," Schadler explains. "We narrate during our cruises so the kids can learn about how the river was run back in Mark Twain's time—before the locks and dams—and how it is run today. The kids really enjoy going through a lock and dam, and want to know how that works."

But the biggest thrill of riding the river, admits Schadler, is being able to steer, a privilege the captain tries to extend to every child who travels with him.

"We invite the kids up to the pilothouse. If

---

## FAST FACTS

■ Waterskiing was invented on the **Mississippi River** in 1922.

■ The name **"Mississippi"** comes from the Ojibwe Indians. They called the river **Messipi** or **Mee-zee-see-bee,** which means **"big river"** or **"father of waters."**

■ Mark Twain wasn't Samuel Clemens's only pen name. He also went by **Thomas Jefferson Snodgrass** when he wrote articles for the *Keokuk Post.*

■ At its broadest point, the Mississippi River stretches more than **seven miles** wide.

---

there aren't a lot on board, I let them each drive the boat," he says. "I want them to go home and tell their friends, 'I drove an 800-passenger paddlewheel boat down the Mississippi.' "

After riverboat cruising—on an overnight excursion or on an hour-long sightseeing tour—head to Hannibal for land-based Huck and Tom adventures.

Cindy Lovell, executive director and "Twainiac-in-Chief" of the Mark Twain Boyhood Home and Museum, suggests starting with a hike up Cardiff Hill. "There are 244 steps to the top, so it's a fun workout," Lovell explains. "This is where Sam

---

**BOOKS FOR KIDS**
■ *Steamboat! The Story of Captain Blanche Leathers* by **Judith Heide Gilliland** (2000)This is the true story of the first female steamboat captain, Blanche Douglass Leathers. Told in a colorful picture-book format, the story follows her from childhood, when she first sees and becomes enamored with a steamship, through adulthood, when she breaks through gender barriers

## Know Before You Go

and finally earns her chance to navigate one.

■ *The Adventures of Tom Sawyer* and *Adventures of Huckleberry Finn* by **Mark Twain** (1876/1884) These classics, written as a series, follow the lives of Huck and Tom as they grow up alongside the Mississippi

River. The two boys encounter trouble, close calls, and interesting characters, yet emerge with a greater understanding of the world around them. Classic American coming-of-age tales with heavier themes and more offensive language than was used at the time they were written (including the "N" word), these books are best suited for children age ten and up.

Clemens and his friends played and explored, and is described in detail in *The Adventures of Tom Sawyer*. The hill now includes a commemorative lighthouse (built in 1935) and looks out over the Mississippi River where Sam and his friends would fantasize about adventures on the river."

From Hannibal's shoreline sidewalks and parks, kids can spot Jackson's Island, the place where Tom, Huck, and Joe Harper spent a few nights when they ran away, and also where Huck and Jim bumped into each other and began their journey down the river. The Hannibal-based *Mark Twain Riverboat* offers sightseeing cruises past the island, which is still undeveloped and uninhabited (except for mosquitoes, turtles, eagles, and other wildlife).

"It doesn't take much imagination to picture Tom and his pals lounging under a shade tree enjoying a good story," Lovell explains. "Another place where kids can be part of the adventures is the Mark Twain Cave. This is where Tom and Becky got lost and where Tom and Huck later found $12,000 in gold. The cave story continues in *Adventures of Huckleberry Finn*. Tom and his gang meet there, and Mark Twain, writing as Huck, gives a detailed description of how they entered the cave through a hole on the hill, which still is visible today."

On the guided cave tour, kids learn both historical facts and about Twain's fictional accounts. From there, they can head to the Twain museum complex to learn about the real people behind the fictional characters, engage with all the interactive exhibits— including a raft and a whitewashing bucket—and listen intently as the Twain storyteller-in-residence recounts Huck and Tom's wildest adventures.

"Twain's memory for detail is widely known, and when kids explore the houses, ride the riverboat, and tour the cave, the books spring to life. Although his books are called 'fiction,' most of what Twain wrote was based on real people, places, and events. Hannibal is where the stories started," Lovell concludes. ∎

# CONNECTIONS

**Mark Twain Boyhood Home and Museum**
*www.marktwainmuseum.org*
Visit this website and learn about Mark Twain's childhood, family, and career. Discover fun facts about his pen names, his fashion choices, and more. Then, plan a trip to see his boyhood home in the town of Hannibal, Missouri.

*Mississippi River Quest*
This three-part National Geographic special features the journey of three modern-day explorers as they attempt to travel the entire Mississippi River. Familiarize yourself with the river's present-day twists, turns, and secrets as you follow Marcus, scientist and environmentalist; Stephen, professional outdoorsman; and Bill, filmmaker and blogger. Buy the DVD at *www.shop.nationalgeographic.com/ngs/ product/dvds/adventure-and-exploration/ mississippi-river-quest-dvd-r.*

**Steamboating the Rivers**
*www.steamboats.org*
This comprehensive website has information on all things steamboat: news, history, photographs, book recommendations, and more. It also hosts a forum where steamboat enthusiasts, veterans, and newcomers alike can meet and chat about their experiences. Click on the "Links, Webcams" sidebar for links to the websites of almost every steamboat company operating today.

# Boundary Waters

*Solitude and Self*

The Boundary Waters area of northeastern Minnesota is the ancestral homeland of the Ojibwe people. With no electricity or Wi-Fi, and offering only the slimmest chance of getting a cell signal, the million-plus acres of untamed land and water that parents and kids can explore there today is little changed from the 1400s, when the Ojibwe first traveled these waterways in birchbark canoes.

For kids tethered 24/7 to smart phones and other electronic devices, such a trip may mark the first time they've really experienced *true silence*, which, wrote William Penn, founder of Pennsylvania, "is the rest of the mind, and is to the spirit what sleep is to the body, nourishment and refreshment."

Managed by the U.S. Forest Service

along the U.S.-Canadian border due west of Lake Superior, the Boundary Waters Canoe Area Wilderness (BWCAW) provides such nourishment and refreshment.

Although adventure seekers treasure it for its scores of trails, primitive camping sites, and more than 1,500 miles of canoe routes, it's the silence of nature and hearing their own breathing and heartbeats, maybe for the first time, that can make this place so magical and meaningful for children.

"This place changes people," says local outfitter and dad Steve Nelson. "Parents who have been in the Boundary Waters as children come back with their own kids. It's a phenomenal experience to share. The wilderness calls you. It really does." Hearing that call takes patience and a willingness to surrender time, agendas, and expectations to the natural rhythms of life in the wild. When Nelson takes families into the BWCAW, he tells the kids to get up early and silently, grab a cup of hot chocolate, and then sit on the shore to watch the flora and fauna of the Boundary Waters wake up. "When the parents and children sit there, they are going to hear loons wailing off in the distance and birds chirping nearby," he says. "They might see fish come up and grab bugs sitting on the surface, and turtles resting on the rocks. They are watching, listening, hearing, and appreciating their surroundings in a way that isn't possible in a city."

Nelson advises first-time visitors with kids to find a base camp, and then explore from there a little at a time. "I've had some parents take kids on a marathon trip, and the kids come back saying, 'I don't ever want to do that again,' " he says. Life in

## FAST FACTS

■ To become airborne, **a loon must run nearly a quarter mile** across the surface of a lake while frantically flapping its wings. Once in the sky, however, **it flies easily,** sometimes reaching speeds close to 90 miles an hour.

■ The **Boundary Waters Canoe Area Wilderness** (BWCAW) is one of only two protected canoe areas in the United States. The other is located in Kenai, Alaska.

the BWCAW is challenging enough—carrying supplies in and out, muscling canoes over portages from one lake to the next—so keeping it basic empowers kids to build skills and confidence at their own pace. Memories here are made in small moments shared, not total miles covered.

"There was a family with three boys who would go out into the wilderness for 20 days at a time," Nelson recalls. "When I asked the dad why he took the trip year after year, he said, 'Number one, it is one of the most inexpensive vacations. Number two, and more important, is who are my kids going to talk to out here? It's just my wife and me, so they *have* to talk to us.' " ■

---

**BOOKS FOR PARENTS**..................
■ *Boundary Waters: The Grace of the Wild* by Paul Gruchow (1999)
This collection of essays presents a writer's musings on humanity's relationship with nature as he hikes, canoes, and camps across the BWCAW, both in isolation and with friends and students.

**BOOKS FOR KIDS**.........................
■ *Leave Only Ripples: A Canoe Country Sketchbook* by Consie

## Know Before You Go

**Powell (2005)** The story of one family's canoe trip in the Boundary Waters, as told through drawings and prose.

**MUSIC**..................................
■ *Ms. Yonson Turn Me Loose* by **Leroy Larson and the Minnesota Scandinavian Ensemble (2006)** The Minnesota Scandinavian

Ensemble has spent more than 30 years resurrecting and performing the folk music of the northern Midwest's early European settlers. The group, whose members all come from Scandinavian or Scandinavian-American families, has appeared on public radio's *A Prairie Home Companion.* This album's folk dances and comical dialect songs provide a window into Minnesota's cultural heritage.

# Mount Rushmore

## *Honoring Greatness*

**K**ids will never forget their first look at the massive Mount Rushmore National Memorial, but it's discovering the stories behind the 60-foot-tall granite faces—who they are, why they were chosen, how they got there (lots of dynamite, 400 men, and 14 years)—that makes a road trip here truly transformative.

South Dakota mother Jean Patrick, who's written two children's books—*Who Carved the Mountain? The Story of Mount Rushmore* and *Face to Face with Mount Rushmore*—suggests using the long drive through Custer State Park in the Black Hills to the Crazy Horse Memorial to spark a kid's natural curiosity.

"Bring along a photo of Mount Rushmore in the car, and challenge the kids to think of as many who, what, where, when, how, and why questions

**BOOKS FOR KIDS**
■ *Face to Face with Mount Rushmore* **by Jean L. S. Patrick (2008)** This interactive guide to the history of Mount Rushmore features quizzes, trivia, photographs, interviews, and answers to questions kids ask.

■ *The Little House Cookbook* **by Barbara M. Walker (1989)** Learn to cook what the plains pioneers ate with this book containing 100

## Know Before You Go

recipes for meals taken straight from the pages of Laura Ingalls Wilder's Little House books. Though all recipes have been updated so the dishes can be prepared in a modern kitchen, each contains a brief description of how Laura's family would have prepared it.

**MUSIC**
■ *Spirit of South Dakota* **by Orange Tree Productions (1997)** Recorded on site at Mount Rushmore National Memorial, Badlands National Park, Wind Cave National Park, and Custer State Park, this album features American classics, regional favorites, and original songs performed on piano, violin, and acoustic guitar.

as possible based on the image," recommends Patrick. "By asking questions ahead of time, kids will be wondering about all sorts of things by the time they arrive. As a result, they will be ready to absorb the information the exhibits and the rangers have to offer. When I talk to school groups about the memorial, kids always ask me, 'Why are those guys up there?' "

The fact that the "guys"—George Washington, Thomas Jefferson, Abraham Lincoln, and Theodore Roosevelt—were selected by sculptor Gutzon Borglum in 1927 to represent specific components of the first 150 years of U.S. history—birth, expansion, preservation, and development, respectively—gives kids a logical starting point for their own research at Mount Rushmore and beyond.

The memorial is compact, making it easy for kids to complete the free Junior Ranger Trainee (ages 3 to 5), Junior Ranger (ages 5 to 12), or Rushmore Ranger (age 13 and up) programs in less than two hours—unless they get absorbed in the history behind the 56 symbols of states and territories flying high along the Avenue of Flags.

Kids can pick up the age-appropriate ranger activity booklets—and feel the power of the dynamite blast simulator—at the Lincoln Borglum Visitor Center. Tour the museum, then hit the half-mile Presidential Trail loop for a closer look at the faces.

Kids will delight in seeing up the nostrils (no, they're not hollow, and yes, Washington's nose is longer), and perhaps have a close encounter with one of the resident Rocky Mountain goats. The trail leads to the Lakota, Nakota, and Dakota Heritage Village—leave time to let kids play in the authentic tepee—and the Sculptor's Studio, which houses the

actual working model Borglum used to carve the memorial. Kids love that his original plans called for Jefferson to be to Washington's right, but unstable rock forced Borglum to take an explosive do-over—blasting the first Jefferson to smithereens and recarving his face between Roosevelt and Lincoln. ∎

# CONNECTIONS

**Black Hills Badlands**
*www.BlackHillsBadlands.com*
Mount Rushmore isn't the only reason to spend time in western South Dakota. From the Badlands to the Black Hills to the site of the Battle of Wounded Knee, the region offers many other attractions. This website provides basic travel information on what to do.

**Mount Rushmore National Memorial Society**
*www.mtrushmore.org*
The Mount Rushmore Society, a fund-raising organization, has partnered with the National Park Service to enhance the preservation of the memorial. Update yourself on current goings-on at Mount Rushmore by checking out the society's events listing and quarterly newsletter (both available on its website). While at Rushmore, be sure to take advantage of the society's audio tour, which leads visitors on a 29-stop journey through the history and geology of the memorial. Visit the society's online bookstore, which sells Rushmore-related memorabilia and helps fund the memorial's educational and interpretive programs.

**Mount Rushmore Dining**
*www.MountRushmoreDining.com*
After your visit to Rushmore's visitors center and museum, you'll want to digest all of the history you've consumed over a nice meal. Check out this website for information about many of the area's restaurants.

# Great Sand Dunes

## *North America's Wild Dunes*

There's no mystery to what kids will love about Great Sand Dunes National Park and Preserve. It's the sand, sand, and more sand, including North America's highest dunes—650-foot High Dune and 750-foot Star Dune.

Dirk Oden, a local parent, teacher, and former seasonal interpretive ranger who leads youth group trips to remote areas of the 100,000-acre park, suggests using the sculpted sand behemoths as a magnet to draw in kids to all the ecological zones represented here—alpine tundra, desert, grasslands, wetlands, dunes, forests, alpine lakes, and 13,000-foot peaks.

"Great Sand Dunes is an amazing place. The best time to go is early June, when Medano Creek is running wide yet shallow through the main access area—the creek dries up later in the summer,"

### INSIDER TIP

Most of Great Sand Dunes is open to horseback riding or use of pack animals (mules or llamas)—an excellent way to see the backcountry. Several providers offer guided horseback trips, including Zapata Ranch, owned by the Nature Conservancy, and Baca Grande Stables, which offers eco-educational trips.

Oden explains. "Catch a children's program to get an introduction to this wonder and then let your children play and explore in and along the creek. Build sand sculptures and chase fingers of the creek as they mysteriously advance and retreat, or explore further, making sure to take the time to roll down at least one of the dunes." (By the way, there are no poisonous animals or insects to fear in the dunes.)

> "The sand-hills extended up and down the foot of the White Mountains about 15 miles, and appeared to be about 5 miles in width. Their appearance was exactly that of the sea in a storm, except as to color, not the least sign of vegetation existing thereon."
> —*Zebulon Pike journals (1807)*

Though a challenging hike, kids can make the High Dunes climb—about one to two hours up and 45 minutes down—to get a hawk's-eye view of the surrounding Sangre de Cristo and San Juan Mountain alpine peaks.

Don't be fooled by the splotches of snow on surrounding tors, though. This place is often scorching. Surface sand temperatures can rise to 140°F on summer days. Visit in late spring, when the dunes aren't too hot to climb.

Oden suggests attempting the climb early in the morning, when the weather is cool, the wind is low, and the kids are of full energy. Take plenty of water and have them wear tennis shoes or hiking boots to protect their feet when the sand gets as hot as you know where. Beware: The winds can top 40 miles an hour, but it is these winds that give the dunes their shape.

Don't make any promises, but come prepared to (legally) slide, ski, sled, or board down any unvegetated areas of the dunes. The kids will want to join in if the weather allows any X Games–worthy boarding action on the sand.

Conditions are best after rain (dry sand is too soft) and even better when it snows. Sand board rentals are available in Alamosa, but kids would be extra pumped to conquer the dune with their own snowboard, skis, or rigid plastic sleds.

For some indoor fun, check out the Discovery Room at the visitors center. It features interactive exhibits such as a geology rock and mineral table, small lightning tube, and video microscope. Plan ahead to attend the special Junior Ranger Day each summer, during which kids can learn about the park environment, primitive skills, and crafts. ∎

## BOOKS FOR KIDS

■ *Apache Children and Elders Talk Together* by E. Barrie Kavasch **(1999)** The ancestors of the modern Apache camped and hunted in the San Luis Valley where the Great Sand Dunes sit. The Library of Intergenerational Learning of Native Americans has put together a book that reveals the key aspects of Apache culture, including the importance of community and family, through excerpts of conversations between children and older members of the tribe.

## Know Before You Go

■ *Billie the Buffalo Goes to Great Sand Dunes National Park* by Judith Stone; photographs by Mark Niederquell **(2009)** In this second installment in the Billie the Buffalo adventure series, Billie journeys to Great Sand Dunes National Park and Zappa Falls, where she wades through Medano Creek, climbs the tallest dune in the park, and watches children play. Photographs provide a stunning visual narrative.

## MUSIC

■ *Navajo Healing Songs of the NA Church Vol. 2* by Jimmy Night, Jr. **(2010)** This Canyon Records CD/MP3 collection of healing songs features traditional songs from one of the several Native American communities that have left their mark on the cultural fabric of south-central Colorado. Sung without the accompaniment of water drum or gourd rattle, these purely vocal performances inspire thoughtful contemplation and meditation.

# Mesa Verde National Park

*Ancient Cliffs of Majesty*

**W**hen President Theodore Roosevelt established Mesa Verde in 1906, it became the first national park created to "preserve the works of man."

More precisely, the southwestern Colorado park protects the remnants of stone neighborhoods constructed by the ancestral Puebloan, the people who lived on the Mesa Verde ("green table") from A.D. 600 to A.D. 1300. There are more than 4,000 known archaeological sites here, the most recognizable—and most appealing to kids—being the 600 cliff dwellings built high within the canyon's sheltered alcoves.

Climbing up, down, over, and through this ancient jungle gym community will delight any child. It is the story of the people who built the structures, though, that helps kids to grasp what makes Mesa Verde truly amazing: the engineering, the history, the traditions, and the culture.

### INSIDER TIP

With no major cities in the area throwing off artificial light, Mesa Verde is an ideal location for stargazing. Clouds rarely obscure the night sky, which is often full of stars with the Milky Way clearly visible. Head to the Montezuma or Mancos Overlooks along the Main Park Road for the best views.

To help prepare her sons for their first Mesa Verde visit, Colorado teacher and mom Betsy Henry sat down with the kids to look through history and travel books related to the site. Developing a basic appreciation for the civilization before traveling and seeing photos of the cliff dwellings helped build excitement.

"When they recognize what they are seeing, it has a lot more interest to them," observes Henry. "We also had talked about ancient Rome and Greece, so to discover some ruins in our own country and state was really neat for them. Another helpful educational tool is the park's Junior Ranger booklet. You can download and print it off the Mesa Verde National Park website (www.nps.gov/meve) ahead of time to prep the kids about what they are going to see."

Advance research empowers kids to choose the dwellings they want to visit. For most, the obvious choice will be the biggest and most photographed: Cliff Palace. Although most of the park's cliff dwellings contained one to five rooms, archaeologists have determined that this domicile or ceremonial space had 150. The place is accessible via guided tour, and the steep, uneven trails require navigating multiple steps and ladders. There are no height or age restrictions, however, so adventurous kids who are up to the challenge can climb to the top and experience a rewarding sense of accomplishment.

Young explorers particularly will enjoy being the first to "discover" Cliff Palace, an honor reserved for those who get up early enough to land tickets for the day's first tour. "We were in the first group and were the only people in the Cliff Palace at the time,"

## FAST FACTS

■ Today, **24 tribes have a relationship with Mesa Verde,** including the Pueblo of New Mexico, the Mountain and Southern Ute of Colorado, the Hopi of Arizona, the Ysleta de Sur Pueblo of Texas, and the Navajo of Colorado, Arizona, and New Mexico.

■ The **gray wolf, brown bear,** and **Mexican spotted owl** found in Mesa Verde National Park are threatened or endangered species.

■ A **4¢ stamp** featuring a picture of **Cliff Palace** in Mesa Verde National Park was issued on September 25, 1934.

says Henry. "It was quiet and magical, and the kids imagined that they were the first ones coming into the dwelling in the 1800s—they had discovered it. The crows were flying in and out, and, from our research, the kids had learned that the crows are thought to carry the spirit of the Native Americans, so that added to the whole experience. Cliff Palace had everything the boys could have wanted—mystery, adventure, native culture, and, of course, lots of climbing." ■

### BOOKS FOR KIDS

■ *Mysteries in Our National Parks: Cliff-Hanger: A Mystery in Mesa Verde National Park* by Gloria Skurzynski and Alane Ferguson (2007) This book is another in the Landon family, National Park mysteries series. When the family journeys to Mesa Verde National Park, they take along their foster child, and scam artist, Lucky. While the search goes on for a dangerous cougar, the tale takes the reader through the landscape and history of this massive archaeological park.

## Know Before You Go

■ *The Ancient Cliff Dwellers of Mesa Verde* by Caroline Arnold (author) and Richard R. Hewett (author and illustrator) (2000) Colorful photographs of cliff dwellings and stories of the ancestral Puebloan provide a glimpse into their unique dwellings, crops, tools, and daily life. Chapters on the discovery of Mesa Verde in the late 19th century by ranchers give insight on the park's early stages and its transformation into a national park.

### MOVIE

■ *The National Parks: America's Best Idea* by Ken Burns (2009) A visual journey through some of America's most impressive historical narrative of our national parks. The series includes the story of the discovery of Mesa Verde by ranchers Richard Wetherill and his brothers in 1889; the government's denial of a request to make it a national park; and the controversy that arose when archaeologist Gustaf Nordenskiöld attempted to ship artifacts from the site back to Sweden.

# Petrified Forest National Park

## *A Land Before Time*

**P**etrified Forest National Park is truly the land before time—tell the kids that the fossilized plants and animals found here date back to pre-dinosaur days.

Stretching north and south between Interstate 40 and Highway 180 in northeastern Arizona, the area contains one of the world's largest concentrations of petrified wood, 200-million-year-old fossils, and archaeological objects documenting 13,000 years of human history.

It's also one of the most convenient places to walk with kids into the Painted Desert badlands—the erosion-striped mudstone and clay slopes, mesas, and buttes located primarily within the Navajo Nation.

Although striking, the badlands backdrop quickly can become boring to a kid watching the view roll by from the passenger seat. It's only by stepping into the "forests" (large accumulations of petrified logs), and seeing and feeling the petrified

---

### FAST FACTS

■ A Spanish explorer is thought to have named the vast badlands landscape **Desierto Pintado** (Painted Desert) because the hills looked like they were painted with the colors of the sunset.

■ **Petrified Forest National Park** has one of the most diverse collections of prehistoric pottery fragments in the Southwest.

■ On clear days in the Southwest, especially on crisp, cold winter days, you can see landscape features almost **100 miles away**.

---

material, that kids realize the "wood" they saw from a distance is mostly silica—rainbow-colored quartz.

Park paleontologist Bill Parker suggests visiting the most kid-friendly of the park's "forests"—Crystal Forest, accessible via a short hike.

"The logs and views are most spectacular here, and kids can get really close to the wood," he says.

"Touching the petrified wood and seeing the other fossils is an important part of the process of understanding. It helps kids realize that the Earth and life in general has changed significantly through the eons. Petrified Forest is one place where they can step back in time and experience this firsthand."

Parker recommends scheduling the Crystal Forest hike when a ranger-led program is taking place, so kids can get answers to their most pressing questions: Why do the logs look like they were cut with a saw? (Silica naturally breaks on an angle.) What kinds of trees were these? (Mainly coniferous, tree ferns, and ginkgoes.) Can I take a piece home? (Not from the forest, because it is protected, but area gift shops sell wood from other deposits.)

After an active Crystal Forest hike, kids will be ready to focus on the fossil animal exhibits (including early dinosaurs) at the Rainbow Forest Museum. The ranger talk helps kids learn about life during the late Triassic epoch, when the trees and animals they are seeing as fossils were actually alive.

"Walking among the fossil logs and seeing the fossils in the museum should help kids realize that millions of years ago northern Arizona was a very different place," Parker adds. "The colorful badlands and sandstone formations are remnants of a sizable river system that flowed through the area more than 200 million years ago. Very diverse plants and animals lived alongside these rivers and streams. When they died, their remains were buried and preserved by river mud and sands.

"Attending the ranger programs will help kids make this connection," he concludes, "and get them to appreciate that the Earth has a long and interesting history that is recorded in rocks and fossils." ∎

# CONNECTIONS

**Arizona Office of Tourism**
*www.arizonaguide.com/places-to-visit/
arizona-parks-monuments/
petrified-forest-national-park*
For a complete Arizona guide, visit the state's Office of Tourism website to see all that the Southwest has to offer. You'll find a simple guide and overview of the Petrified Forest and information on other notable destinations, such as the Hoover Dam and Lake Havasu.

**National Geographic**
*http://travel.nationalgeographic.com/travel/
national-parks/petrified-forest-national-park*
National Geographic's website maps out a guide that includes all the main attractions, such as Rainbow Forest Museum and Pintado Point.

**National Park Service**
*www.nps.gov/pefo*
The National Park Service provides a comprehensive overview of Petrified Forest, including daily activities, trip planners, and children's programs. Have the youngsters read some of the stories on early civilization and petroglyphs, the stone drawings that are thought to be 600 to 1,100 years old.

# Grand Canyon

## *Eons in a Rock Sandwich*

For too many kids, seeing the Grand Canyon—277 river miles long, up to 18 miles wide, and a mile deep—is just an hour spent staring out over the abyss, posing for photos, and jostling with other tourists for prime viewing spots without ever dipping a single sneaker below the rim.

Yet, below the rim, says botanist and wilderness skills expert Mike Masek, is precisely where kids need to go to begin to appreciate the Grand Canyon's natural, geologic, and historical wonders.

"The Grand Canyon is not just an object to be seen, it is an *experience* to relish for a lifetime," Masek explains. "Each child should spend time hiking below the rim. The immensity of the canyon makes people think *big*. While this is rewarding, the true nature of the canyon comes alive upon closer inspection."

Taking a day hike or participating in a ranger-led hiking program gives kids the chance to safely examine little treasures they would miss from the rim, like the fossils in the rock layers, lizards

---

**BOOKS FOR KIDS**
■ *A Grand Canyon Journey: Tracing Time in Stone* by Peter Anderson (1997) This overview of the multibillion-year geological history of the canyon begins by profiling rock layers at the canyon's rim and continues downward to the valley floor. Interspersed is information about the flora, fauna, and early human inhabitants.

■ *"Hey Ranger!" Kids Ask Questions about Grand Canyon National Park* by Kim Williams Justesen (2007) Both educational and entertaining,

## Know Before You Go

this book offers answers to questions children ask rangers at the Grand Canyon every day. Ready-to-color illustrations accompany its text.

**MUSIC**
■ *Hopi Katcina Songs & Six Songs* by Hopi Chanters, produced by Smithsonian Folkways (2010) A collection of songs first recorded by Jesse Walter Fewkes, head of the Bureau of American Ethnology

and Archaeology. The tunes were performed at Hopi ceremonial events held during his visits to Hopi reservations.

■ *Music of the Grand Canyon* by Nicholas Gunn (1995) Drawing on both New Age and traditional Native American influences, this album's original compositions feature melodies performed by master flutist Nicholas Gunn, synthesized nature sounds, distant chanting, and tribal rhythms played on electronic percussion.

basking in the sun, and desert wildflowers and wildlife, Masek adds.

"As they are walking down the trail, have the kids stop and look back up to see the work that went into building the trail," he advises. "Point out the transition from one rock layer to the next. Encourage them to think about the different body responses they experience when descending and climbing."

Both Masek and Flagstaff-based wilderness guide and forester Brad Ball suggest taking the South Kaibab Trail to Cedar Ridge, a three-mile round-trip hike that's appropriate for kids, yet still offers a 360-degree view of the inside of a canyon.

"What's unique about this trail is that it follows a ridgeline, while most of the other trails follow fault systems," says Ball. "This creates these classic panoramic views. Plus, it is the right length for kids—they could hike

down and back up in about three hours—and it's a maintained trail, so it is moderate by Grand Canyon standards. Below the rim, the Grand Canyon is a pretty rugged place, so you have to keep that in mind when visiting with kids."

The iconic Grand Canyon experience is the overnight mule ride down to the Colorado River; riders must be at least four feet seven inches tall and weigh less than 200 pounds. The ride can be physically taxing, especially in the heat of summer.

# CONNECTIONS

**Hiking the Grand Canyon, TUA Outdoors**
*www.tuaoutdoors.com*
Using this iPhone app, navigate the Grand Canyon's network of hiking trails. With maps, trail descriptions, day hike recommendations, and climate and weather information, it eliminates the need to weigh down your backpack with easy-to-crumble paper brochures.

**Kids Can Travel**
*www.kidscantravel.com*
This website offers suggestions for kid-friendly accommodations, restaurants, and hiking and rafting trips.

**National Geographic Kids
Grand Canyon Brainteaser**
*www.kids.nationalgeographic.com*
Before your trip, have your kids take the Grand Canyon Brainteaser quiz on this website's geography games page.

**Grand Canyon Association**
*www.grandcanyon.org*
This not-for-profit organization works to support research and educational programs of the national park; its site has an events listing and park news page that are both worth a visit.

As an alternative, Ball suggests taking one of the National Park Service–sponsored North Rim one-hour or half-day mule rides designed specifically for kids age seven and up. In addition to being accessible to children, the trips typically are available on the day of arrival, unlike the overnight treks, which can fill up more than a year in advance.

Grand Canyon naturalist guide Jake Slade says the key to making any Grand Canyon visit memorable for kids is choosing activities that match the child's natural interests.

"The first time I came here I was 12 and I was bored out of my mind," he recalls. "Now I live here, because as an adult I was able to get down into the canyon and explore. So if your child is interested in science and nature, or loves to hike or ride bikes, or maybe is interested in history or Native American culture, there are resources here to facilitate experiential learning in that area."

Before you visit, Slade suggests browsing the Grand Canyon Field Institute (GCFI) programs that will be offered during your stay. The GCFI, a non-profit partner of the national park, supports education, the arts, research, and other programs for kids age six and up. The single-day "Meet the Canyon" class can be scheduled in advance and customized to fit a family's specific interests and fitness levels.

Although Slade agrees that the Grand Canyon is best experienced below the rim, he encourages parents also to walk with their kids along the Trail of Time, a paved, interpretative South Rim trail starting just west of the Yavapai Geology Museum in the Grand Canyon Village area. The geologic time line leads backward in one-million-year increments

## FAST FACTS

■ Although **fossilized reptile footprints** are visible on many surfaces throughout the Grand Canyon, no fossilized reptile bones have ever been discovered here.

■ The Grand Canyon's **oldest rocks,** located at the bottom of its inner gorge, are nearly **1.8 billion years old.** That's more than one-third of the age of the Earth itself.

toward the oldest rock in Grand Canyon, 1,840 million-year-old Elves Chasm gneiss.

"We humans are pretty egotistical about time, and a long time to us isn't a long time for the Grand Canyon," says Slade. "The time line represents 2,000 million years of Earth history, and is a good visual to give kids a better idea of what one million years really means. When kids understand how old these rocks are and how the canyon was made, it all starts to make sense."

Because summer at the Grand Canyon typically is hot and crowded, wilderness guide Ball suggests a spring (mid-March to mid-April) or fall (mid-September to late October) visit to give kids a cooler, quieter environment for that life-changing initial encounter.

Although most kids can identify the Grand Canyon in a photo, says Masek, no child can begin to understand the place until he or she visits: "No previous experiences can prepare children for the canyon. It really cannot be compared to anything else. The mind quits working in the usual way, and becomes mesmerized, not so much by the thing that is the canyon, but by the experience." ■

# Arches National Park

## *A Visual Wonderland*

**T**his park is way better than any video game," says 13-year-old Alex Schaefer as he clambers up the base of Double Arch, one of more than 2,000 sandstone arch formations that form the filigreed landscape of Arches National Park. "I really like that I can get so close to—and even sit under—many of the arches. And the sandstone rock is so smooth and curvy that it makes climbing super fun."

These words—music to many parents' ears—sum up what thousands of visitors experience each year at this most interactive of national parks.

"You really can't beat Arches for broad appeal," says Alex's father, Wolfgang Schaefer. "The rock formations here—arches, windows, fins, spires, buttes, towers, domes—and the rich colors of the sandstone make it a visual and recreational wonderland. It's a video game come to life."

Five miles north of the adventure town of Moab, in eastern Utah—and just 40 miles from vast Canyonlands National Park—Arches was born of a unique geology that, eroded by winds, rains,

• • • • • • • • • • • • • • • • • • • • • • • • • • • • •

### INSIDER TIP

Head up to Delicate Arch, an easy hike that leads to a rock formation that resembles cowboy chaps. The hike itself, which begins at Wolfe Ranch parking lot, yields sweeping views of red rock and, at one point, borders the edge of a rock cliff. Delicate Arch teeters on the rim of a sandstone bowl and provides breathtaking views of the La Sal Mountains, especially during the late afternoon when one can watch the orange glow of the sunset slip into the horizon. Don't miss a stop at Frame Arch on the way, located in the cliff above the last 50 yards of the trail.

• • • • • • • • • • • • • • • • • • • • • • • • • • • • •

and ice, has yielded the richest concentration of arch and "window" formations in the world. Headliners include Double Arch, two immense arches that share a common support column; Landscape Arch, one of Earth's longest arches; Balanced Rock, a boulder balanced at an unlikely angle on a stone spire; a congregation of arches known as Devils Garden; and Fiery Furnace, a warren of passageways between stone fins and walls that plunk you right into your own action adventure (and are best explored on a guided hike).

The superstar of them all? Delicate Arch, a monolith rising at the center of its own natural amphitheater that may be the most photographed arch on the planet and is best viewed at dawn or sunset, when the sun's rays seem to fire up the salmon-hued sandstone from within.

"Compared to the mega parks—Grand Canyon, Yellowstone, and nearby Canyonlands—Arches is so easy and accessible," says Schaefer. "The 36-mile scenic loop road takes you to the main sights and trailheads, and many of the trails are the perfect length—less than a mile—for kids."

"Plus here you can really see how the Earth is always changing," adds son Alex. "We went to find

## FAST FACTS

■ **Arches last for a short period** in terms of geologic time. On August 4, 2008, the 71-foot-long, 33-foot-wide **Wall Arch collapsed.**

■ Native Americans roamed through the park, but **never inhabited it year-round.** They left behind petroglyphs as evidence of their presence.

■ In order to be classified as an arch in the park, the opening must be **at least three feet** in any direction.

■ Known for his book *Desert Solitaire* about Arches National Park, author Edward Abbey also wrote *The Monkey Wrench Gang,* a fictional tale set in the parks of the Southwest.

■ Portions of the movie *Thelma and Louise* were filmed in Arches National Park, as was Steven Spielberg's *Indiana Jones and the Last Crusade.*

Wall Arch after seeing it in photos—and it wasn't there. A ranger told us that it collapsed in 2008—and that parts of Landscape Arch have also fallen off. It's sad that Wall Arch fell, but new stuff is forming here all the time—only much more slowly than in a video game." ■

## BOOKS FOR KIDS

■ *The Illuminated Desert* by Terry Tempest Williams and Chloe Hedden (2008) Magnificent paintings and poetic text bring to life the red-rock canyons, ancient peoples, and wildlife of Southern Utah in this award-winning alphabet book for young readers.

■ *Cactus Desert* by Donald Silver and Patricia Wynne (1997) This book encourages kids to discover the rich array of wildlife that lives in the

## Know Before You Go

deceptively still, arid desert landscape. Young explorers learn how to spot tortoises, beetles, and lizards, as well as how to watch out for rattlesnakes and scorpions. Fun facts reveal how plants and animals cope with the extreme temperatures.

## BOOKS FOR PARENTS

■ *Desert Solitaire* by Edward Abbey (1968) Called the "Thoreau of the

American West," Abbey captures the stark beauty of the desert in this memoir of his time as a ranger at Arches National Park. He recounts trekking through uncharted canyons, trying to capture a wild horse, camping on a 13,000-foot mountain, and rafting down the Colorado River. An outspoken environmentalist, he also rails against the destruction of nature and advocates the preservation of wilderness as "a necessary part of civilization."

# Yellowstone National Park

## World's First National Park

"National parks are the best idea we ever had," wrote American novelist and environmentalist Wallace Stegner. "Absolutely American, absolutely democratic, they reflect us at our best rather than our worst."

When President Ulysses S. Grant signed the bill creating Yellowstone Park in 1872, it became the world's first national park—and a boon to family explorers past and present. Now the National Park System includes 397 areas (58 designated as "national parks"), encompassing more than 84 million acres. But Yellowstone, whose two-million-plus remote and rugged acres encompass half of Earth's geothermal features, stands as the first—an enduring testament to the mission statement etched on the giant stone Roosevelt Arch at the park's North Entrance: "For the benefit and enjoyment of the people."

"Yellowstone always gives me hope that this country is capable of protecting an area of the

### INSIDER TIP

To avoid the crowds at Old Faithful, take the kids on a moonlit adventure under the stars and watch the geyser as it spews water up to 180 feet in the air. Or walk up Geyser Hill for a view of its impressive size.

park's size, because we did it at one point. Ask kids to imagine what would have happened if we hadn't," says David Gafney, a former Yellowstone interpretive ranger, a seasonal interpretive ranger, and author of *Yellowstone, Grand Loop Drive Interpretive Road Guide*. Spanning Wyoming, Montana, and Idaho, "it's a high volcanic plateau that is inspiring because of its size, wildness, and location. Kids can look in all directions and be surrounded by higher mountains, and everywhere they turn there is tremendous diversity—wildlife, geysers, and geothermals, a petrified forest, and the Grand Canyon of the Yellowstone."

Because Yellowstone is so huge, Gafney suggests breaking up the visit into kid-captivating daily chunks, such as a day each for mammals, thermal features, and waterfalls. This is similar to the format followed by Yellowstone for Families, a three-day, small-group program offered by the nonprofit Yellowstone Association *(www.yellowstoneassociation .org).* The association also has naturalists for hire who can re-create some or all of the program's activities for individual families.

"A lot of people think Yellowstone is only Old Faithful, wolves, and bison, and that's all their kids get to see," says the association's Rebecca Kreklau. "Participating in a program created specifically for kids opens up the whole family's perspective, and lets everyone experience everything that is out there without wearing them out. We go out wildlife-watching and have laser guns so kids can take temperatures of thermal features. We show younger kids how to track earthworms, and show older kids some of [painter] Thomas Moran's work to help them see how his art helped to create this park."

Whether you choose a guided tour or strike out on your own, the key to helping kids enjoy Yellowstone is to create an itinerary that brings what interests them into focus.

"A lot of times the wildlife is out there, but it is hard to find it if you don't know what you are

## BOOKS FOR KIDS

■ *Yellowstone (Ready-to-Read) Level 1* by Marion Dane Bauer; **illustrated by John Wallace (2008)** From the Wonders of America series, this book focuses on the geologic elements found in our first national park. The vivid watercolor illustrations provide a glimpse into a world filled with bison and bubbling mud puddles. An illustration of the Earth's crust reveals its different layers and unusual features like fumaroles.

■ *"Hey Ranger!" Kids Ask Questions about Yellowstone National Park* by **Kim Williams Justesen; illustrated by Judy Newhouse (2005)** A look into all the funny and smart questions kids often ask rangers, this educational guide also offers cool facts and ready-to-color

## Know Before You Go

illustrations. Read about how rangers answer questions such as "What time do you let the animals out for feeding?"

### BOOKS FOR PARENTS

■ *Lost in My Own Backyard: A Walk in Yellowstone National Park* by **Tim Cahill (2004)** Local writer Cahill has spent a quarter of a century exploring the vastness of Yellowstone. In this offbeat adventure, Cahill wanders the remote backwoods and encounters bison, spends a night admiring moonbows across waterfalls, and gets spooked in the Goblin Labyrinths, all the while musing over the park's history and former explorers.

## MUSIC

■ *Canyon Trilogy* by R. Carlos Nakai **(1993)** The haunting music of R. Carlos Nakai evokes an array of moods—from lament to joy—and reflects his ties to the spiritual Native American world. Nakai's cedar flute echoes throughout the canyons and valleys of the Southwest.

■ *The Sounds of Yellowstone* by **Various Artists (1995)** Musicians accompany recordings of actual sounds from Yellowstone on this tribute to the natural music of the park. Listen to birds chirp alongside a breezy violin in a track called "Centennial." Other ambient sounds on the CD include Old Faithful's eruptions, elk communicating through their distinctive bugle call, and boiling mud pots.

looking for," explains Kreklau. "It is tough when kids are all excited about seeing animals and then don't see any. That rock you think you see on the hill might actually be a wolf. With a guide, you can learn what is there from day to day and how to see it, and what time of day to go out."

To maximize your child's wildlife spotting, Gafney suggests investing in some high-powered binoculars and heading to Hayden Valley and Lamar Valley for a day devoted to animals. Let the kids know that early morning is best for wildlife viewing, says Kent Taylor, a certified tour guide with the National Park Society. Because they'll want to see the animals, it could be a bit easier to get them to go to sleep the night before and get them out of bed in the morning.

"Keep a scorecard to check off the animal species you see in the park, striving to find as many types of animals as you can," Taylor adds. "And consider purchasing a DVD of common Yellowstone animals to show in your vehicle while traveling through the heavily forested areas of the park, where wildlife sightings are limited."

Every kid will be metaphorically blown away watching Old Faithful shoot 3,700 to 8,400 gallons of hot (204°F) water into the sky—the perfect time to talk to kids about the power of the geysers and the scalding temperatures of the pools, mud pots, and other thermal features. Stay on the boardwalks and trails to avoid burns and other injuries. A cooler water source that kids need to experience as well,

## FAST FACTS

■ During the American Civil War, Gen. Philip Sheridan and his men sometimes used **Old Faithful geyser** as a place to clean their laundry, using the bursts of hot air and steam.

■ **President Theodore Roosevelt** buried a time capsule beneath the Roosevelt Arch at the North Entrance of the park. It contained a **Bible, local newspapers, and a picture of himself.**

■ **Hoodoo Basin,** located at the head of the Lamar Valley, is marked by its strange volcanic hoodoos (formations that resemble human figures), which are known to visitors as **Goblin Labyrinths.**

says Gafney, is the Lower Falls area of the Yellowstone River.

To give kids unobstructed views of the 308-foot drop in the falls, Gafney recommends taking the Uncle Tom's Trail near Canyon Village down the south side of the Grand Canyon of the park to a safe viewing platform.

"It's a fabulous trail that kids would love; metal stairway part of the way and right near the lower falls," he says. "The kids can see osprey nesting well into the summer there, and they just might witness a rainbow rising out of the canyon. Even without the rainbow, the canyon is incredibly colorful. Any kid lucky enough to see that will be awestruck."

Adds Kreklau, "Yellowstone is our classroom and it is such an amazing teacher. You just have to open kids' eyes to it." ■

"Today, just as in 1872, Yellowstone's capacity to whet man's sense of wonder and refresh his spirit remains ageless and undiminished."—*President Richard Nixon*

# ꙩierra Nevada Parks

## *Caves, Caverns, and Canyons*

California's side-by-side, southern Sierra Nevada national parks—Sequoia and Kings Canyon—collectively are known as the "land of giants."

And for good reason: Everything here is super-duper-size, from 14,494-foot Mount Whitney (tallest mountain in the lower 48 states, partially located in Sequoia) to the cloud-climbing trees, including the world's largest single-trunk tree—the 275-foot-tall General Sherman sequoia in Sequoia's Giant Forest (where kids will love riding through the "Tunnel Log" cut through another 275-foot tree that fell along Crescent Meadow Road in 1937).

The giant attractions, although spectacular, are obvious and easily viewed from the passenger seat of the family car. That's why junior explorers in particular will delight in discovering the flip side of the parks, where more than 200 marble caves are hidden under the surface.

Steve Fairchild, who grew up in Kings Canyon and now leads family cave and canyoneering tours here, says the views and ecosystems underground are different from anything kids will see up top.

"Kids are amazed when we tell them that what they find inside the cave is what it looks like from under a giant coral reef," he says. "About 100 million years ago we had gigantic coral reefs that were pulled underneath the continent and pushed up into the Sierra to the spot where they now stand. They understand immediately that they are seeing something that few kids get to see."

The year-round 55-degree temperatures make caves comfortable, living classrooms in which kids can learn by seeing, asking questions, and, most important, doing, adds Fairchild.

He designs kid-friendly tours of nearby Boyden Cavern and of natural river caves and canyons downstream. Additional cave tours are offered at Crystal Cave. Sequoia-size, underground expeditions available to young Kings Canyon visitors—including Pirate River Cave Adventures, where kids rappel down canyon walls—are designed to help convey basic geology and speleology knowledge while building outdoor skills.

"On the world scale, Boyden Cavern is not big, but it is a perfect size for kids," says Fairchild. "They can crawl beyond the trail with the guides, explore, and then pop back out on the trail. Kids have an innate sense of adventure, so when they go down in the lower section of the cave, they can't believe they are allowed to go somewhere so wild—no handrails, no cement, just boulders and a stream bed. They look back up at mom and dad and say: 'We get to go down *there?*' They can't believe it. That makes the trip for them."

Californian Michelle McCoy says the caves are one of the major reasons why her family chooses to camp in the heart of Kings Canyon each summer. In Boyden Cavern, McCoy explains, her two sons learned about and to appreciate the forces of nature at work around them.

"By following the stream that flows through the mountain to the opening in the cliff, my boys could see that a tiny flow of water holds a significant amount of power to carve out a cave," she says. "When they came out of the cave, they saw the Kings River below them and made the connection that this rush of water carved out the deep canyon." ∎

---

## BOOKS FOR PARENTS & KIDS

■ *Yosemite, Sequoia & Kings Canyon National Parks* by Danny Palmerlee and Beth Kohn (2008) Choose the perfect itinerary for your family's experience level and interest. This guidebook suggests various kid-friendly hikes—such as exploring the moss-covered sequoias on the Hazelwood Nature Trail—whether you're traveling through the backcountry or rock climbing.

## BOOKS FOR KIDS

■ *Who Pooped in the Park? Scat Tracks for Kids: Sequoia and Kings Canyon National Parks* by Gary Robson; illustrated by Robert Rath

## Know Before You Go

(2006) Follow Michael and Emily on an adventure through Sequoia and Kings Canyon National Parks as they explore a variety of wildlife. Young readers will learn about black bears, spotted bats, brush rabbits, and mule deer through their droppings.

## BOOKS FOR PARENTS

■ *Best Easy Day Hikes: Sequoia and Kings Canyon National Parks* by Laurel Scheidt (2011) Small enough to bring along on your hike, this handy guide provides maps and detailed descriptions of 20 family-friendly hikes ranging from an hour to a half day. Classics such as Crescent Meadow, the General Grant Loop, and Tokopah Falls provide opportunities to inspect the flora and fauna.

## MOVIES

■ *The Underground World of Sequoia National Park* (2004) Go below and explore the caves of Sequoia. Learn about the geologic formations in caves such as Lilburn, Palmer, and Hurricane Crawl. Kids will enjoy the stories of human cave exploration and the images of the colorful, natural wonders.

# Big Sur

## *Great American Road Trip*

Novelist and painter Henry Miller called Big Sur "the face of the Earth as the creator intended it to look."

A serpentine, roller-coastering stretch of California's Highway 1 brings kids face-to-face with Big Sur's primal, coastal wonders—sheer cliffs plunging into the thundering Pacific; migrating pods of orca, humpback, gray, and blue whales; thousands of northern elephant seals molting, resting, and breeding on the beach at Piedras Blancas Viewpoint; and rare California condors—North America's largest soaring birds—coasting on the wind currents in search of their next meal.

Riding the 90-mile route from just south of Carmel down the central coast to San Simeon can be a rite of passage from little kid to big kid. Because, although the pace is leisurely, the corkscrew turns can induce motion sickness in rookie road-trippers. Younger kids may need a few milder car treks under their seat belts before attempting Big Sur. More seasoned kid road warriors experiencing Big Sur for the first time—ideally from the backseat of a

convertible—likely will finish the trip with a different view of the world and their place in it. For as longtime Big Sur resident Miller also wrote, "One's destination is never a place, but rather a new way of looking at things."

Help kids create a digital scrapbook of the journey by encouraging them to take photos along the route. Professional photographer and dad Kevin Lozaw, who has made the drive with his three young daughters, suggests stopping three miles south of Carmel—just north of Big Sur—at Point Lobos State Natural Reserve.

"This is my favorite destination along the central coast," he says. "It has just the right amount of space—big enough to spend a few hours and not so big that your kids can get lost. The terrain is diverse, there's lots of wildlife—birds, sea lions, seals—and cool, weird-looking trees, including a giant tree called the General."

Walk the Sea Lion Point Trail, where kids can snap shots of seaside gardens, harbor seals basking on the rocks, and the Carmelo formation, a wave-carved conglomerate of coves, crevices, and shelves created from rock and sand dating back about 60 million years.

Make time for a visit to Whalers Cove to discover the small cabin built by Chinese fishermen during the height of the whaling and abalone industry, suggests travel writer Nancy D. Brown.

"Our two kids liked climbing in the whale pots where whalers melted whale fat long ago," she recalls. "There also are whalebones outside of Whalers Cabin Museum—a tiny shack of a museum, but fun for kids to explore. This area is an opportunity to explain our connection to the sea and why it is important to respect natural resources. Once abundant abalone have all but disappeared and are now protected due to overharvesting."

Spending time at Point Lobos lets kids expend a bit of energy before strapping in for the wild ride ahead. Although there aren't many gas stations along the way—fuel up and pack a picnic or snacks in Carmel—there are plenty of scenic vistas at which to stretch legs, take photos, and use binoculars to scan the ocean for whales. Before heading over the Bixby Creek Bridge—one of the world's highest single-span bridges at 260 feet—pull into the overlook on the north end so kids can capture the money shot.

It's possible to cover the entire route in a few hours, or a full day if you stop to explore, but Highway 1 through Big Sur is a road best taken slowly. No one on the route is looking for the fastest way from point A to point B, so relax, focus on the road—especially in summer when lumbering RVs can set a snail's pace—and let the kids' sense of wonder reveal little discoveries around every precipitous bend.

# CONNECTIONS

**Big Sur: Wild California**
*www.nationalgeographic.com*
The National Geographic Channel investigates the causes behind a recent resurgence in wildlife along Big Sur. Via video, you can cavort with mountain lions, swim with sea lions, and stand captivated by soaring condors in this visually stunning look into the late natural history of one of the most biologically diverse sections of the California coast.

**Big Sur & Monterey Bay: Cruising Highway 1 from San Simeon to Santa Cruz**
Written by a Monterey Bay native, this iPhone app and electronic guidebook provides an insider's perspective on more than 110 top destinations and best-kept secrets. The app is updated regularly and, with more than 700 professional photographs of the region, can also serve as a souvenir to help you remember the beauty of Big Sur.

**Carmel-by-the-Sea's Official Travel Website**
*www.carmelcalifornia.com*
This village offers a level of sophistication rarely seen in towns three or four times its size. A regularly updated events calendar, compilation of suggested travel itineraries, photo gallery, and comprehensive directory of contact information for restaurants, spas, and hotels make this website a go-to guide.

Devoting at least two days to the drive gives kids more time to get out of the car and into nature. Make sure everyone wears sturdy footwear, packs a jacket or sweatshirt, and sticks close to an adult during the dramatic photo-op stops. Summer is the busiest season, as well as the time when morning fog is more likely to obscure ocean views. If possible, schedule an early fall visit, when the typical forecast calls for clear blue skies, warm temperatures, and lighter vacation traffic.

Kid-friendly lodging options range from luxury resorts to primitive tent sites. Meet in the middle at Treebones Resort, a family-run yurt community surrounded by the Los Padres National Forest and the Pacific. Kids age six and up are welcome to bunk with their parents in one of four fully furnished family yurts—sturdy structures modeled after nomadic Mongolian tents. Rates include a free breakfast buffet (waffles, homemade granola, and fresh fruit), free Wi-Fi in the lodge, and unlimited stargazing.

State parks offer the least expensive overnight option, but campsites fill up months in advance, so plan accordingly.

Whether you want to camp or simply need a hike break, stop at Julia Pfeiffer Burns State Park, where kids

## FAST FACTS

■ Buildings in **Carmel-by-the-Sea** lack street addresses and mailboxes. All mail is picked up at the town's central post office, and building locations are identified by cross street names.

■ **Unlike the eagles and hawks** they are so often compared to, **California condors** do not have sharp talons. Because they are scavengers and not birds of prey, they never evolved claws capable of killing or grasping things.

can follow the trail to a cove and see a waterfall dropping 80 feet into the sea. While there, give the kids the time and freedom to explore the redwood groves.

"Have the kids select the biggest tree they can find, give it a bear hug, and guess how old the redwood tree is," advises Brown. "If a park ranger is available, he can explain how old these trees are and how the tree rings equate to the age of the tree. There are also plaques on the trails that go into more details about the flora and fauna. Our kids got a kick out of our picture-taking antics with the giant redwoods—a teachable moment that demonstrates our connection to redwood groves and nature." ■

**BOOKS FOR KIDS**

■ *California Condors: Saved by Captive Breeding* by **Meish Goldish (2009)** Following a century of habitat destruction and relentless poaching, only 22 California condors remained alive in 1987. Today, they number more than 350. This installment in the America's Animal Comebacks series chronicles this triumphant rebound, made possible by captive breeding.

## Know Before You Go

■ *Redwoods* by **Jason Chin (2009)** While waiting for a subway, a boy finds a book about redwoods on the platform and begins to read it. The book transports him to a redwood forest in California. Though fiction, this illustrated title contains factual information about the giants.

**BOOKS FOR PARENTS**

■ *Big Sur* by **Jack Kerouac (1962)** In this classic of American folk literature, a celebrity author from the East Coast makes three trips to a town in Big Sur to escape the pressures and responsibilities that come with fame. His nervous breakdown during his final sojourn is thought to parallel author Jack Kerouac's own mental struggles.

# Muir Woods

## *Redwood Giants*

John Muir called the Marin County woods named for him "the best tree-lover's monument that could possibly be found in all the forests of the world."

Located only 11 miles north of the Golden Gate Bridge near San Francisco, Muir Woods puts some of nature's most colossal creations within reach of little feet, hands, and imaginations.

"Muir Woods is home to a grove of giant redwood trees that reach to the sky and surround you in a way that is best experienced in person," says David Shaw of the Golden Gate National Parks Conservancy. "Redwoods grow taller than any other tree species in the world. The average age of the redwoods here ranges from 400 to 800 years old, and many ancient specimens have been around for more than a millennium."

Although the towering, ancient trees will make

### INSIDER TIP

During summer peak season, most parking spaces are full by 9 a.m., so arrive early. Weekday trips are advised to avoid park congestion. The best times of the year to visit are during the spring and fall months. Most of the year, Muir Woods is damp and cold, with highs only reaching 70°F on summer days. Expect rain from November through April.

kids feel extra small, learning the story of who protected the woods can help children stand a little taller.

William Kent, the man who donated the 298 acres to create the Muir monument among some of the most valued real estate in the world, grew up in Marin and played in similar redwood groves. That childhood experience inspired him to save the redwoods as an adult.

"You know that I have not lagged behind in the work of exploring our grand wildernesses, and in calling everybody to come and enjoy the thousand blessings they have to offer."—*John Muir*

"Young people can learn about young William Kent when they visit here," says interpretive ranger Timothy Jordan. "Kent's early connection with nature fostered his love of the outdoors. As an adult, he witnessed the destruction of many Bay Area redwood forests. This, with the writings of John Muir, inspired Kent's conservationism."

Walking (and playing) in, on, and around the redwoods will help kids understand why young Kent was so mesmerized by the trees. Ranger Jordan encourages children to lie down and look up at the treetops, hug a redwood tree, touch the bark, and start a nature journal like John Muir.

"Have kids find a redwood spray the same age as them; count the rings in trees and learn how to measure a tree; sit inside of a hollow redwood tree on Fern Creek; see ladybugs clustering; and teach someone else about Muir Woods," he advises.

After all the interaction, the kids just may be ready to rest—at least for a moment. Take this time

## FAST FACTS

■ Some of the redwood trees in Muir Woods are **taller than the 305-foot Statue of Liberty.** The tiny seed that they grow from is no bigger than a tomato seed, and it takes about 125,000 of them to equal a pound.

■ A plaque in Muir Woods' Cathedral Grove recognizes the May 19, 1945, signing of the **United Nations organizational charter.** Delegates from 48 countries met beneath the giant redwoods to hold a memorial for Franklin D. Roosevelt, who had died one month earlier.

■ A live redwood that is knocked over will attempt **to continue growing.** If undisturbed, the limbs pointing up will **become trees of their own.** This is the source of groups of trees seen in rows.

■ When **heavy rains** during winter break open the sandbar at Muir Beach, the surge of fresh water that travels from **Redwood Creek** to the ocean lets the endangered coho salmon know that it's time to return to the stream of their birth to spawn.

to "be quiet and listen to the sounds of the forest," says Shaw. "Encourage kids to think about how these trees are more than 1,000 years old, and have stood quietly through year after year of rain, fog, sun, and sometimes even snow." ■

---

**BOOKS FOR KIDS**
■ *John Muir: Young Naturalist* by Montrew Dunham (1998) This book, designed for middle-school children, begins with Muir's life as a seven-year-old boy in Scotland and covers his first few years in America and his exploration of the national parks.

**BOOKS FOR PARENTS**
■ *The Wilderness World of John Muir* by John Muir; edited by Edwin Way Teale (1954) A revealing

## Know Before You Go

look into conservationist John Muir's journals as he traversed the wilderness on foot with only stale bread and tea, this book is both an anthology and biography. It contains inspiring descriptions of Muir's travels through America's national parks. His stories give readers a glimpse into the life of one of the most famous wilderness pioneers.

**MUSIC**
■ *Muir Woods Suite* by George Duke (1966) Jazz legend George Duke used to camp in Muir Woods as a young boy. In this orchestral album, his renowned keyboard playing conveys his memories of the massive redwoods and the sounds and smells of the forest. You'll hear the expressiveness of jazz mixed with classical instruments in bass and drum solos and songs such as "Phase 6 (Love Theme)."

# Hawaiian Volcanoes

*Forged by Fire*

For kids, watching Kilauea's fire-red lava drizzling down the side of the volcano and sizzling into the ocean conjures up images of a mammoth wizard's boiling cauldron, a sci-fi planet shaped out of mysterious goo, or, true to Hawaiian tradition, the goddess of fire—Madame Pele—making her presence known by breathing fire.

The mystical and magical forces at work on the Big Island's lush 330,000-acre Hawai'i Volcanoes National Park extend far beyond two of the world's most active volcanoes—Kilauea and Mauna Loa—but it is the volcanic wonders that mesmerize kids, says Julie Mitchell, general manager of the community-based Friends of Hawai'i Volcanoes National Park.

"From steam vents, steaming bluff, and sulfur banks to the fuming vent at Halema'uma'u Crater, nothing is more exciting than seeing the Earth as alive and dynamic," Mitchell explains. "The volcanic forces that shaped the Hawaiian Islands are

## BUY WORTHY

Pick up some **block prints** from the Hawai'i Volcanoes National Park bookshop in Volcano village. Skilled artisans carve **intricate designs on bamboo strips** and transfer them to blocks. The prints depict local themes such as the Hawaiian hibiscus and ukulele playing. Each block print is signed and numbered by the artist.

visible here in a way that can help kids envision how much of the world was formed."

Seeing the living, breathing volcanoes inspires amazement, creativity, and tons of rapid-fire questions from curious young adventurers. To help kids understand what they are seeing, Mitchell suggests heading first to the Kilauea Visitor Center to watch a movie about the volcano, explore the interactive displays, listen to the sounds of the rain forest, and see dioramas of creatures who live in the park.

While there, pick up a copy of the *Junior Ranger Handbook: A Guide to Discovery and Exploration of Hawai'i Volcanoes National Park*. By working through the booklet to earn the Junior Ranger badge, kids learn how scientists measure changes in the volcanoes, can see and touch different types of lava rock at the park's Jaggar Museum, watch seismographs track earthquake activity, and learn the sacred stories of Kilauea's and Hawai'i's gods and goddesses.

Park education specialist Joni Mae Makuakane-Jarrell says the goal of the Junior Ranger program—and of all the ranger-led activities—is for kids to "have fun as they explore, discover, and fall in love with the park. In this ever changing landscape, you never know where or when an eruption will be seen on the Kilauea or Mauna Loa volcanoes. Here, the very ground you walk on is a *wahi kapu* (a sacred place) and the home of the fire goddess, Pelehonuamea."

To help prepare kids for what they might see, Makuakane-Jarrell suggests having them check out the live webcam of the park's current eruptions ahead of time on the U.S. Geological Survey's Hawaiian Volcano Observatory website at

## FAST FACTS

■ Some **23,000 petroglyphs** are located at Pu'uloa, **"long hill,"** which is considered a sacred place by the Hawaiians. Traditionally, parents carved holes into the rock and put the umbilical cords of their newborn babies to ensure long lives for the children.

■ Since 1983, **Kilauea** has constantly erupted. As a result, the lava flows have added more than **500 acres of new land** to the southern shore of the volcano and covered 8.7 miles of highway.

■ Although known for its **bountiful butterflies,** only two types are actually **native** to Hawai'i: the **Kamehameha butterfly,** Hawai'i's state insect, and the **Blackburn's blue.**

hvo.wr.usgs.gov. While watching the images from the park, Mitchell suggests talking to kids about how volcanic activity changes from moment to moment. "There's no predicting when lava may or may not be visible, but the stunning volcanic landscape is always on view," she says.

After equipping kids with basic volcano knowledge at the visitors center, pile them in the car for the epic trek up near the simmering summit caldera. The 11-mile Crater Rim Drive is a loop with plenty of scenic pull-offs, at which kids can take short walks

## BOOKS FOR PARENTS & KIDS

■ *Volcanoes of the National Parks of Hawaii* by Gordon A. Macdonald and Douglass H. Hubbard, Jr. **(1997)** This kid-friendly guide is filled with pictures from Mauna Loa, Kilauea, and Haleakala, along with explanations of how the island was formed and lists of recorded volcano eruptions. At 64 pages, it's small enough to take along while exploring the park.

## Know Before You Go

### BOOKS FOR KIDS

■ *High Tide in Hawaii (Magic Tree House #28)* by Mary Pope Osborne **(2003)** Siblings Jack and Annie rush to help save families on the island from a tidal wave in this fast-paced adventure that's part of the Magic Tree House series. The story also introduces children to traditional Hawaiian customs like eating poi and making *kapa*.

### MUSIC

■ *Alone in IZ World* by Israel "IZ" Kamakawiwo'ole **(2001)** With one of the most recognizable voices in Hawai'i, Kamakawiwo'ole exemplifies the peaceful nature of Hawai'i's music culture. The CD consists of the singer's most recognizable songs.

and hone their budding photography skills. The drive passes through desert, tropical rain forest, and the caldera floor—making it easy for kids to experience the park's diversity in only a couple of hours.

As you make the drive, take time to stop at the clearly marked trails, nature paths, and displays so kids can see, feel, and hear nature at work all around them.

"We look to encourage a child's appreciation for that which is unique to Hawai'i," says Makuakane-Jarrell. "Children can hike beneath towering tree ferns, through an underground lava tube, and over fields of ropy *pahoehoe* (lava flows). They'll feel the steam and catch a glimpse of Hawai'i's rare birds. And on a clear night, they can see the glow from the lava lake created by the eruption at the summit of Kilauea in Halema'uma'u Crater."

Mitchell says that getting out of the car and onto the trails is the best way to bring the inspiring scenery down to a level kids can absorb without feeling overwhelmed.

"When kids meander through the towering tree ferns, have them try to spot a red *'apapane* bird flickering through the rain forest," she advises. "When they walk through the cool, dripping wet (and 500-year-old) Thurston Lava Tube, ask them to imagine what it was like when red-hot lava was flowing through it. And when you take a stroll along Devastation Trail, ask the kids to try to figure out how and why the landscape looks as barren as it does."

The reason, it turns out, connects back to the volcanoes. The eruption of Kilauea Iki in 1959 obliterated the rain forest. Learning the history while walking the half-mile paved trail reinforces the message that volcanoes—no matter how scenic and inspiring—are unpredictable forces that can't be controlled (not even by parents, teachers, or other adults). That thought can be scary to a kid, but more likely, it will seem extremely—and powerfully—*cool*. ∎

# CONNECTIONS

**Hawai'i Volcanoes National Park**
*www.nps.gov/havo*
Visit the National Park Service website before your trip for up-to-date information regarding weather conditions and services in the park. Print out a handy trip planner with suggestions of what to see and do based on how much time you can spend in the park. Find out where to best see lava flows (the park's eastern boundary or the end of Chain of Craters Road). Test kids' knowledge of what to do in a dangerous situation with the "Don't Be a Lava Loser" packet.

**National Geographic**
*http://travel.nationalgeographic.com/travel/ national-parks/hawaii-volcanoes-activities*
This website's travel section provides information that will help you plan a successful trip from sea level to summit. In "What to Do at Hawai'i Volcanoes," find recommendations such as the 12-hour van tour with Hawaii Forest and Trail or the 45-minute helicopter tour out of Hilo that flies above the Pu'u 'O'o vent, with views of lava flowing into the sea. Smart Traveler advises bringing binoculars to watch honeycreepers siphon out nectar from flowers.

**Leigh Hilbert**
*www.hawaiianlavadaily.blogspot.com*
Blogger Hilbert shares what's going on in the Big Island. See photos of the Kilauea volcano's active craters and video of molten lava.

# Denali

## *The High One*

On December 2, 1980, President Jimmy Carter put pen to paper preserving 79.53 million acres of Alaska wilderness. In just one day, the unprecedented Alaska National Interests Lands Conservation Act (ANILCA) he signed into law created ten new national park properties, increased the size of three others, and set aside additional public acreage for the U.S. Forest Service and U.S. Fish and Wildlife Service.

Of the new parks—including Gates of the Arctic, Glacier Bay, Katmai, Kenai Fjords, Kobuk Valley, and Lake Clark—13.2-million-acre Wrangell-St. Elias National Park and Preserve instantly became the nation's largest.

Most of Alaska's newest parks are pretty remote and rugged, so to help kids begin to comprehend the enormity of what the legislation achieved (and to launch loftier discussions about the American democratic process, how laws are made, and land use), take them to

**INSIDER TIP**

Instead of hiking Denali in midsummer as most do, come in late May or early June. At this time of year, the wildlife is more active as birthing season comes to a close, rainfall decreases, and the trails are less crowded.

the most famous park (and one of the more accessible ones) included in the law. Originally called Mount McKinley National Park when it was established in 1917, Alaska's first national park was renamed and expanded by ANILCA as Denali National Park and Preserve.

The area is named after the Athabaskan term for "high one." Its massive centerpiece—20,320-foot-tall Mount McKinley, or Denali—is North America's tallest peak, requiring a near backbend for kids to be able to look high enough in the sky to see the top, which is often obscured with clouds from the severe weather on the mountain.

Because the sheer size of the peak

"The top of Mount McKinley was thrilling, but there's nothing on earth more exciting than the eyes of a youngster at the instant of discovery."—*Bradford Washburn, author and climber*

and the six-million-acre park can make kids feel extra small, Anne Beaulaurier, program coordinator at Camp Denali and North Face Lodge, suggests engaging in earthbound activities.

Start with the hands-on, educational exhibits at the Denali Visitor Center and Murie Science and Learning Center, followed by a bus ride out to the Eielson Visitor Center.

"The kids can keep their eyes open for wildlife and ask the bus driver lots of questions. On the way, hike in the Thorofare Pass area on the open alpine tundra," says Beaulaurier.

Although spotting moose, caribou, grizzly bears, sheep, and beavers from the bus or trail is a natural highlight for kids, Beaulaurier says joining a guided hike allows them to learn from trained naturalists and absorb Denali in a more meaningful way.

"Let kids romp around, lay on their bellies, and explore the world that is even smaller than they are," she advises. "When they see squirrel holes, they can investigate them. They can follow animal tracks and experience the joy of tundra by rolling on its spongy surface.

"Then have kids dig a hand down through the moss and into the cold soil in search of permafrost, and bring a thermometer to measure the temperature of the ground," concludes Beaulaurier. ∎

## BOOKS FOR PARENTS & KIDS......
■ *The Kids from Nowhere: The Story Behind the Arctic Educational Miracle* by **George Guthridge (2006)** In 1982, Guthridge took a teaching post in a failing school on the Bering Sea's remote St. Lawrence Island. His book chronicles the struggles he and his students experienced on their path to a state championship in a difficult academic competition.

## BOOKS FOR PARENTS.................
■ *Arctic Spirit: The Albrecht Collection of Inuit Art at the Heard Museum* by **Ingo Hesell (2006)** Sculptors from Alaska, Canada, Greenland, and Siberia have garnered international acclaim for their ivory and soapstone carvings of far north animals. The book features photographs of prominent

# Know Before You Go

pieces in one of the world's most important collections of such carvings, and offers an authoritative history of Arctic art and in-depth interviews with leading sculptors.

## BOOKS FOR KIDS...........................
■ *Buried Alive (Mysteries in Our National Parks)* by **Gloria Skurzynski and Alane Ferguson (2003)** The 12th book in the series takes the family to Alaska to study the number of wolverines in Denali National Park. While on a dogsled ride into the backcountry, the children face the danger of an onrushing avalanche.

■ *Running With the Big Dogs: A Sled Dog Puppy Grows Up in Denali*

*National Park, Alaska* by **Lori Yanuchi; illustrated by Wendy Brown (1999)** This book tells the story of a husky puppy who dreams of pulling the sled of a winter patrol ranger.

## MUSIC
■ *Drums of the North* by **Pamyua (2005)** In the first strictly Yupik album ever recorded and winner of the 2007 Aboriginal People's Choice Music Award, Pamyua—one of Alaska's best regarded Native American music ensembles—joins forces with high school students from Anchorage's Alaska Native Heritage Center to bring you haunting drum-and-chant-accompanied dance melodies from the indigenous communities of the western part of the state.

# Alaska's ⚓nside Passage

## *Last Frontier by Ferry*

The Alaska portion of the Inside Passage (a coastal navigation route extending from Puget Sound, Washington, north to the Alaska Panhandle with a stop at Prince Rupert, British Columbia) packs kid-favorite, last-frontier adventures into a 500-mile stretch of narrow straits and protected coves through the Tongass National Forest—the world's largest contiguous temperate rain forest. The passing scenery is pure great white north—tidewater glaciers, glistening orca and humpback whales,

**BOOKS FOR PARENTS & KIDS**......
■ *The Inside Passage to Alaska* **by Art Wolfe (2008)** A boat excursion from Seattle to Glacier Bay captures Alaska's islands, untamed forests, and massive glaciers. Kids learn about the Inside Passage through photographs, facts, fun quotes, and reflections.

**BOOKS FOR PARENTS**......
■ *Alaska's Inside Passage* **by Kim Heacox (1997)** This compilation by award-winning photographer Kim Heacox includes a meltwater pool in Skagway, a Native American

## Know Before You Go

Chilkat dancer, immense icebergs, and isolated communities on the coastal route.

■ *Inside Passage: Living With Killer Whales, Bald Eagles, and Kwakiutl Indians* **by Michael Modzelewski (1997)** An inspiring tale of one man's sojourn into the wild; desiring to be closer to nature, Michael Modzelewski sets out from Vancouver to experience the paradise of Swanson Island. The

explorer spent 18 months on the island and chronicles his stories of living in isolation during severe weather conditions, swimming with whales, and his relationship with the wilderness and Kwakiutl Indians.

**MOVIES**......
■ *Journey Along the Inside Passage* **by Richard Olsenius (2008)** This thrilling documentary presents a firsthand account of traveling along the coastline from Puget Sound, British Columbia, to Juneau, Alaska.

mist-shrouded fjords, cascading waterfalls, iceberg-laden waters, and snow-white mountain goats precariously perched atop towering cliffs.

This is the main thoroughfare for all types of craft, but the ice, islands, and wildlife here are best experienced at a slower, more personal pace.

Rather than seeing the Inside Passage from the deck of a giant cruise ship, try the more authentically Alaska blue and yellow Alaska Marine Highway System (AMHS) passenger/cargo ferries. This allows for the freedom to choose what your child wants to see—including the intricate Tlingit totem poles and the native craftsmen who carve them—says Anchorage mom Erin Kirkland, who spent two weeks exploring the Inside Passage by ferry with her husband and two young sons. A plus: Summer trips come with interpreters from the Forest Service and the Fish and Wildlife Service who often make presentations about the wildlife and coastal environment with kids in mind.

"AMHS offers both the up close experiences with Mother Nature along the various routes, coupled with a healthy dose of Alaska characters," says Kirkland. "Kids love the ferry, and not just for the ride. Where else can a child stand on a top deck with the salty wind spraying in his or her face while saying good night to a bald eagle who insists upon escorting the ferry through a narrow passage? Or laughing as a hundred or more Dall's porpoises leap and dance in the boat's wake? AMHS is no tour boat, but the staff knows the landscape, water, and the state's many creatures, and do their darnedest to make sure kids know them, too." ■

# CONNECTIONS

**Alaska Marine Highway System**
*www.dot.state.ak.us/amhs*
Designated a scenic highway, the ferries wind through more than 1,000 coastal islands, large and small. Rangers are on board and there are a multitude of programs for kids. Make reservations early (up to a year in advance) as this is a popular way to travel.

**Sitka National Historical Park**
*www.nps.gov/sitk*
The oldest national park property in Alaska, Sitka was originally designated a "federal park" in 1890. On the site of the 1804 battle between the Tlingits and Russian fur traders, the historical park showcases the Russian Bishop's House, a modern visitors center with original totems and trails through a temperate rain forest.

**Totem Bight State Park**
*www.dnr.state.ak.us/parks*
Located just north of Ketchikan, Totem Bight hosts a re-created 19th-century clan house and 14 totem poles arranged along a self-guided interpretive trail.

**White Pass & Yukon Route Railroad**
*www.wpyr.com*
Located in Skagway, a stop along the Inside Passage, the White Pass & Yukon Route Railroad still provides an easy journey following a path the sourdoughs took on their way to find their fortunes in the mountains of Alaska. A journey taken by tens of thousands on their way to the gold fields during the 1890s Alaska gold rush, today's trip is made in one of the restored railcars named after the lakes and rivers of Alaska, Yukon, and British Columbia. Trips range from three to six hours.

# Glacier Bay

## *Domain of Show and Ice*

**N**o roads lead from Juneau to Glacier Bay, so for kids, getting there—either by air or water—pumps up the adventure quotient and offers a whale's- or bird's-eye view of how the Earth has changed since the last ice age.

On the trip over or through Glacier Bay National Park and Preserve, let the kids know that the shorelines and islands they see were covered by ice 200 years ago. Gliding back from the bay to the glaciers gives kids a visual time line of the melting ice through views of the vegetation.

Point out to them that the land nearest the bay (where the ice first receded) is lushly forested, while the plants and trees shrink and thin out as they move toward the barren ice face. The new vegetation has provided ample nutrition for wolves, moose, mountain goats, ptarmigan, and brown and black bears to survive. The sea also supports a new—in

geologic time, less than 200 years old—food chain for salmon, bald eagles, harbor seals, harbor porpoises, humpback whales (which summer here after wintering near Hawai'i), and killer whales.

Of course, the monster ice blocks in motion provide the biggest "wow" moments for wide-eyed kids. The park has nine tidewater glaciers, each of which emits a thunderous roar when it "calves"— chucking thousand-year-old icebergs (some up to 200 feet high) into the water. "What can compare to watching a tidewater glacier calve into the

"The tidal fluctuations in Glacier Bay can be as high as 25 feet! Be sure to keep this in mind when you decide to enjoy an after-lunch nap on the beach during your next paddling adventure."—*Did You Know?* *National Park Service website (www.nps.gov/glba)*

ocean?" says Steve Schaller, Glacier Bay's supervisory park ranger. "Glaciers have a tremendous influence on the land, and most kids have only seen this activity on television. Glacier Bay is one place on Earth that they can still experience the power of a calving glacier." Cruise ships ply the bay, but a one-day charter tour boat offers a more intimate sightseeing experience and can travel closer to the shore.

For an even closer look at the richness of the area, head to Bartlett Cove to take the kids on a guided kayak tour of the glacier-nourished water, vegetation, and marine life.

"Bartlett Cove is a protected cove with calm waters and a great place for kids to learn about sea kayaking," says Glacier Bay sea kayak outfitter Leah Okin-Magowan. "What appeals to kids about kayaking is that they are up close and personal to all the amazing things they saw from the boat. From a kayak, the whales are far more massive and the breath of a porpoise is magical.

## FAST FACTS

■ Among the living creatures that depend on the glacial ice for existence are **ice worms.** The worms of Muir Glacier (located at the end of Muir Inlet) were first written about in 1887.

■ There are more than **1,500 sea otters** in the waters of Glacier Bay.

■ Only **two cruise ships** per day are allowed to enter Glacier Bay National Park.

■ Although most glaciers are shrinking, the **Johns Hopkins Glacier** continues to grow.

■ The average age of the ice at the toe of the glaciers here is **75 to 200 years.**

■ A **Glacier Bay humpback whale** can weigh up to 50 tons.

"Kids can run their fingers through the kelp line while looking at all the baby sea creatures," summarizes Okin-Magowan, "and they take with them—for the rest of their lives—an understanding of the wonders of Glacier Bay." ■

---

**BOOKS FOR KIDS**..........................
■ *Totem Tale: A Tall Story From Alaska* by Deb Vanasse; illustrated by Erik Brooks (2006) This book tells of a magical night when the animals on an Alaska totem pole came to life. It introduces children to the role these iconic structures play in the cultures of the Glacier Bay region's indigenous communities.

**BOOKS FOR PARENTS**...................
■ *Kodiak Kreol: Communities of Empire in Early Russian America* by Gwenn A. Miller (2010) Many forget that the first white explorers

## Know Before You Go

of this part of Alaska arrived from the east. Reminders of imperial Russia's presence in Glacier Bay are visible in Sitka, a Kodiak Island town whose architectural centerpiece is an onion-domed Orthodox cathedral. This book explores places created by and left behind by this colonization movement.

**BOOKS FOR PARENTS & KIDS**......
■ *The Tlingit Encounter With Photography* by Sharon Bohn Gmelch

(2008) This book explores the impact of photography, brought to Glacier Bay in the 19th century by Russians and Americans, on the evolution of the modern cultural identity of the Tlingit, the region's original inhabitants.

**MUSIC**...........................................
■ *Glacier Bay* by Dennis Hysom (2001) This installment in Dennis Hysom's Last Great Places on Earth series sprinkles original electronic orchestrations with recordings of Glacier Bay's natural sounds, including whale songs, wolf cries, and wave crashes.

# Canadian R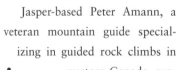ckies

*Bounty of Beauty*

Encompassing 69,498 square miles and five national parks (Banff, Jasper, Kootenay, Waterton Lakes, and Yoho), the Canadian Rockies are pure Canada: jagged peaks and protected wilderness, emerald green lakes and crystal clear waterfalls, grizzlies and glaciers, wildflowers and woodland bison. With so much to do and see in an area the size of Oklahoma, it can seem daunting to determine how to introduce this rugged and remote landscape to children.

Jasper-based Peter Amann, a veteran mountain guide specializing in guided rock climbs in western Canada, suggests starting with a feature intrinsically interesting to any kid—ice. And the most famous ice

here isn't just any frozen water. These are glaciers made from sky blue ice that is doubly appealing to kids because it is leftover from the last ice age.

"Visiting the Columbia Icefield gives kids an appreciation of how much things are changing in a natural worldscape," says Amann. "Much of North America's water is stored on glaciers, and from a peak in the icefield water flows into three different oceans—Arctic, Atlantic, and Pacific. You can tour the icefield by (motorized) snow coach, but it would be better for kids to take a glacier walk with a certified guide. Kids can see the wonders of the glacier, feel cold air rushing down the mountains, see water disappear into the bedrock, and experience something they can't do in many other places."

The 100-square-mile, 1,000-foot-deep Columbia Icefield is the largest reservoir of ice and snow in the Canadian Rockies. The most accessible glacier in the icefield is Athabasca, between Lake Louise and the town of Jasper on the Rockies' grand boulevard—the 142-mile Icefields Parkway.

Traveling the highway, which crests two mountain passes (Sunwapta and Bow Summit), becomes even more engaging for kids when they can follow along on a topographical map. Tracing the ridge route (paralleling the Continental Divide) with a finger helps them understand that they aren't simply taking one of the world's most spectacular drives, but more important are riding down the backbone of the North American continent along Canada's highest road.

Amann's recommended trail for kids is the Athabasca Glacier Forefield Trail (65 miles south of Jasper), so named because it crosses the glacier's

---

### FAST FACTS

■ Kootenay National Park is Canada's only national park where you can find both **glaciers and cactus plants.**

■ **Snow Dome,** a mountain in Jasper National Park, is considered by many scientists to be one of only two places in North America from which runoff flows toward **all three of the continent's oceans.**

■ **Grizzly bears** may be western Canada's most fearsome predator, but **elk** have injured and killed more humans here.

---

forefield—the rocky, barren area exposed by glacial melt. The trailhead is directly across from the Columbia Icefield Center, where interactive exhibits teach kids how glaciers form, grow, and retreat.

Although the glacier descends imperceptibly from the slope, kids will delight in the fact that they will get to stand on moving ice. And though it's possible to walk a mile to the edge of the three-mile-long glacier from here, heed the posted warning signs and don't let kids (or adults) trek onto the ice without an experienced guide, says Amann.

---

**BOOKS FOR PARENTS & KIDS** .....
■ *The Canadian Rockies: Pioneers, Legends, and True Tales* by Roger W. Patillo (2006) Kids and parents alike will enjoy these accounts of exploration and discovery in Canada's forbidding western wilderness.

**BOOKS FOR KIDS** .........
■ *Wayne Lynch's Canadian Rockies Wildlife for Kids* by Wayne Lynch (2011) One of Canada's most widely published wildlife photographers, Lynch has compiled a

## Know Before You Go

selection of photographs of animals that roam the Rockies— each accompanied by descriptive captions.

**BOOKS FOR PARENTS** .................
■ *A Taste of the Canadian Rockies* by Myriam Leighton and Chip Oliver (2002) This book prepares the dishes served in the region's resorts, including recipes from the kitchens of Banff Springs Hotel,

Château Lake Louise, Emerald Lake Lodge, and Mount Assiniboine Lodge, among others. It also contains a selection of photographs by Douglas Leighton, a leading Rocky Mountains landscape photographer.

■ *The Mounties* by Elle Andra-Warner (2009) Look into the early years of the Northwest Mounted Police. Legendary leaders are celebrated alongside its unsung heroes in this read about the enduring symbol of the Canadian west.

A glacier isn't an outdoor skating rink. Dangerous and potentially deadly crevasses lurk ahead, along with slippery footing and other obstacles.

"In the vast backcountry of the Canadian Rockies, it is the profound sense of wildness and how apart from civilization we actually are that immediately overcomes and impresses a child," says adventure travel specialist Dan Austin, who designs and leads Canadian Rockies tours. "Putting on crampons and walking out onto a living glacier is the best classroom ever. Where I witness the most wide-eyed amazement in our youngest travelers is when they venture out onto the massive Athabasca Glacier with one of the region's most accomplished mountaineering guides. Not only do kids walk on the glacier; they also learn all about what created the glacier and what challenges lay ahead for its survival."

Because winter lingers in the Canadian Rockies, Austin recommends a late July or August visit to ensure that hiking trails and roads are open; this is also prime wildlife viewing time.

"What kid won't be thrilled at sighting their first mother bear with cubs, soaring eagles, or a pack of black wolves?" says Austin. "The frequent elk or moose sightings are icing on the cake. Outfit the kids with a broken-in pair of hiking shoes, a two-piece rain suit, a journal, and point-and-shoot digital camera. It's great for them to create a log of what they see. Revisit it when you get home, and find out more about animals using educational wildlife books and movies."

Banff artist Max Elliott, author of the children's book *Canadian Rockies ABC* (2010), says that although the Rockies truly are where the wild things are, kids also will respond to—and remember for a lifetime—the calmer, smaller encounters.

"The Canadian Rockies allow children and adults alike to experience rare moments of aesthetic arrest—the sighting of a wild animal, northern lights in the night sky, or a majestic mountain touched with alpenglow," she explains. "Though adventure is key to attracting children to mountain places, I think that these quieter experiences also inspire imagination and a deep respect for nature. I had the experience as a child of being deeply impressed by a glacier hike, and vowed then to return to live in the Rockies someday. Banff National Park has now been my home for close to 30 years." ∎

## CONNECTIONS

**Canada's Tourism Authority of the Rockies**
*www.canadianrockies.net/familytravel*
This website has a section devoted to family travel, offering insider information on restaurants, accommodations, and outdoor activities that are particularly popular with children and their parents.

**Nature Canada**
*www.naturecanada.ca*
For authoritative information on the fragile state of the Rockies' endangered species, like the grizzly bear and woodland caribou, visit the website of Nature Canada, a member-based nonprofit conservation organization. Your kids may have an interest in joining its Nature Explorers online community, where young people meet to exchange ideas about conservation issues.

# Dinosaur Provincial Park

*North America's Bone Yard*

On the drive southeast from Calgary to Canada's badlands, eerie hoodoos (lifelike rock pinnacles rising up from the Red Deer River Valley) first signal to kids they've time-traveled back 75 million years. Although mesmerizing, this haunting wind-and-water carved landscape is but a gateway to a real *T. rex*–size dinosaur adventure.

Dinosaur Provincial Park—a UNESCO World Heritage site—is the final resting place of countless dinosaurs. During the late Cretaceous period, when the now semiarid region was a swampy coastal plain, dinosaurs thrived in the warm, subtropical climate.

Today, what remains of the dinosaurs—most impressive to kids are the bones—lies scattered naturally throughout the preserved areas of the park for kids to discover.

"The most amazing thing you first notice is the amount of dinosaur bones out there. It's the

real deal—no cement dinosaur statues here. You step on actual dinosaur bones, and sometimes you see a giant bone sticking out of nowhere and think, *shouldn't that be in a museum?*" says family travel writer Jennifer Merrick, who made a pilgrimage to the park with her nine-year-old son. "As soon as you get out to the fossil fields, kids will find dinosaur bones right, left, and center. There are so many dinosaur bones that soon kids won't even look for them any more because they're so common. Instead, kids start searching for microfossils, dinosaur teeth, and crocodile scute, the bony plates under the skin of prehistoric amphibians."

More than 40 species of dinosaurs have been discovered at the park, and although hundreds of specimens have been removed for display in museums, kids won't notice or care.

What will supremely disappoint them, though, would be driving all the way out to the park and for them not to be able to participate in its hands-on Fossil Safari.

Because most of the area is a protected natural preserve, access to the fossil sites is restricted and guided tours are limited—so make reservations well in advance, particularly if visiting during July or August. Try to get tickets for the Prep Lab tour. Here in a working lab are shelf upon shelf of fossils; this is where the technicians brush and pick at the bones.

During the two-hour fossil-finding program, kids learn what to look for and then are set free to dino-hunt, without digging or pocketing any treasures, of course.

Helpful human and printed guides assist kids in identifying what they've found. These moments of discovery bring dinosaurs back to life, even for older kids who have relegated their models and books to storage in the attic.

"Being there rekindled my son's love of dinosaurs," adds Merrick. "After visiting the park, we stopped for one last look from the edge of the canyon. My son pointed out toward the badlands, saying, 'Mom, look there's an *Albertosaurus* [a bipedal predator who roamed western North America more than 70 million years ago].'

"He was picturing what it must have looked like when the dinosaurs walked there," Merrick continues. "Learning about the history and the time period made the dinosaurs come to life. When we got back home, he got out his dinosaur books again." ■

---

**BOOKS FOR KIDS**..........................
■ *Paleoimagery: The Evolution of Dinosaurs in Art* **by Allen A. Debus and Diane E. Debus (2011)** This highly detailed children's book with illustrations of prehistoric dinosaurs, such as the *T. rex,* also includes stories on how artists have created paintings and sculptures of dinosaurs based on the scientists who reconstruct the prehistoric animals.

■ *National Geographic Kids Ultimate Dinopedia* **by Don Lessem; illustrated by Franco Tempesta (2010)** The perfect preparation manual for a trip to Dinosaur Provincial Park. Everything kids want to know about the creatures before you go.

## Know Before You Go

**BOOKS FOR PARENTS**...................
■ *Dinosaur Provincial Park: A Spectacular Ancient Ecosystem Revealed* **by Philip J. Currie and Eva B. Koppelhus (2005)** The two editors—a vertebrate paleontologist and a palynologist—provide insight on the ecosystem home of the late Cretaceous fossils. This book provides a scientific overview of the park's major fossil excavations, its history, and its flora and fauna. Deft illustrations show the park's wildlife.

**BOOKS FOR PARENTS & KIDS**.....
■ *Dinosaur Country: Unearthing the Alberta Badlands* **by Renie Gross**

**(1998)** The author explored the Red Deer River badlands to provide this historical overview of the site and its well-preserved dinosaur skeletons. Maps, charts, and drawings provide a comprehensive guide, with topics on the dinosaurs that roamed the region and excavations made during the great Canadian dinosaur rush.

**MOVIE**...........................................
■ *Great Canadian Parks—Dinosaur Provincial Park* **by Good Earth Productions (1996)** This DVD provides an overview of the park's cultural history and restricted areas. The wildlife, hidden treasures, and natural environment are brought to life through stories told by explorers and researchers.

# Musk🌀ka
## *Land of Loons and Lakes*

If you're looking for an unplugged place that's a world away from powerhouse Toronto, Canada's largest city, head two hours north—via Highways 400 and 11—by car to Muskoka, the heart of Ontario's "cottage country."

Families have gathered here for generations to revel in true wilderness that has somehow resisted the blandishments of modern times.

The 2,500-square-mile area includes 8,699 miles of shoreline, 17 historic towns and villages, and countless waterfalls bordered by the granite peaks of Algonquin Provincial Park to the east and the 30,000 islands of Georgian Bay Islands National Park to the west. It attracts more than 2.1 million visitors annually.

Spend the day in the region, paddleboarding on Lake Muskoka or exploring the Riverwalk and shops of Canada's waterfall capital, Bracebridge. Canoe,

sail, windsurf, kayak, or waterski on the region's more than 1,600 lakes. Plan an August visit to catch Algonquin Provincial Park's educational Thursday evening wolf howls, starring—weather permitting—the reclusive, inhabitant, four-pawed chorus.

Muskoka has just over 50,000 regular residents, with another 100,000 seasonal property

"I was first invited there when I was 12, and was instantly captivated by the scenery and the lovely weathered cottage that held within its walls the essence of a different era."—*Novelist Gabriele Wills*

owners usually summering there. Cottages are easy to rent and relatively cheap—a steal if you team up with other families. Or you can head to a place like Peninsula Lake's Pow-Wow Point Lodge, a 91-year-old, all-inclusive resort featuring simple summer pleasures like campfires, canoeing, and volleyball.

Muskoka is a throwback to an earlier time when families just hung out with no agenda and didn't rely on man-made amusements to distract them or their children.

"You can spend real time with your kids, seeing a simpler life through their eyes," says Kyle Jones, a mother of three who spent summers in Muskoka as a child and parent.

Let the kids make their own fun, use their imagination, and just play, so banish the electronics and revel in how self-directed kids can be, she advises.

"I remember the smell of pine with soft sand and needles underfoot, early mornings watching the sun burn off the mist on a glassy lake, hearing the loons float by, standing outside in sweats wondering if it really was going to be warm enough to swim in the lake that day—it always was," says Jones.

"I recall jumping off rock faces into deep, cold lakes, the laughter and bonfires and s'mores at night (and searching for the perfect marshmallow roasting stick by day)," she continues. "Having ant races, painting rock bugs, playing x's and o's in the sand. Boating to the marina for ice cream, watching canoe races, tubing, feeding the chipmunks, catching frogs and minnows, having pinecone races in the water, bathing in the lake, and swimming across it for the first time while parents canoed behind, sunning on the deck with friends, barbecuing everything—especially the first fish I ever caught (nothing tasted as good), seeing the night sky from a dock in the pitch black, and playing board games while listening to the rain. And running around barefoot all day (lunch seemed to consist of watermelon, popsicles, peaches, or whatever you could take on the run).

"There is so much to do," she concludes. "I always hoped all that fresh air would make the kids sleep in, but it never happened." ■

BOOKS FOR PARENTS..................
■ *At the Water's Edge: Muskoka's Boathouses* by John de Visser and Judy Ross (1997) Award-winning photographer joins forces with leading lifestyles journalist to take you in and around several Muskoka boathouses (covered docks where the region's vacationers store their sleek motorboats and vintage wooden launches). Exploring buildings constructed from the Victorian era through today, the book provides an architectural history overview of this unique feature of Muskoka's cultural landscape.

# Know Before You Go

BOOKS FOR PARENTS & KIDS.....
■ *Ghost Towns of Muskoka* by Andrew Hind and Maria Da Silva (2008) This well-researched book takes a look into the history of the vibrant communities that once inhabited now abandoned settlements in the Muskoka wilderness, most of which sprang up during a late 19th-century logging boom. Haunting photographs of the ghost towns' dilapidated surviving buildings complement the book's narratives.

■ *Muskoka Flavours: Guidebook & Cookbook* by Brenda Matthews and Dwayne Coon (2001) This collection is of regional Ontario recipes—watercress soup, wild rice and corn chowder, maple mousse, and butter tarts. Selections come from the kitchens of cottage country's favorite inns and restaurants. Each is accompanied by a profile of its parent establishment. An Ontario map orients you to the geography of the Muskoka area and shows the location of every place mentioned in the book.

# Saguenay Fj◉rd

## *Meeting Place of Whales*

Little-known fact: One of the world's longest fjords is in North America. It's true: Saguenay runs 62 miles from the heart of Canada's Quebec Province to Tadoussac, which in 1600 became France's first trading post in Canada. There it joins the St. Lawrence River, just a two-and-a-half-hour drive north of Quebec City. If you visit the area in winter, there's no experience quite as challenging or as fun for families as dogsledding.

Drive along the Ste.-Marguerite River, cloaked in pan ice and immense bricks of tumbled ice to Ferme 5 Etoiles, a 700-acre working farm in Sacré-Coeur-Saguenay that rescues and nurtures injured and orphaned wildlife (there's also a rustic cottage for rent here).

You'll see red- and white-tailed deer; a cluster of bison; Moe and Destiny, a pair of rescued moose; and Jacob, a young, 140-pound timber wolf, who jumps, cavorts, and nips at a handler who feeds him dog kibbles.

If you're lucky, Gilles, who lives here, will set up a sugaring table packed with ice. He'll pour the family puddles of fresh *sirop d'érable* (maple syrup) on the ice. It will freeze almost immediately; you'll roll it up on a Popsicle stick—a delicious Quebec tradition.

But don't come just to see the animals. Come to follow them—on a sled. Go over a rise to a snowy clearing crowded with some 50 malamutes and huskies. Sleds—they look like souped-up kids' sliders—await, each anchored with a snow brake and yoked by a complex series of cables to four dogs, which lie panting off heat in the subzero weather. They are born to run.

Sign a waiver of liability and a guide gives

● ● ● ● ● ● ● ● ● ● ● ● ● ● ● ● ● ● ● ● ● ● ●

## INSIDER TIP

To be a true Canadian, you would have had poutine once or twice in your life. You can find this dish at many restaurants and even at a few fast-food joints. It is a combination of French fries, fresh cheese curds, and brown gravy. During your time in Canada, be sure to try this classic Quebec-invented recipe.

● ● ● ● ● ● ● ● ● ● ● ● ● ● ● ● ● ● ● ● ● ● ●

you a slam-bang, condensed version of how to be a musher: "Place feet on either side of the sled, but ride on one and drop low when negotiating a corner. Jump on the thin foot brake when you want to slow—or stop (pressure is everything). Lean forward when going downhill. Don't let the dogs tangle the leads. It's really much easier than it seems." Two guides will lead the way, ready to help if your sled topples over or you fall off. Children under ten must sit in the sled basket, while an adult "drives."

As you approach your sled, the four canines attached to it—could be Volk, Loup, Canuck, and Tintin—erupt into a keening melody of howls and yelps. You step onto the back of the sled, grab the handles, and you're off.

You loop across a flat, open field on a clear trail, then enter dense forest with just a thread of trail. The dogs pull hard, desperate to make speed. The curves become sharper. You fight to keep your balance, to stay with the dogs as they turn. You hit a steep, winding downhill. Sometimes the dogs will just stop and you find yourself yelling, "Mush!"

After 45 minutes, you arrive at a yurt with six bunks, a fireplace, and a table and chairs—and a stunning view of the Saguenay.

The return trip is uphill. You end up running behind the sled as the dogs strain against gravity.

There is a short roller coaster of ups and downs and sharp turns—one over a brook that is a bit hair-raising—and then you are in the flat. For 20 minutes, the dogs hurtle for home. You clatter into camp.

"It is an exhilarating experience," says Roch Anctil, head of Boutique Voyages. "It's best for teens because they can actually stand up and drive the sled. But for any young one just being out in the snow and the fresh air in the middle of the wilderness—it's the experience of a lifetime."

More than 900 feet deep and 2 miles wide in places, the Saguenay fjord is also one of the best places in the world to see whales. Thirteen different species ply these krill-rich waters, including the blue whale—at up to 100 feet long, the world's largest. But the nearly 500 beluga whales, which breed in cold waters near Tadoussac and

# Yum!

■ **Café Bohème** Eat at this bistro located in historic Tadoussac's original general store. Kids will love its desserts (try the chocolate *croustillant*),

and they can borrow books and toys to use while dining.

■ **Restaurant Chez Georges** For some regional food in Chicoutimi, head here. Since opening in 1960, this landmark serves home-style favorites and also has a kids' menu that includes chicken and pasta.

> "A deep and powerful watercourse that is the river and road of the Kingdom and the lands of the Saguenay."—*Explorer Jacques Cartier (1535)*

live here year-round, are most readily spotted. The whales are up to 20 feet long, travel in pods, and communicate with a cacophonous mix of clicks, whistles, and clangs.

At the confluence of the Saguenay and St. Lawrence River is the Saguenay-St. Lawrence Marine Park, and there are strict prohibitions about approaching the whales, but the viewing is easy. Head out in a sea kayak or Zodiac, or take one of the ubiquitous whale-watching tours. Or just eyeball the whales from the Pointe-Noire viewing platform.

If you've never taken the family camping—too buggy, the ground is too hard, what if it rains?—a great place to introduce kids to the concept is about a mile from Tadoussac's crowds deep in the wilds of Saguenay Fjord National Marine Conservation Area. Head for a classic eight-room family chalet run by Parcs Quebec overlooking Baie-Ste.-Marguerite, home to belugas year-round. In warm weather, it's an easy four-mile drive through dense forest; in winter, access is only by ski, snowshoe, or snowmobile—impractical for most families.

At Camp Rustique Anse-de-la-Barge, the emphasis is on rustic—it's as close to camping as you can get while still staying in a shelter. You bring your own water, food, cooking gear (there's a propane stove), candles or hurricane lights, and bedding or sleeping bags (the place offers bare mattresses). There is no power and just an outhouse. Wood is piled outside to stoke the fireplace on cool nights. On a summer evening, you sit on the open porch counting belugas as the sun bleeds into the water.

"It is easy to feel that you are as far from civilization as possible," says the park's director Daniel Groleau. "Kids really respond to the wildness. They can explore the forest by day and go down to the shore. When it gets dark it's eerily quiet, except in winter when the ice creaks and groans. And the stars are clearer than you'll ever see in the city. It can't be much different from when the French were running the fur trade along this river in the 1600s." ∎

## FAST FACTS

■ The fjord blends **fresh water** and **seawater** that comes from the Atlantic Ocean. Because the densities are different, kids can observe two different layers in the water, similar to oil and vinegar. **This also allows both freshwater and seawater marine life to live together.**

■ **Blue whales** found in the fjord can grow to the size of about **25 elephants** and can blow water spouts up to **33 feet high.**

■ The rocks here along the Canadian Shield are believed to be around **950 million years old.**

■ Along the fjord, **the winter ice moves with the tides.**

■ Pierre Chauvin built the first trading post near today's Tadoussac in 1600, and young **French explorer Samuel de Champlain** came in 1603.

# Lighthouse Route

## *Where Pirates Rule*

Twenty-plus lighthouses stand sentry along Nova Scotia Lighthouse Route, the 220-mile Halifax-to-Yarmouth coastal drive paralleling the South Shore first charted by Pierre du Gua, Sieur de Monts, and Samuel de Champlain in 1604. Weatherworn fishing villages, secret sea caves, and tranquil coves harbor treasures and tales of legendary explorers, rum runners, and privateers.

The latter refers both to large wooden-hulled ships and the men who sailed them. These private, legal pirates of sorts were authorized by the British in the late 1700s to defend maritime communities by raiding enemy American supply vessels. British North America's leading privateer port, Liverpool, is midpoint along the Lighthouse Route.

Plan an early summer visit so kids can experience the musket fire, precision marching, and living-

history military encampment of Privateer Days, centered on Fort Point Lighthouse Park.

"Walking through the re-created King's Orange Rangers tent city is transforming for parents and children," says Phaedra Charlton-Huskins, economic development officer for the local Regions of Queens Municipality. "The child reenactors share with kids what it was like to grow up in Liverpool during the heyday of privateering, when children were drafted and part of the military."

For a look at the life of a lighthouse keeper's child, let the kids loose at hunchback-shaped Fort

"I have travelled around the globe. I have seen the Canadian Rockies, the American Rockies, the Andes and the Alps and the Highlands of Scotland; but for simple beauty, Cape Breton outrivals them all."—*Alexander Graham Bell*

Point Lighthouse. Here they can race to the top of the tower to toot the loud, hand-crank foghorn, and then descend to the compact living quarters to view the video recollections of a keeper's child who moved to the lighthouse at age five.

"Kids think it's a playhouse, but it was an actual house. Seeing where the families lived helps them understand the struggles of lighthouse keepers," adds Charlton-Huskins.

Outside, join a walking tour of Perkins House Museum. Costumed interpreters lead the way, but the kids really start to listen when the resident hologram ghosts appear out of nowhere to recount portions of privateer Simeon Perkins's detailed journal.

Every lighthouse and hamlet along the South Shore has seafaring tales. In Old Town Lunenburg, a UNESCO World Heritage site 40 miles east of Liverpool, the stories are shared by local old salts—retired fishermen and sea captains—who answer questions and swap fish stories aboard the *Theresa E. Connor*. Canada's oldest salt bank schooner is moored wharf-side at the waterfront Fisheries Museum of the Atlantic.

Kids can spend a couple of hours climbing around the museum's maritime vessels; counting the lobsters and eels in the aquarium; watching the wooden-boat craftsmen and scallop shuckers; and soaking in the ocean smells, textures, creatures, and shells—all within a child's reach at the Tidal Touch Tank. ∎

## BOOKS FOR PARENTS

■ *Lighthouse Island: Our Family Escape* by Bill Baker (2004) Baker recounts his adventures purchasing Nova Scotia's uninhabited lighthouse on Henry Island and rebuilding much of its deteriorating structure. The 150-acre retreat is described through his personal tales, historical context, and photographs.

## BOOKS FOR KIDS

■ *My Home Nova Scotia* by Anne Rosen and Jeff Cox (2011) A story for young travelers of the province's land and landscape. From the lighthouses of Lunenburg to the beaches of Peggy's Cove, look at the place in rhyme and

## Know Before You Go

illustrations designed to stimulate the traveler's imagination.

■ *B Is for Bluenose: A Nova Scotia Alphabet* by Susan Tooke (2008) Become a Nova Scotia expert by learning about the culture and wonders of the place. This alphabetized book answers questions such as: Who were the first people of Nova Scotia? What massive star-shaped fortress can be found in Halifax? And what type of water plant provides food and shelter for wildlife and also lessens erosion? Along with fun facts, kids will love the whimsical illustrations.

■ *Blizzard of Glass: The Halifax Explosion of 1917* by Sally M. Walker (2011) The story of the famous 1917 collision of two ships in Halifax Harbour and the explosion that resulted, followed immediately by a major snowstorm.

## MUSIC

■ *Lovely Ernestina: Songs of the Sea* produced by Whaling City Sound (2005) Sing along to songs in the style of 19th-century seafarers aboard a Nova Scotian ship. The chantey chorus-style songs will have the entire family stomping their feet to the music of dueling violins with catchy lyrics based on maritime themes.

# Avaln Peninsula

## *Continent's Easterly Edge*

There's a storybook charm to Newfoundland's Avalon Peninsula that resonates immediately with kids.

The fairy-tale floating icebergs, giggle-inducing town names (Cupids, Paradise, Heart's Desire), and quirky summer time zone—1 hour and 30 minutes ahead of the eastern daylight time—will convince young travelers that this easternmost edge of North America was created just for them.

There is plenty of history to soak in here—including the provincial capital of St. John's, one of the oldest English cities in North America—but it's the water and whales that captivate kids, and

### BOOKS FOR KIDS...............................

■ *Fables, Fairies and Folklore of Newfoundland* by Alice Lannon and Mike McCarthy (1991) Kids will love reading about the magical side of the island known as "the rock" and all its interesting but unusual features. Explore your superstitious side and read the tales of "Big Black Bull of Hollow Tree," "The Harbour Grace Prophecy," "The Thing from the Sea," and "The Fairy Captive."

## Know Before You Go

### BOOKS FOR PARENTS...................

■ *Newfoundland and Labrador Book of Everything: Everything You Wanted to Know About Newfoundland and Labrador and Were Going to Ask Anyway* by Martha Walls (2007) This book features thousands of interesting facts and stats about the island and its unusual place-names (Goobies, Joe Batts Arm, Come-by-Chance). Notable Newfoundlanders catalog their

favorite Newfie words, and artist Gerald Squires shares his best memories from growing up on Exploits Island.

■ *The Iambics of Newfoundland: Notes From an Unknown Shore* by Robert Finch (2008) This travelogue takes readers through the close-knit community and natural environment of the island. Finch's beautiful sketches accompany the vivid tales, which are humorous but also chronicle the hardships many families faced.

## INSIDER TIP

Head to Witless Bay Ecological Reserve for whale-watching. From Mobile, venture out on the 35-foot *Molly Bawn* sailboat, which heads to the four-island oasis, nearly 25 miles south of St. John, to see massive humpbacks. But whale-watching is only half the fun. Witless Bay is also a breeding reserve for seabirds. Kids will be amazed as thousands of shrieking birds fly by in unison—kittiwakes, murres, Leach's storm-petrels, and puffins all reside on the island.

the walkabilty that keeps them out of the car. Like the winding coastline, spring and winter weather here is rugged and rocky. And June, although good for iceberg viewing, can be cold and foggy. Schedule a summer (July and August) or fall (September) visit to enjoy outdoor activities with less wind and more sun.

Hit the water to introduce kids to peninsula life at sea level. Experienced preteen kayakers may be able to go solo, but this is the North Atlantic, so opting for tandem boats—child sitting in front and guide in back—is the safer choice. And not focusing on paddling will give kids the chance to absorb the sights and sounds of the surrounding ocean.

"It's an incredible experience for a child because he or she can get so close—within 20 to 30 feet—to the humpback whales or the icebergs," says Shannon Guihan, who grew up on the Avalon Peninsula and led sea kayak tours here. "It's just the child, the ocean, the guide, and the whale."

Launch out of Witless Bay to give kids an offshore peek at the Witless Bay Ecological Reserve, summer breeding ground for more than two million seabirds, including North America's largest Atlantic puffin colony. Back on shore, head to St. John's and

ice cream at Moo Moo's Dairy Bar. Guihan adds, "St. John's is cool for kids because it is small enough to walk around. From downtown, you can walk past little jelly bean–colored wooden row houses to Signal Hill overlooking St. John's Harbour."

Allow plenty of time to explore. Kids will want to head underground at the Johnson Geo Centre, a geological interpretation center built in a natural rock basin (the exhibit area's exposed rock walls are 550 million years old), and climb Cabot Tower at the Signal Hill National Historic Site—the spot where Guglielmo Marconi's first transatlantic wireless signal was received in 1901. To help kids appreciate the military significance of the fortifications here—and witness the rousing fife and drum concert—visit during the Signal Hill Tattoo (July 1 to mid-August), when costumed actors bring the Royal Newfoundland Regiment of Foot circa 1795 back to full, musket-firing glory.

For some fun, visit the town of Cupids, established by John Guy as England's first colony in Canada. Tour the plantation remnants, a functioning archaeological dig. The Cupids Legacy Centre displays treasure from various digs, including silver coins, bottle shards, and 150,000 other artifacts. ■

## FAST FACTS

■ The peninsula was **named for the Isle of Avalon** from Arthurian legend by Sir George Calvert, an early settler.

■ More than **20,000 gannets roost atop a 300-foot-high rock** just yards from shore at Cape St. Mary's Ecological Reserve, in the southwest corner of the Avalon Peninsula.

NORTH AMERICA

Sea of Cortes

MEXICO

Central Highlands

Old Havana

CUBA

PUERTO RICO

El Yunque

Atlantic Ocean

Antigua

GUATEMALA

Canopy Tours

COSTA RICA

Galápagos

ECUADOR

Amazon River

PERU

Machu Picchu

BRAZIL

SOUTH AMERICA

Pacific Ocean

Rio de Janeiro

Map Key

◻ Selected point of interest

0        1,000 miles

0        1,500 kilometers

# Caribbean, Mexico, & South America

......................................

# El Yunque
## Mountain Cloud Forest

**N**amed for the Taino god Yuquiyu, who was said to rule from his mountaintop home, El Yunque on the island of Puerto Rico is the only tropical rain forest in the U.S. National Forest system. Located in the Luquillo Mountains on the eastern side of the island, the 44-square-mile park features lush mountain cloud forest along its steep slopes.

"I still bring family and friends to El Yunque as one of the top attractions when people come visit me in Puerto Rico," says Adriana Partida, who grew up outside San Juan. "The rain forest is absolutely gorgeous—as you climb to higher ground you almost feel like you are walking in the clouds, since there are days when the fog is very thick."

After feeling the cool mist of La Coca Falls, a straight sheet of water that falls 85 feet to tumbled boulders, older children will enjoy the hike along the 2.5-mile El Yunque Trail to Cerro El Toro, the highest point in the park at 3,533 feet.

Keep an eye out for some of the park's 240 species of trees, 23 of which are found only in El Yunque,

### INSIDER TIP

Locals flock to Fort San Felipe del Morro in Old San Juan every Sunday to fly kites. The 16th-century citadel guarded the entrance of San Juan Bay from seafaring enemies. The broad, windy plain in front of El Morro forms the perfect stage for kite flying, with dozens of brightly colored chiringas taking to the air every week.

and 1,500 types of bromeliads. Colorful bird species include the Puerto Rican lizard-cuckoo, the elfin-woods warbler, and the endangered Puerto Rican parrot. Listen for the distinctive two-note chirp of the coqui, a thimble-size tree frog native to Puerto Rico.

Karen Bate visited El Yunque with her daughters, Madeline, Veronica, and Sarah, then 13, 16, and 18. "They loved it. It was hot, wet, and steamy, and began to rain just as we arrived," Bate says. "They had a lot of fun looking for the rare Puerto Rican parrot and, of course, the tree frogs. They've always adored the tree frogs and they would yell, 'Coqui! Coqui!' outside their grandmother's windows in Puerto Rico all night long. The hunt for the parrots and frogs was an adventure—maybe they'd be the ones who spotted these hard-to-see creatures."

This biodiversity of Puerto Rico, which straddles the line between the Atlantic Ocean and the Caribbean Sea and is about the size of Connecticut, extends to the island's surrounding ocean, where the warm waters and encircling mangroves of several bays form ideal conditions for dinoflagellates, microscopic organisms that glow brightly when slightly disturbed. Motorboats damage the dinoflagellates' ecosystem, so many companies offer kayaking trips to the bioluminescent bays at La Parguera, Fajardo, and Vieques.

"I've been to the Fajardo bioluminescent lagoon more than six times in the past eight years," Partida says. "It's really an extraordinary and fun experience. You start in the ocean, kayaking at night—without moonlight is even better—through a trail of mangroves, and as you come into the bay, you start seeing how your paddle glows in the dark more and more. Sometimes, you can even see the trails where the fish are swimming."

Located just off the eastern coast of Puerto Rico, Vieques is the largest of the Spanish Virgin Islands. Its Phosphorescent Bay at Puerto Mosquito, on the largely

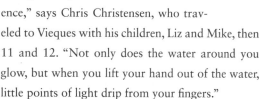

undeveloped southern side of the island, allows the bioluminescence to shimmer brilliantly in the absence of city lights.

"Swimming with bioluminescence was a magical experience," says Chris Christensen, who traveled to Vieques with his children, Liz and Mike, then 11 and 12. "Not only does the water around you glow, but when you lift your hand out of the water, little points of light drip from your fingers."

"I swam slowly, mostly backward so I could look down and watch the glowing around my arms and body," his son, Mike, remembers. "Sometimes I would just sweep my arm across the water, just under the surface, a long clean stroke to get the glow going."

Children can learn about evolution and adaptation from the dinoflagellates, says Fernando Gilbes-Santaella of the University of Puerto Rico. "They can understand how important it is to preserve and well manage these bays," he says. "It is a beautiful way to show them the wonders of our planet and how important it is to study and protect them." ∎

---

**BOOKS FOR KIDS**..................
■ *Sweet Dreams: El Yunque Dreams* **by Jo Anne Valle (2011)** Islita's grandmother teaches her about Puerto Rico through dreams, taking her on a journey to the beautiful rain forest of El Yunque.

**BOOKS FOR PARENTS & KIDS**......
■ *Natural Puerto Rico* by Alfonso **Silva Lee (1998)** Puerto Rico is

## Know Before You Go

known for its indigenous coqui. But Puerto Rico's variety of animals goes far beyond its famous frog to the snails, lizards, birds, and other nonhuman species of the island. This book shows the fauna with beautiful photos and provides scientific descriptions written for young adults.

**MUSIC**..................
■ *Jibaro Hasta el Hueso: Mountain Music of Puerto Rico* **by Ecos de Borinquen (2003)** *Música jíbara* is the national music of Puerto Rico, originating from the *jíbaros*, rural mountain dwellers who live in the heart of the island. The simple melodies are usually performed on the *cuatro*, a Puerto Rican lute, or the *güiro*, a Taino Indian percussion instrument crafted out of a gourd.

# Old Havana

## *Afro-Cuban Culture*

To get an inside glimpse of daily life for the average Cuban, you and your kids should skip the hotels and stay in one of the hundreds of *casas particulares* sprinkled throughout Havana, the Cuban equivalent of B&Bs and one of the few forms of private enterprise permitted by the country's socialist government.

Besides costing a fraction of a hotel, staying inside the home of a Cuban family puts your family in the middle of a residential neighborhood, where you will awake to the sounds of daily life—street vendors calling out "*¡pregones!*" to advertise their wares, children playing ball in the street, and salsa music blasting from open windows.

"Staying with a family was critical to get the cultural rhythms," says Mark Goehring, father of two who visited Havana with his children. "The kids got to see the day-to-day life and practice some of their Spanish with people who really cared for them."

Also, staying in a home gives parents and kids alike a chance to hear the Cuban perspective on living in a socialist society.

"The owners of our particular *casa* were both born just after the revolution and we often talked politics," Goehring adds. "The kids learned about [revolutionary leader] Che Guevara from his often-present image around town. We actually had a 'Che-spotting' game."

Live like a Havanan outside the home by visiting the places Cubans take their own kids, like the Coppelia ice cream parlor; El Cinecito, a movie theater that exclusively screens films for kids; or La Colmenita, a children's theater company housed in the Teatro Nacional.

Stroll the streets of Old Havana, and you will inevitably encounter strains of *son*—the old style of Cuban music made famous by the group Buena Vista Social Club—wafting down the colonial streets from bars and cafés where live bands play.

Music is at the heart of

Cuba's culture, and Cuba's African heritage is at the core of its music. Unlike in North America, where drumming was often banned in slave communities, "in Cuba, the conditions existed for an explicitly African culture to flourish into the present day," notes Ned Sublette, author of *Cuba and Its Music* (2004). "Maybe one of the most important lessons Cuba can teach a visiting child from the United States is the same lesson it can teach adults: the richness of Afro-Cuban culture. In Cuba one quickly sees that there are other modes of black-white social relations than the ones North Americans have internalized."

The best place to get an authentic taste of Afro-Cuban culture is at the weekly *Sábado de Rumba* (rumba Saturday) held in the shady patio of El Gran Palenque, home of the Conjunto Folklórico Nacional, the national folklore ensemble founded by the Cuban state in 1962. The show starts with a performance of the more traditional Afro-Cuban music and dance styles associated with Santeria, and ends with a high-energy rumba that gets

foreigners and Cubans alike up and dancing. Kids will experience firsthand how Cubans like to have a good time.

Music is a way to end any day in Havana, so as the sun sets, stroll along the Malecón, the seaside walkway—there guitar-bearing troubadours will serenade you and your kids for a tip. ■

---

**BOOKS FOR PARENTS**
■ *Cuba: After the Revolution* by **Bernard Wolf (1999)** This photo essay presents a glimpse of daily life in contemporary Cuba, focusing on 12-year-old Havana resident Ana Moreira and her family. The accompanying narrative gives an overview of the politics, economics, diversity, and social history of Cuba.

**MOVIES**
■ *Viva Cuba* (2007) This independent Cuban film tells the story of two children, best friends Malú and Jorgito. When they learn that

## Know Before You Go

Malú's mother plans to leave Cuba and take Malú with her, the two run away together to the eastern side of the island. Winner of the Junior Prize at the Cannes Film Festival, *Viva Cuba* explores the issue of emigration from the literal point of view of the country's children.

**MUSIC**
■ *Cuba* by **Putumayo Presents: Various Artists (1999)** This compilation brings together a sampling

of *son,* a soulful, energetic genre that was the precursor to salsa. Featuring stars such as Ibrahim Ferrer and Irakere, this album will get you moving to a Cuban beat.

■ *Rumba Caliente 88/77* by **Los Muñequitos de Matanzas (1999)** Arguably the best rumba group to come out of Cuba, Los Muñequitos de Matanzas has been around since 1952 and still tours internationally. The group has been instrumental in the preservation of Afro-Cuban traditions, and received a Grammy Award nomination in 2001.

# Sea of Cortés
## *The World's Aquarium*

**Z**ada can spot a bird nest in a split second, turn over low-tide rocks carefully to find brittle stars, and will tell you the difference between sea lions and seals," says Nancy Jones, who, with her husband, Ethan, and daughter, Zada, six, has lived on a sailboat in the Sea of Cortés for nearly three years. "She thrives on nature, and the Sea of Cortés is the place to be for the most hands-on experiences with nature, both on land and in the water."

Also known as the Gulf of California, the Sea of Cortés stretches 700 miles along the northwestern coast of Mexico, hemmed in by the stark desert landscape of the Baja California peninsula. As the Joneses have found, there is no better place to witness the magic of Earth.

"Some days the milky pale blue sky matches the water and a horizon line can't be found," observes Jones. "Zada will comment on the beauty of it, or count the gradation lines from the various mountain ranges as they go from dark to faint gray, eon to eon."

The deep green waters here hold such astonishing biodiversity that the region has been called a natural laboratory for studying marine species, and oceanographer Jacques Cousteau called it the "world's aquarium."

More baleen whale species can be found in this sea than anywhere else in the world, from gray

## OBJECTS OF WONDER

At times called devilfish, **manta rays** are true wonders of the sea. Ghosting along on blue-black fins that can reach a wingspan of nearly 30 feet, these filter feeders are friendly to humans. In the Sea of Cortés, they can be seen swimming and leaping clear out of the water.

whales to humpbacks to blue whales, the largest living animal. Bottlenose dolphins, manta rays, and sea lions abound.

"One thing you can see in the Sea of Cortés, and something that always surprises people, is sometimes you'll be sailing offshore and you'll observe the whole sea torn up with chop. And it's dolphins—hundreds and hundreds of dolphins, all swimming together," says James Glover, who has lived in Baja California Sur for 25 years and publishes the *BajaInsider*.

"It is such a rich sea," says Flip Nicklin, who has been traveling to the region for more than 50 years, since his childhood spent between San Diego and Ensenada, Baja California. A *National Geographic* photographer and marine biologist, Nicklin is one of the world's leading photographers of whales.

"The spirit of the sea comes from looking at these animals," he says. "To look into the eye of a whale—it takes us so far beyond ourselves and our basic needs. For the world to have these big animals that make us look puny, you need all the rest of the ocean to work and be healthy. That's a great message for kids."

Thousands of gray whales migrate from Alaska's Bering Sea to the Sea of Cortés every year to mate and give birth in the warmer waters. The 6,000-mile journey can take them two to three months to complete, and is one of the longest migrations of any mammal. They can be seen spouting, breaching, and slapping their tails all about Baja California from January to March.

"With all the issues of the sea, there's probably not more iconic animals than whales and dolphins," Nicklin says. "Gray whales and humpbacks were taken to the edge of extinction, but now they've recovered—it's a hopeful story for kids to be part of."

Whale sharks congregate near Bahía de los Ángeles. The largest fish in the ocean, they can grow to more than 40 feet in length—but as filter feeders,

# CONNECTIONS

**BajaInsider**
*www.bajainsider.com*
This online news magazine is a one-stop resource for living and traveling in Baja California. It provides details on the prime destinations in the region, accommodations and restaurants, fishing reports, diving and sea kayaking companies, and essential information, such as passport requirements for Mexico. Be sure to visit the Adventures section to read personal stories of readers who've cruised through the Sea of Cortés and swum with sea lions.

**Nature Conservancy**
*www.nature.org/ourinitiatives/regions/
northamerica/mexico/placesweprotect/
gulf-of-california.xml*
Visit this website to learn more about the challenges facing the Sea of Cortés and its rich wildlife, and just why it's so crucial as an ecosystem. A separate section is devoted to the Baja California peninsula and its rare Mediterranean habitat, the only example in North America and one of only five worldwide.

**American Cetacean Society**
*www.acsonline.org/factpack*
This site provides quick facts on whales and dolphins. Species found in the Sea of Cortés, such as the gray whale, humpback whale, bottlenose dolphin, and blue whale, all have their own page.

they're harmless and even friendly toward swimmers. "When kids find out they can literally swim within inches of a giant animal, it teaches them to not be afraid of animals, and the planet," Glover says.

"We daily had whale sharks swimming by our boat in Bahía de los Ángeles," Jones says. "Zada jumped into the water and got a close look at an incredibly spotted shark. She made eye contact with the shark and soon it slowly, with its big tail low in the water, started swimming. The shark went out 30 yards, circled, and came back to the dinghy with Zada right beside him the entire time. During this whole interaction with the whale shark, Zada had a huge grin on her face. She knew it was a filter feeder and that it would not eat her."

A large colony of sea lions welcomes visitors at Islas Islotes, off the shore of La Paz. Kids will be delighted with the inquisitive pups that love to imitate swimmers. "The sea lions seem as interested in kids as the kids are in the sea lions," Nicklin says. "Just play around, and they play with you," Glover adds. "If you do a somersault, so will the sea lions."

One of the best ways to encounter marine animals is by kayak, quietly traversing the calm waters.

Many companies in Loreto and La Paz offer sea kayaking tours around the desert islands of Isla Carmen, Espíritu Santo, and Coronado, whose profile is dominated by a dormant volcano.

"I love the silence of kayaking," Glover says. "While you're paddling, the visibility in the water is amazing. You can see manta rays, huge balls of baitfish like mackerel and sardines, maybe even sea horses. You're not going to observe that in a powerboat."

The rocky, arid islands also support hundreds of species of birds and reptiles, such as blue-footed boobies, pelicans, and iguanas. Tidal pools shelter hermit crabs and sea anemones, while exotic-sounding species, such as tiger reef eels, butterflyfish, and zebra morays, twine around coastal coral reefs. There's never a lack of creatures for curious children to discover. ∎

**BOOKS FOR PARENTS**..................
■ *Sea of Cortez: A Cruiser's Guidebook* by Heather Bansmer and Shawn Breeding (2009) This painstakingly researched guide is a must for sailors and cruisers in the region, detailing the many remote anchorages in the Sea of Cortés. The authors don't stop at navigation—they also provide city maps, point out the best hiking trails and dive spots, and describe marine and terrestrial animals in the area.

## Know Before You Go

■ *The Log from the Sea of Cortez* by John Steinbeck (1951) In 1940, Steinbeck and a close friend, the author Ed Ricketts, spent six weeks exploring the coves and examining the marine life of the Sea of Cortés. The result is this endearing travelogue filled with Steinbeck's vivid imagery and musing on the wonders of nature

and science, the remote coastal communities of Baja California, and the travails of life at sea.

**BOOKS FOR PARENTS & KIDS**.....
■ *The Girl of the Sea of Cortez* by Peter Benchley (1983) The author of *Jaws* paints a friendlier picture of the sea in this book, in which a young girl must protect an offshore seamount—and the manta ray that lives near it—from the fishermen who would destroy it.

# Central Highlands
## *Miracle of Butterflies*

The Aztec believe that when we die our souls become butterflies. So you could say that there's one place where souls gather in the billions during one of Earth's greatest natural events—a 2,500-mile monarch butterfly migration that starts in Canada and the northern United States and ends in a 60-square-mile part of central Mexico's volcanic highlands.

For you and your kids to witness this miracle of nature, head to the tiny town of Angangueo, with its cobbled streets and white-stuccoed, red-roofed buildings, where you land on the doorstep of a boreal forest overtaken by clouds of monarchs. For at least 10,000 years, these butterflies—each weighing no more than a fifth of a penny—have traveled with uncanny accuracy to a place they've never before visited. In migrating monarchs' six- to nine-month life cycle, they begin the return trip before dying somewhere along the way—which means their offspring must repeat the amazing journey without parental guidance.

The butterflies arrive in fall and winter in central Mexico, where conditions are perfect for

## GET INVOLVED
......................................

■ **MONARCH MOTEL:** One way kids can have fun and help the monarch population is to start a little conservation area in the backyard. Have them plant a milkweed tree and even a butterfly bush to help attract butterflies. Then before they know it, there will be new-generation monarchs right before their eyes.

breeding—neither too cold nor hot, dry nor wet. One of the best places to see them is at El Rosario Monarch Butterfly Sanctuary, the closest to Mexico City (129 miles) of four public monarch refuges.

At the site, you hike an hour upward to 10,000 feet. It sounds like an ordeal—but it is a multi-generational experience, something of a pilgrimage. "I was surprised that most of the visitors were Mexicans themselves," says Annie Griffiths, both a mother of two and a photographer who has documented the monarchs. "I saw visitors so elderly that they were carried up on stretchers by family members and porters."

Here some 150 million butterflies stud pines like ornaments, overwhelming branches in great rustling clumps. The power of their numbers is staggering.

"This experience turns photographers into children," says Griffiths. "You can't shoot fast enough, and yet it's a tremendous challenge to take a picture that gives outsiders a sense of the sheer volume of butterflies that gather. No question, this is one of the great natural wonders of the world."

The monarch sites are a natural classroom. "Talk to kids ahead of time about a butterfly's life cycle," says Griffiths. A monarch remains motionless until it mates in spring, laying its eggs on milkweed plants on which fledgling caterpillars feed. Explain how a butterfly develops through four stages: from egg to caterpillar to chrysalis to the gossamer black and orange creature so familiar to most kids.

"And emphasize how much the Mexicans have done to protect their forests," says Griffiths. Harm a single butterfly and you're fined 500 pesos. In the last decade, Mexico has tripled the size of protected areas, and illegal logging—which threatens the butterflies' forested lifeblood—has dropped 48 percent since 2008.

"And make them aware of migrations around the world and how this one is so miraculous," she

### FAST FACTS

■ The **male monarch** has a black spot over a vein on both hind wings. Females don't have any spots.

■ **Monarchs are poisonous.** They won't harm humans, but they do harm their predators, such as birds, mice, lizards, and frogs.

■ During the monarchs' time in Mexico, they **fill the trees in the sanctuaries.** Sometimes so many butterflies fill a branch that it becomes **invisible and has been known to break.**

adds. The monarchs are one of Earth's few creatures that can latitudinally and longitudinally reorient themselves; so fine-tuned are their instincts that they can flawlessly funnel through narrow channels of airspace to their destination.

"Apart from the wonder of seeing millions of butterflies, which kids seem to universally love," says Griffiths, "families can teach their kids about the biology of this amazing migration, as well as environmental lessons about preserving forests and the crushing results that can happen due to climate change." In 2002, 70 percent of the butterfly population was wiped out by a freak winter storm.

Everyone who speaks of meeting the monarchs comes away blessed and astonished. "The thing that really surprises kids," Griffiths reports, "is when a mass of butterflies take flight. They actually make a lot of noise."

The butterflies ultimately make a personal connection as one, or maybe more, alight on your child. "Instill in kids how delicate these butterflies are," says Griffiths, "and that the best way to have a close encounter is to sit still and let them land on you." ■

### INSIDER TIP

Be sure to pack good walking shoes. No matter how you get to the butterfly reserve, you will be doing a lot of walking. Also pack a sweatshirt. It gets cold at night and when you climb to a higher altitude.

# Can⋆py Tours
## *Soaring Through Treetops*

Trips into the "canopy"—the layer of branches and leaves formed by the tops of trees—in the rain forests of Costa Rica started as a way to study the biodiversity of cloud forests and rain forests in the 1970s. Today, tours of the trees are mostly just for fun, and you and your children can savor the flora and fauna from above in several ways.

"My favorite is the hanging bridges walkway that combines a walk through the rain forest floor with hanging bridges that cross valleys, so you can look down on the treetops," says Jenny Jensen, who leads tours for Global Family Adventures. "You can go at your own pace and have a better chance of seeing wildlife."

An aerial tram tour is a great alternative, however, for families with smaller children who lack the stamina for rigorous hikes. In the Monteverde region, Sky Adventures features an aerial tram as well as hanging bridges. And daredevils age eight and up can even fly above the forest on zip lines.

Near the town of Santa Elena, Selvatura Park also has well-maintained zip lines available to

# Yum!

■ **Morpho's Café** In a jungle-themed interior, this restaurant serves everything from hamburgers to typical Costa Rican cuisine.

■ **Monteverde Cheese Factory** Take tours for those age seven and up, which include samplings of several varieties of cheese such as Swiss, Gouda, and smoked Provolone, as well as cured meats and ice creams.

■ **Stella's Bakery** This place offers breakfast, lunch, and dinner items such as pancakes, quiche, soups, sandwiches, and salads, as well as tantalizing pastries.

■ **Tree House Café** The kids will get a kick out of this spot in the town of Santa Elena, where a massive tree grows through the center of the restaurant. Enjoy locally made ice cream at the shop across the street.

younger children (age four and up). Don't expect to see much wildlife as you quickly whiz through the forest. Selvatura, however, also boasts attractions such as a butterfly garden as well as a 1.9-mile treetop walkway.

"Kids really like this walk," says Jensen of the latter. "Bridges are always fun, and it's cool to look down on the treetops and see the tree ferns from above—they look like green stars. We often spot monkeys from the walkway."

After working up an appetite, grab a bite at a *soda,* a small restaurant that offers affordable plate-of-the-day type meals. "You can get *batidos,* which are Costa Rica's answer to milk shakes," says Jensen. "Have your child pick a fruit and ask for the drink '*con leche*' (with milk) or '*con agua*' (with water), and they'll mix it in a blender for him or her."

Although travelers frequently visit the area around Monteverde and Santa Elena to see Costa Rica's world-famous cloud and rain forests, other parts of the country also host canopy tours.

Ron Hynes of Ridgefield, Connecticut, for example, visited the Poás Volcano area with his wife, Stacy, and children Ethan, 11; Amelia, 9; and Eliot, 8. The children loved the zip line tour, but they also enjoyed staying at the eco-friendly Peace Lodge, hiking, and visiting La Paz Waterfall Gardens, a rescued wildlife preserve.

"They were able to take away a lot of learning about nature and how fragile it is," reports Hynes. "The guides did a great job teaching them about the need to preserve and protect."

Another area Jensen recommends for families

# NEST

■ **Hotel Atardecer**
*Montezuma*
Run by a Costa Rican family, this clean and affordable hotel is walking distance to Santa Elena's center. Some of the larger rooms sleep five. Breakfast is included.
www.hotelatardecer.net

■ **Hotel Arco Iris Lodge**
*Monteverde*
Near downtown Santa Elena, the Arco Iris has landscaped grounds and comfortable cabins. Two-bedroom cabins are a good option for families.
www.arcoirislodge.com

■ **Hotel Fonda Vela**
*Monteverde*
An upscale option for families who want to be closer to the Monteverde Cloud Forest Reserve. Look for birds through the restaurant's big windows.
www.fondavela.com

■ **Peace Lodge at La Paz Waterfall Gardens**
*Poás Volcano area*
Luxurious and eco-friendly, these lodgings are on the grounds of La Paz Waterfall Gardens Nature Park. The hotel is located near Costa Rica's Poás Volcano National Park.
www.waterfallgardens.com

who want to see animals is the lowland rain forest, especially around Puerto Viejo de Sarapiquí.

"The canopy isn't as dense and there are fewer tourists, so you can see a lot more wildlife—coatis, iguanas, monkeys, sloths, and so on," she advises. "You're almost guaranteed to see animals in the lowland if you take some time to look around with a guide." ■

# Antigua & Beyond
## *Central American Dreamscape*

In the villages of Guatemala, shamans and their inherited rituals remain an integral, and intimate, part of the way of life. It's these holy priest-doctors, usually men, who act as intermediaries between the natives and Maya deities.

For kids and parents, glimpsing these old customs requires a total immersion into the world of natives. "Meeting a shaman is a quest—it has to be from within, and you have to have a good reason," says John Heaton, owner of the Quinta Maconda Inn in Antigua and purveyor of tours throughout Guatemala.

Shamans perform private ceremonies for anyone who seeks spiritual guidance—visiting families included. It's a practice that, much like that of the local people, exists where Christianity mingles with Maya paganism.

José Francisco Coutiño Garcia, a Maya priest with 30-some years of experience in Guatemala, says shamans are glad to talk with kids, "especially if they are interested in the Maya traditions."

During ceremonies, shamans perform ritualistic burnings of offerings on cement floors—from symbols made out of sugar and eggs to candles, chocolate, incense, and flowers.

"With these materials, we make a sacred fire

## OBJECTS OF WONDER

 Instead of collecting change in piggy banks, Guatemalans stash away extra quetzals in **ceramic coin banks** shaped like *tecolotes* (owls). Artisan-made owl banks line the walls of Antigua's Doña María Gordillo's Dulcería, a 130-year-old candy shop.

to ask for peace and love, or for a special request," Garcia says. The burning of candles symbolizes the "harnessing of life force," explains Omar W. Rosales, author of *Elemental Shaman: One Man's Journey into the Heart of Humanity, Spirituality, and Ecology* (2009). "Red candles are burned for love, blue for health, green for money, yellow for good luck, white for purity and marriage."

Resist the urge to attempt to explain the ceremony to young participants, Heaton advises. Instead, quietly watch the scene unfold together, and discuss the experience afterward.

"A kid tends to be really sensitive to what he sees, and he may not want his parents to tell him what he's observing," he says. "He may perceive something his parents don't even understand. The connection the shaman has during his ritual is powerful. As the fire burns, the shaman reads the flame and flicks his fingers, and the flame responds."

Children can relate to (and engage with) that tangible connection between shaman and flame. "To be visually acquainted with the world of shamanism can shift their paradigms into a new reality—which can be very different from the world they live in," Heaton concludes.

Leading by example, parents can help establish an unprejudiced and reverent attitude. "If you say,

## BUY WORTHY

Craft markets abound with artisans who sell **vibrant** *huipils* (loom-woven blouses) emblazoned with embroidered birds, flowers, and geometric shapes. On the finest examples, the **bright embroidery** matches on the front and back panels.

## FAST FACTS

■ **Of Guatemala's 13.8 million citizens,** children 14 and under account for 38 percent, whereas just 4 percent of the population is over the age of 65.

■ Slightly smaller than the state of Tennessee, Guatemala **sits at the confluence of three tectonic plates** and is home to more than 30 volcanoes, including Tajumulco, Central America's highest at 13,845 feet. Twelve miles southwest of Antigua, Fuego Volcano has been considered in near-constant eruption—spewing smoke, steam, and rocks—since the Spaniards arrived in 1524.

'Look at how amazing and cool this is,' and approach everything with a joyous, open way," says traveler and writer Carl Hoffman, "then kids will perceive things that way too."

Kids and adults alike will marvel at Guatemala's Technicolor dreamscape. Hoffman describes visiting the country as "a magical mystery tour—like falling through the keyhole of Wonderland."

In villages and cities, local women still wear brightly colored *huipils* (handwoven smocks) and balance baskets on their heads. City vendors hawk fresh pineapple slices, and stray goats and roosters loiter alongside centuries-old stone fountains. Colorful stucco houses—splashed aqua, lime, burnt orange, bubblegum pink—line cobblestone lanes; even churches are painted cheery shades of yellow and tangerine. The aroma of hand-flattened tortillas wafts through kitchen windows.

"It's a bit like being at a circus," Hoffman adds. "There are all these crazy, wonderful colors, and people are always letting off fireworks and banging things, and having parades."

Start your tour in Antigua, the onetime colonial capital that the Spanish founded in 1543 and ordered abandoned in 1776, in the wake of devastating earthquakes. With its shady courtyards and preserved colonial architecture, Antigua serves as a foreigner-friendly gateway to Central America's most populous country; it's also a UNESCO World Heritage site.

But for a closer look at the local way of life and a possible existential encounter, leave the comforts of Antigua for the rustic villages scattered across the country. Villagers maintain a deep respect for Maya heritage, and that is where you will find priest-healers, or shamans, for spiritual guidance.

Take the bumpy, hours-long drive, for example, to Santiago Atitlán, a village on the shores of stunning Lake Atitlán—considered one of the world's most beautiful bodies of water—in the highland region of southern Guatemala. Santiago is home to the Lord of the Lake, aka Maximon, a pre-Columbian effigy. A rotating roster of families serves one-year terms to watch over Maximon, actually a four-foot-tall, moustached puppet-deity carved from wood.

Typical offerings to Maximon include Gallo beer, aguardiente liquor, and cigarettes, so a ceremony with Maximon is intended for a mature audience. Even so, kids will surely appreciate Maximon's flamboyant persona and layered adornments that include dozens of wildly colored scarves, two cowboy hats, and a gaggle of wool shawls.

North of the lake on Route 15, Chichicastenango is home to Pascual Abaj, an ancient stone altar in the center of a hilltop clearing. Shamans linger near the altar; if you are in a reverent mood, ask one to perform a private ceremony for your family. ■

## CONNECTIONS

**National Geographic**
*http://travel.nationalgeographic.com/travel/
countries/guatemala-guide*
Delve into the geography and culture with this guide. Learn about Maya ruins, the country's long civil war, and today's struggles; click through photos of the country's people and places.

**National Geographic Kids**
*http://kids.nationalgeographic.com/kids/places/
find/guatemala/*
Kids can navigate the country with this interactive guide, which presents easy-to-understand facts and alluring photographs. Young explorers can also watch a video of a bat falcon make a dazzling midair catch over Maya ruins.

**Nim Po't**
*www.nimpot.com*
Learn about Guatemalan textiles, such as *huipils*, at the "virtual retail museum" of a bricks-and-mortar consignment warehouse for Maya textiles in Antigua.

**Visit Guatemala**
*www.visitguatemala.com*
The website of Guatemala's tourist board features visitor highlights, from the modern capital of Guatemala City to the Maya Highlands, plus Caribbean beaches, volcanic landscapes, and forest ecosystems. Get inspired with photo albums, videos, and the sounds of the marimba.

**Guatemala on the Web**
*www.guatemalaontheweb.com*
This site offers general tourist information, including places to visit, things to do, and articles about local cuisine (from tortillas to candies).

# Galápagos
## *Nature Close Up*

There is a common misconception among parents that a holiday to the Galápagos Islands isn't for your kids—because they "won't remember a thing."

"Not so," says Francesco Galli Zugaro, who first came to the Galápagos in 1993 and ran tours there aboard the S.S. *Eclipse* for four years before recently establishing Aqua Expeditions, a cruise company on the Amazon River in Peru. "These experiences will leave a lasting impression that can shape the way kids understand the world they live in. Children—and parents—can enjoy the timelessness of the islands."

Though the magic of the Galápagos can touch any child, Galli Zugaro says that age does make a difference. "Families with kids under seven best experience the Galápagos by staying in a land-based hotel and taking day trips to nearby bays and coves," he advises. Those with children eight and older should take a cruise for the diversity of experience. "My kids were in seventh heaven at a simple tide pool, at seeing hundreds of dolphins from the ship's bridge," says Galli Zugaro. "But the experience of a lifetime was swimming with

> ## BUY WORTHY
> **Tagua nut carvings, or vegetable ivory,** are good, authentic souvenirs because the tagua nut—which is harvested from mainland palm—is the **sustaining source of income** for many small communities.

sharks in Tortuga Bay. Galápagos sharks almost never attack humans. My kids, experiencing the wonder of their size and agility, reconsidered their preconceived notions of sharks. And it stimulated their courage and sense of adventure."

So imagine a trip to the Galápagos, where, Galli Zugaro says, "I can stare, close up, into a blue-footed boobie's eyes and have it look back at me with equal curiosity." You're in Charles Darwin's fables, the place where he developed his theory of evolution, an Equator-hugging, evolutionary petri dish 600 miles off the west coast of Ecuador on a weeklong voyage aboard an elegant 48-passenger boat.

"Visiting the Galápagos Islands permits children to contemplate how each island's specific environment generated subtle variations in species," says

Galli Zugaro. "Each island has different characteristics—for example, some are made of pure volcanic rock while others have white-sand beaches. Kids must understand the pure chance and probability of millions of opportunities occurring, so as to allow two similar species landing on one island being able to adapt and evolve accordingly—perhaps in completely different ways depending on the conditions. And consider what these creatures had to endure: The mere thought of an iguana living through an ocean trip on driftwood to land on arid terrain—and surviving through adaptation—is mesmerizing."

Ninety-seven percent of the Galápagos archipelago's 19 islands is a park—fiercely protected by Ecuador and a phalanx of international agencies. Here you walk the straight and narrow. Straying from the marked trails is forbidden lest you stumble into turtle nests or the private domain of some rare creature.

There's no more wondrous place on Earth for families to amuse (and educate) themselves. Kids come face-to-face with creatures in the wild—their parents seeing, firsthand, that offspring who might go slack-eyed when deprived of their electronics at home are perfectly eager to walk miles over baking lava to stand transfixed by a gnarly looking iguana or a scuttling Sally Lightfoot crab.

"You can look at a picture in a guidebook for five minutes," one child traveler says, "but you can look at the real thing in nature for an hour and still not get bored."

On a trip to the Galápagos island of Fernandina,

---

## GET INVOLVED

········································

■ **LONESOME GEORGE:** Francesco Galli Zugaro has created Fundación Scalecia (*see www .fundacionscalecia.com*), which educates children about the environment and leverages Lonesome George—the last member of a Galápagos turtle species that will disappear when he dies. Scalecia provides up to six scholarships a year from sales by Lonesome George and Company, an apparel line.

---

you enter the shockingly cold water in wet suits. The guide, Klaus Fielsch, explains that hot water stifles life, but cold water often abounds in nutrients. You see how that plays out in nature when you find yourselves floating amid an armada of sea turtles jawing great chunks of seaweed. A turtle flippers by, a cloud of blue fish swarming its back ("Cleaning," explains Fielsch). Then one, two sea lions join in, and you have a bobbing tête-à-tête. You plunge into the water—arching, tumbling, flipping, and angling to keep up with the sea lions as they flit through the ocean. They have clearly come to frolic. They torpedo and barrel-roll and tickle your face with their whiskers.

On Genovesa Island, you find bushes thick with male frigatebirds, their red throats inflated like beach balls, wings extended to six and a half feet, cries rattling the air as come-hither females wheel overhead looking for potential mates. Everywhere red-footed boobies perch like lawn ornaments. Carpets of black, gargoyle-faced marine iguanas molt in the baking sun, higgledy-piggledy, atop one another.

On Santiago Island, you take a hike through

lava fields and encounter a five-week-old seal yelping for its mother. "Not just a seal," corrects Fielsch. "A fur seal. Otherwise, it's a little like calling a sea horse a horse." Another pup lies wedged in a crevice, while casting a calm eye at a five-year-old child hovering

## CONNECTIONS

**Ecuador Travel**
*http://ecuador.travel*
The official website details the Galápagos Islands and provides tips on flights, when to visit, and how to select the best sea cruises. Discover a special section devoted to the islands' unusual wildlife.

**National Geographic Expeditions**
*www.nationalgeographicexpeditions.com/ expeditions/galapagos-family-cruise/detail*
The "Galápagos Family Odyssey" offers families a ten-day trip on board a National Geographic expedition ship. Highlights: hiking to the top of Isla Bartolomé's volcanic cone, snorkeling with sea turtles and sea lions, and a visit to Lonesome George.

**Galápagos Islands**
*www.galapagosislands.com*
Sponsored by the Galápagos Conservation Trust, this company provides a wide array of tours to the islands, from cruising to diving to adventure trips.

**Galápagos National Park**
*http://galapagospark.org*
An interactive map directs visitors to dozens of land and sea sites, noting what activities are allowed at each site, and which require special permits. It also shows how tourists can sustainably visit and avoid harming its fragile environment. Kids can learn about research projects in the Galápagos in the science section, which lists studies on topics from sea lion colonies to the movements of striped marlins.

over it. The seal, like all Galápagos creatures, is oblivious to threat. "We can get so close because they have no reason to be afraid," says Fielsch. "There's no natural predator on land here larger than a hawk."

As you approach the swamps of Bartolomé Island, Fielsch points out a cluster of tiny penguins. Of these creatures usually found in the Antarctic, he says, "Consider this: Where else in the world but the Galápagos would you find penguins at the Equator—near a mangrove swamp?"

On Santa Cruz, you spot a motionless tortoise the size of a dishwasher and an only-in-the-Galápagos bright yellow land iguana with the grin of an eager sales clerk. You walk single file to avoid stepping on turtle eggs, buried in the sand. Later, after snorkeling, you watch Darwin's struggle for survival in real time—three baby turtles emerge from their eggs under a merciless sun. The lead turtle scuttles toward the surf. The others follow, agonizingly in the heat. The turtles slow. The first seems disoriented. The second stops and struggles. The third keeps on, its tiny head bobbing. Here, you can talk about survival of the fittest with kids.

"The Galápagos is a place so unique and important to us all because what is there is nowhere else," says Galli Zugaro. "Before the 1960s, the islands didn't have today's environmental protections. Animals introduced by man, like goats and rats, were destroying the natural habitat and food for endemic species. Today, because the islands are protected, the Galápagos teach kids to interact respectfully with animals and observe the positive consequences of caring for the environment." ∎

# Amaz✷n Basin

## *Jungle Wonderland*

**T**here is so much to experience," says Julie Dubin, co-founder of Global Explorers. "Just the idea of traveling the Amazon is exciting to kids—and adults—and it delivers. To live it, feel it, breathe it, see it, taste it. It's very alive. It is not an armchair experience. Kids might see or hear a species not yet identified by scientists. The Amazon still feels unexplored—so children can imagine themselves as explorers."

The Amazon is the world's largest river by volume, carving through a basin that, if superimposed on North America, would cover almost all of the continental United States. It still harbors undiscovered tribes and supposedly is home to legendary creatures like Sach'amama, a giant black boa, and an old dwarf named Chullachaqui, who can take many devious forms to lure people deeper and deeper into the forest until they are lost.

The pure scale of the river is astonishing—28 miles wide, on average, when the water is at its highest, a half mile when it drops to its lowest ebb. At its most swollen during the rainy season, the mouth of the Amazon can be 300 miles across, dumping 7.1 million cubic feet of water a second into the ocean—60 times the discharge of the Nile and 11 times that of the Mississippi.

One of the best ways to get kids into the depths of the Amazon is to take a boat trip out of Iquitos, Peru, the largest city in the world inaccessible by road, situated 2,300 miles from the river's mouth on the Atlantic Ocean and reachable only by boat or air.

Two of the newest boats plying the river are the luxurious *Aqua* and its bigger sister ship, the *Aria*, both of which sail from Iquitos. The *Aqua* accommodates 24 travelers and a 24-person crew that includes pilots and naturalists who know the jungle intimately. The *Aria* hosts 32 guests.

"When you put your hand in a flowing stream, you touch the last that has gone before and the first of what is still to come."—*Leonardo da Vinci* (The Notebooks, *1508–1518*)

The *Aqua* and *Aria* take three to seven days to tour the Pacaya Samiria National Reserve, the second largest rain forest reserve in Peru and one of the world's most diverse. It is home to anacondas, manatees, pink dolphins, jaguars, anteaters, giant otters, tarantulas, and more than 500 species of birds. It is a five-million-acre monster that has only 92,125 inhabitants and sees fewer than 6,000 tourists a year.

The Amazon has its own soundtrack: layers and layers of hoots, warbles, grunts, yelps, buzzes, clicks, splashes, and a chiming background choir that is mesmerizing. Kids will learn to recognize the bark of the toucan, the distant roar of a howler monkey, and the banshee cry of a hoatzin.

The place is a riot of fauna. Here you will see birds like purple-throated euphonia, white-headed marsh-tyrant, Amazonian royal flycatcher, and clouds of ani birds with their shiny blue-black feathers.

"Kids will quickly become more interested in birding if you have a good pair of binoculars and an experienced guide," advises Dubin. "Bring along a bird book with color pictures. Make it a game: Have

the guide point out a bird, let the kids spot it through binoculars, and then ask them to identify it using the pictures. Kids are also fascinated by monkeys—they can watch them forever. They are charismatic."

On display: leaping, vaulting, saddleback tamarin monkeys, howler monkeys, and monk sakis, which locals call "Michael Jackson monkeys" for their sashaying style and white-glove paws.

And then there are the pink dolphins, found here. Up to ten feet long, they have a hump rather than a dorsal fin and unfused neck vertebrae that allow them to turn their heads 180 degrees. Local legend holds that the creatures shape-shift at night

## BOOKS FOR KIDS
■ *Jabutí the Tortoise: A Trickster Tale from the Amazon* by Gerald McDermott (2005) Young readers will be drawn to the colorful illustrations that accompany this retelling of a traditional Amazon story, which features jaguars, tapirs, and toucans and explains how the tortoise got his cracked shell.

■ *The Great Kapok Tree* by Lynne Cherry (2000) Butterflies, monkeys, and other Amazon creatures visit a sleeping woodcutter to warn him against chopping down the rain forest trees. Beautifully

## Know Before You Go

detailed illustrations help impart the lesson that all living things are connected.

## BOOKS FOR PARENTS
■ *The River of Doubt: Theodore Roosevelt's Darkest Journey* by Candice Millard (2006) This gripping account narrates Roosevelt's harrowing journey down an unexplored tributary of the Amazon, accompanied by his son Kermit. Beset by disease, lack of food, dangerous river rapids,

and hostile indigenous tribes, the small party barely survived. The author captures Roosevelt's dynamic personality as well as the Amazon's rich early 20th-century biodiversity.

## MOVIES
■ *The Amazon: River of the Sun* (2009) This award-winning film explores how the creatures of the Amazon River adapt to its extreme ebb and flow, from floodwaters that drown trees to droughts that can last for months. Sharp underwater footage features manatees as well as unusual fish species.

into spectral figures that enter villages on foot to steal the loveliest girls. They congregate where muddy brown and tannin black waters meet, and eat plentiful crayfish and shrimp. The creatures are playful, cresting not much higher than the depth of their humps, following the thrum of the engines, growing pinker as they become more excited. They blow and dive, crisscrossing from one side of the boat to the other, clearly using their sonar to coordinate a seemingly calculated strategy to bedevil those trying to get the perfect photo.

The Amazon's visual tableau is stunning, the vegetation so dense and lustrous. You enter a world of stands of gray trees, dribbling thick, ropey lianas, and endless miles of green—blue-green, yellow-green, purple-green—so many variations of green that the most masterly painter would be defeated trying to capture them.

"There are a lot of secrets in these jungles," says Francesco Galli Zugaro, who runs the *Aqua*. "Countless medicinal plants are still waiting to be discovered here." Indeed, researchers now seek out shamans and village elders in search of new medicines.

"The rain forest is the future of the world," one of *Aqua*'s guides says. Wild garlic, a climbing vine, is used to treat asthma, bronchitis, and sinusitis; the fer-de-lance plant (which looks like the snake of the same name) treats poisonous snakebites within two hours of a strike (any later and death comes in the form of bleeding from the eyes, nose, mouth, and ears); in the center of the chakka fruit is liquid jelly used to treat athlete's foot and ringworm; *sangre de grado* (dragon's blood) controls psoriasis, lessens acne, reduces wrinkles, and treats piranha

**INSIDER TIP**

The government regulates most tourist access to the Amazon, and independent travel can be a challenge. Best bet: Book boat tours and stay in local eco-lodge camps.

and mosquito bites; golden button is applied as an anesthesia to treat toothaches, and tarantula and scorpion bites; and lemongrass lowers cholesterol and cures insomnia.

You can stop at Lago Prado, a village of 14 dilapidated, stilted, open structures that house 120 villagers, half of them children. Chickens, a black pig, and runty dogs crowd the settlement. The kids sing songs and accept simple gifts—pens, T-shirts, paper.

"When kids actually have a chance to get to interact with local kids, they almost always walk away from the experience moved by how similar they are to each other," says Dubin. "The Amazon is a place where kids can learn how much people are connected to the natural world. They depend on it. They have to adapt to constantly changing conditions (rain, rising and falling river levels). They have the same basic needs and wants as other humans on the planet—to have enough food and clean water to sustain them, to have a safe place to live, to love and have a family. They may achieve this differently than visiting kids, but the basic motivation is the same. It is important not to romanticize what life is like in rural communities where access to health care, clean water, and other necessities is often lacking. And kids will often be shocked by how few possessions people own and yet they still smile and seem happy." ∎

# Machu Picchu

## *Lost City of Incas*

**H**ere's a cool fact to share with children visiting Machu Picchu in Peru—the place probably would never have been discovered without the help of a kid just like them.

You see, after two years of research to pinpoint the location of the "Lost City of the Inca" and raise money for his expedition, intrepid American historian and explorer Hiram Bingham set off into the Peruvian jungle in 1911 with a fedora planted firmly on his head and nothing more than an educated guess as to where it might be. He eventually only found the spot with the aid of an 11-year-old Quechua Indian boy.

"It fairly took my breath away," Bingham wrote of his first encounter with the ruins in 1911 high in the Andes. "What could this place be?"

A century later we're still not exactly sure *why* this place was constructed on a spot that practically touches the sky—a mystery kids will surely find compelling. Nobody is quite sure when Machu Picchu was first built—educated guesses put it at around 1450—or why it was abandoned a century later.

Researchers still aren't sure what its original function might have been: a place of worship, a royal estate, an astronomical observatory? And nobody can say with any certainty what became of its original inhabitants.

That's why Machu Picchu is "one of those places that *overdelivers*," says *National Geographic Traveler* contributing editor Barton Lewis, who has been visiting there since the 1960s. "No matter what your expectations are, it's more than you imagined. The Inca were the end result of 5,000 years of civilization that started at the same time as Egypt and Mesopotamia. Because of conquest and disease, however, they were only around for 100 years. But they left behind this undisturbed site that is just incredible."

About a third of the ruins have been reconstructed and it's easy to imagine how the city must have looked in Inca times, clinging to the top of an emerald green ridge in the rain forest. A main plaza flanked by stone homes, temples, workshops, bathing areas, and a royal palace, surrounded in turn by stone terraces where maize and other crops were grown. Estimates put the population at no more than 1,000 at any given time. Although the reconstructed temples are the most impressive buildings, Machu Picchu's most important structure is the Intihuatana or "hitching post of the sun," a mysterious abstract stone construction that ancient priests may have used to study the heavens and make astrological predictions.

At the Temple of the Condor, show kids how the large stone in the middle of the structure has been carved to resemble the head and neck feathers of a huge Andean bird, and how the rocks behind are shaped into outspread condor wings. And gazing down on the Temple of the Sun, point out the Serpent Window, which according to legend was used to admit snakes to the shrine.

Part of the fun of Machu Picchu is getting there. Nearly everyone takes the narrow-gauge railway from Cusco to the Urubamba Valley below the ruins. You can hop off the train at the 82-kilometer mark and walk the Inca Trail (26 miles)—the most celebrated hiking route in all of South America—or continue up to the town of Aguas Calientes, where buses shuttle you up a series of steep switchbacks to the mountaintop.

If your kids aren't quite up to the full Inca Trail, an alternative is disembarking at

the 104-kilometer spot and hiking the last four to five hours of the route (8.75 miles).

"That is the single best way to be introduced to Machu Picchu," says Lewis. "You come up really steep steps, almost climbing with your hands. At the crest there's a stone arch. You look down and see the citadel below and it's astounding."

Due to its high and remote location, Machu Picchu requires some preparation, especially when visiting with children. If time permits, take a few days to acclimatize to the trail's altitude that ranges between 6,700 and 12,000 feet above sea level.

"When one sees Machu Picchu for the first time you have to stop and try to gather it in," says Lewis. "Even without knowing the background, cosmology, or history, it's incredibly impressive. The more you observe and see, the more you wonder about it. How *did* these people do this? And to *what* purpose?" ■

# Rio de Janeiro ⚽

## *Culture on the Coast*

Since the release of the animated movie *Rio* (2011), parents and kids might be forgiven for thinking the city on the coast of Brazil is populated by frolicking blue macaws, red-crested cardinals, and yellow canaries that spar with British-accented cockatoos—and yet, feathers do indeed dance both down on the streets and high above Rio.

During the fabled celebrations of Carnival, exotic costumes topped off by feathered headdresses and colorful boas flutter about every corner of the city as part of one of the world's greatest parties—which has evolved into a combination of music, dance, and fantasy that can single-handedly kick-start a universe of creativity for young minds.

The party is only likely to grow wilder as Brazil prepares to host the 2014 FIFA World Cup (which will see Rio hosting many matches), and in 2016, as Rio

holds the first Summer Olympics in South America.

Yet, although there is great benefit from letting kids enjoy the frenetic rhythms of the city, there is ample room for them to discover a more serene, reflective Rio atop the enchantingly named Sugarloaf Mountain (Pão de Açúcar).

Prime postcard material beautifully set in an otherwise entirely postcard-worthy city, the 600-million-year-old, granite-and-quartz peak is not only a "registered trademark" of Rio, but it stands as a beguiling, bold monument to Brazil's nature, history, and tourism. Jutting out of the Atlantic like a stony sentinel, the mountain affords mesmerizing views of the city, the ocean, Guanabara Bay, and the many green-covered mountain droplets that rise within Rio's panorama.

"On the way up to the Pão de Açúcar, one is overcome by a wonderful, magical feeling that can naturally stimulate a child's imagination," says local Rita Vieira de Souza—daughter of a Brazilian ambassador—who grew up in various countries and experienced firsthand the benefits of early immersion into a global education. Now an English teacher with a background in child psychology, Souza says, "One feels that he or she is in a different, fascinating world surrounded by nature—this is amplified in a child's mind."

With cable cars soaring swiftly to the quarter-mile-high mountain, it's not hard to picture where the inspiration for an animated movie featuring birds of a feather flocking together could have come from. Only the third cable-car operation in the world when it opened in 1912, the Sugarloaf

system ushered in a new era of tourism for Brazil as a whole, and enabled millions of visitors (some 37 million by certain estimates) to conquer one of the world's most recognizable monoliths.

It was at the foot of the Sugarloaf that Portuguese explorers founded the city of Rio de Janeiro in 1565. And, just as Rio in its early days was subject to attack by (mostly French) pirates and buccaneers, the mountain guarding Guanabara Bay would be subject to conquest centuries later at the hands of the many mountaineering nationalities that scaled its steep surface—the British (in 1817), the Portuguese (in 1817, one day after the British), and the Americans (in 1851) all planted their flags at the summit.

As an alternative to the cable cars, families seeking a sky-high adventure can opt for a helicopter ride from Morro da Urca, which circles Sugarloaf. Who knows? Your child might even spot a singing blue macaw, like that in the movie, trying to learn to fly. ■

## BOOKS FOR PARENTS

■ *Rio de Janeiro, Carnival under Fire* by Ruy Castro (2004) Part of Bloomsbury's The Writer and the City series, Ruy Castro's entry is a good-humored, good-natured social history of Rio and its colorful inhabitants. Taking on every definable era of the city, from early founding quarrels to contemporary issues, Castro freshly recounts many anecdotes that capture the city's charming and spirited side.

## MUSIC

■ *Brazilian Playground* by Putumayo Kids Presents (2007) The award-winning world music label has compiled an eclectic mix of sounds from Brazil's many genres of music, like samba, bossa nova,

# Know Before You Go

and *forró*. Child-friendly anthems suitable for any carnival take center stage as greats, including Gilberto Gil and Roberta Sá, perform. Putumayo's website also includes a downloadable Brazilian Playground learning guide that parents can use in conjunction with the CD.

■ *Rose and Charcoal* by Marisa Monte (1994) One of the classics of MPB (abbreviation for Brazilian popular music), Rio's own songbird, Marisa Monte, with her soft, seductive voice has crossed Brazilian borders and gained followers worldwide. Released in 1994, this

work is but one of Monte's highly acclaimed albums—but one that encompasses a varied repertoire of songs penned by Monte herself, Paulinho da Viola, and Jorge Ben Jor, to name a few composers and contributing artists. The result is melodic, intense, and satisfying to ears of all ages.

## MOVIE

■ *Rio* (2011) Chronicling the story of Blu, a blue macaw that grows up in Minnesota and then finds himself back in his native city, this animated film is a fun, visual feast suitable for curious, wide-eyed kids (and their parents). The famous Rio backdrop enhances the tale of adventure, love, and self-discovery.

ICELAND

Ring Road

Atlantic
Ocean

West Coast

NORWAY

FINLAND

Helsinki
St. Petersburg

RUSSIA

Loch Ness

Edinburgh

New Trim to Grange
IRELAND

UNITED
KINGDOM

Stonehenge
London

St. Ives &
Penzance

BELGIUM

Waterloo

Berlin

GERMANY

POLAND

E   U   R   O   P   E

Brittany
Paris

Rhine
Valley

Kraków

FRANCE

Tyrolean
Alps

Vienna

AUSTRIA

Bled

SLOVENIA

Venice

Ljubljana

Tuscany

ITALY

A   S   I   A

SPAIN

Barcelona

VATICAN CITY

Amalfi Coast

GREECE

Athens

Mediterranean   Sea

**Map Key**

☐ Selected point of interest

0                           600 miles

0                           900 kilometers

A   F   R   I   C   A

# Europe

· · · · · · · · · · · · · · · · · · · · · · · · · · ·

# Iceland's Ring Road

## *Scandinavian Sagaland*

Iceland is one of the warmest cold countries you'll find—especially so toward children. It seems everywhere you look there are pram-pushing moms and blond-haired kids swarming the capital of Reykjavik. The big hit for children (and adults) will be the city's 18 mostly open-air geothermal pools (82–109°F); most also have slides and fountains. Use a pool visit to introduce the concept of renewable resources. Iceland is on the Mid-Atlantic Ridge, a belt of mountains and rift valleys where periodic eruptions widen the ocean floor. One of the world's most tectonically volatile places, it feeds more than 200 volcanoes and 600 hot springs and heats 85 percent of Iceland's homes. Add to this energy produced by the nation's rivers and streams, and the country essentially gets all its electricity from nature.

The other thermal experience kids will love is a visit to the Blue Lagoon—40 miles from the city. This geothermal spa is built over and around what could

be described as the world's biggest Jacuzzi—a large pool with white mud that kids can smear all over their bodies (for the health benefits and to make a joyous mess). Much of the lagoon is shallow enough for them to stand on the bottom, heads above water.

Next comes the grand journey—the Ring Road (aka Highway 1), 830 miles of majesty that encircles the country and skirts black-sand beaches, volcanoes, imposing fjords, crater lakes, thermal fields, and some of the world's largest glaciers. Prepare your kids for more than eye-filling scenics. But you'll be in the car a lot—so stock up on some Icelandic tapes and books (maybe even some Björk music) to help while away the hours and give your passengers an earful of Norse sagas and eerie folktales. This is a place of the imagination, where we can all have permission to make things up, pretend, and make believe. The locals indulge in that—and you should, too. "We have thousands of stories," says Reykjavik-based guide Geir Rogwaldsson. "Stories of people visible and invisible; giants mean and ugly; dwarfs, gnomes, and little fairies who live in rocks. That's how people entertained themselves in the old days—telling stories through the long winters."

So as you go, invite your kids to imagine the route populated by ice trolls, guardian spirits in the shape of birds and bulls, mermen and mermaids in offshore waters, ghosts, elves and other creatures. To Icelanders these are more than mere myths. Building projects in Iceland are sometimes altered to prevent damaging the rocks where they are believed to live. And throwing rocks is discouraged—you might hit a *huldufólk,* gray-clad "hidden people" said to hate churches, crosses, and electricity.

From Reykjavik the Ring Road can be tackled either way, but driving counterclockwise (starting along the south coast) provides a faster introduction to what makes Iceland so special. Reaching the town of Selfoss, detour inland to the steaming thermal field at Geysir and the Gullfoss, a churning wall of water that plunges more than 100 feet into a narrow crevice. The tectonic forces that give the country its thermal energy are also responsible for its dramatic landscape, the basaltic columns, the tortuously rumpled topography, and the kind of volcanic activity we saw when Eyjafjallajökull blew its top and darkened Europe's skies in April 2010.

Back on Highway 1 continue to Dyrhólaey, a black-sand beach shadowed by volcanic cliffs, and home to one of the island's strangest attractions—an old military amphibious vehicle now used for tours. "Glaciers cover about 12 percent of Iceland and there are quite a few volcanoes beneath," says skipper Thorsteinn Gunnarsson, as he plunges his vessel through whitecaps into the chilly Atlantic. "Over the years the volcanic ash has turned this coast into a black-sand desert. We . . . must be prepared for a volcanic disaster at any time—evacuating our homes, schools, or work in one hour or less."

## BOOKS FOR PARENTS

■ *Iceland: Land of the Sagas* by Jon Krakauer and David Roberts (1998) Icelandic heritage comes to life as the authors walk, climb, and photograph their way through Iceland's majestic terrain.

## MUSIC

■ *Takk* by Sigur Rós (2005) This Icelandic quartet is known for its ethereal sound. Bridging the gap

## Know Before You Go

between ambient and pop, the band has magnetic force in both its English and Icelandic renditions.

■ *Gling Gló* by Björk Guðmundsdóttir and Guðmundar Ingólfssonar (1998) This collaboration of the acclaimed vocalist and a trio playing piano, drums, and bass

allows Björk's voice to enrich the group's smooth jazz sound and warms the Icelandic lyrics for a soothing listening experience.

## MOVIES

■ *Wrath of Gods* (2006) This award-winning documentary tells the story of the extremes a cast and crew endured to film *Beowulf & Grendel* in the wilds of Iceland.

Continuing along the south coast, the drive culminates in a stretch of blue called Jökulsárós, a lagoon filled with hundreds of icebergs calved from the Vatna Glacier. A boat ride brings you to within reach of the bergs, crossing waters that have appeared in such movies as *Batman Begins*.

The fire and ice fade away into majestic fjords as the Ring Road banks along the island's east coast. With its old wooden buildings and family-friendly Skálanes nature center featuring seals, reindeer, and puffins, Seydisfjördur is the place to take a break from driving and arrange a hiking, biking, kayaking, sailing, or fishing trip in a local fjord.

North of Seydisfjördur, the road cuts across a vast volcanic desert and more natural wonders. Among possible detours are the Askja caldera field, Dettifoss waterfall (Europe's most powerful by volume), and the unearthly Leirhnúkur lava field, where kids can traverse the lunarlike landscape where the Apollo astronauts practiced for moon landings. Akureyri, on the north coast, provides a welcome splash of civilization, as well as a rare chance for children to golf under the midnight sun (in summer).

Round a corner, to the west coast, and the landscape becomes green and lush, rather than cold and stony. Just west of Highway 1 awaits the long and fertile Haukadalur Valley, where Erik the Red settled after his family was banished from Norway. "Erik was a bit of a troublemaker," says Alma Gudmundsdottir, one of the living-history actors at a reproduction Norse homestead on the site of Erik's farm. "He was always arguing with his neighbors . . . After murdering three of them, Erik was 'outlawed'—meaning he could be killed without punishment. Rather than

await certain death, he took his family and his livestock and sailed away to Greenland." One of those family members was son Leif Eriksson.

At Haukadalur kids can see a bit of what Viking life must have been. Alma and others, clad as medieval peasants, sit around a smoldering hearth inside a sod house, chatting in Old Norse as if the modern world never happened. "Iceland offers connections to the past found almost nowhere else," says National Geographic fellow Jonathan Tourtellot, who has been to the country six times. "Just tell your children that Icelanders have two letters in their alphabet (thorn and edh) that we don't have but used to, in Old English. And that people go by a first name plus that of the father. Iceland will fascinate kids. They can have a wild adventure in a literate, safe, sophisticated country. And they can hike all day and wind up in a thermal pool." ∎

---

**FAST FACTS**

■ **Glaciers** cover more than 12 percent of Iceland, though the Gulf Stream and warm southwesterly winds moderate the climate.

■ **Foxes** were the only land mammals in Iceland when it was settled. Newcomers imported domesticated animals and reindeer.

■ **Vatnajökull,** or **Vatna Glacier,** covers 8 percent of the country (3,200 square miles) and is Europe's largest glacier.

■ Iceland contains about **200 volcanoes** and produces one-third of Earth's total lava flow.

■ The colors in Iceland's flag represent the elements that comprise the island: Red is for the island's **volcanic fires;** white for the **snow and ice fields;** and blue for the surrounding **ocean.**

# West C❄ast

*Where Fjords Rule*

**H**ere's the ideal (though challenging) trip to unlock Norway for children: In winter—because the true Norway is all about the cold—take a ferry from Bergen to apple-producing Solvorn, in the fjords. It is a peaceful home to some 200 people, with small gabled houses dating from the 1640s, and the Walaker Hotel, the country's oldest family-run lodgings (run by the Nitter family for nine generations since 1691). "The loudest thing here," says its owner, "is when the ferry starts up." It putters past a school of pygmy dolphins and puts in on a side of the fjord that has but 110 inhabitants in winter.

Head on to Jostedal Glacier, maybe in driving snow. "This is the experience of a lifetime," says guide Bjotnar Grov, "but not appropriate for a child younger than ten and ideal for the intrepid: a five-hour, 2,600-foot hike in snowshoes, sometimes through shin-deep powder. In summer you can cut to the chase and take a boat to within an easy walk of the glacier."

But winter is the Norway time to do it. You hear the snap of triggered avalanches letting loose at 215 miles an hour, equivalent to a Category 5

> ### BUY WORTHY
> If you are going to pick up some chocolate, **be sure to grab Freia.** It is made in Norway and comes in many different flavors.

hurricane, as you cross a buried lake, snorting and puffing, wielding poles, and following a guide who breaks a trail in virgin snow. In places, water puddles through thin ice. Occasionally you encounter a wolverine track, an immense boulder vaulted by some massive snow slide, or walking cross-country skiers—a woman pulled by a husky, a man walking solitary and head down.

Finally, you are at the glacier, reached by a tortuous switchback slide. You climb into its dusky, yawning blue mouth. You crawl and shimmy upward through the refrigerated walls, then settle and take deep clammy breaths.

"Here is where you breathe the air of the Vikings," says Grov. "The air released from this ice is 1,000 years old." At one point he demonstrates what ice sounds like when tapped by a small axe.

A 100-pound block shears, shatters, and skitters off. You can only smile. There are sandwiches and hot chocolate. And then it is back through the snow.

Among Norway's fjords, you have a chance to discover a land that happily resists change. It offers that elementalism, that raw "remember when" that all parents yearn to give their kids.

For another adventure, head to the so-called King of Fjords: three-million-year-old Sognefjord Glacier, Norway's longest at 127 miles and deepest at 4,291 feet. There, find Gudvangen, which features a re-created Viking village combining serious research with a facsimile of Viking life: People live as ancient Norse throughout summer, and you can join them around the campfire, row across a fjord in a Viking

# CONNECTIONS

### Fjords.com
*www.fjords.com*
Here is a one-stop location for planning a trip—book hotels, boats, and guided tours. There are also slide shows and videos showcasing the country.

### Norway in a Nutshell
*www.norwaynutshell.com*
For a fast and easy way to plan a trip to the fjords visit this website, for it gives the opportunity to book hotels, excursions, and everything else that you can think of for your trip.

### Norway in HD
*www.norwayinhd.com*
This free podcast is dedicated to the culture and nature of Norway, mostly the fjord region. Videos reveal what makes this place so majestic.

## INSIDER TIP

Despite being the land of perpetual light in the summer, the weather is a factor. So plan ahead and bring a warm jacket or fleece. You might also remember the rain jacket as Bergen has been referred to as "Norway's City of Rain."

boat, revel in their swords and costumes, and learn firsthand about Viking life.

Nature, however, is the true lure here. "It is not a place with lots of amusement parks," says Kristian Jørgensen, Fjord Norway's managing director and father of a son. "You really amuse yourself by getting close to nature. Going as the road takes you. To a place like Preikestolen or Kjerag, amazing spots to hike with children because they see views as impressive as that of the Grand Canyon.

"Children love to canoe or kayak on the fjords, where sometimes small porpoise whales swim alongside," he continues. "Sea raft to see puffins or seals. Watch eagle feeding—toss fish into the air and eagles swoop them up. Sleep under the stars or in cabins where you can meet people and tell stories by the fire. Swim alone in small lagoons that come from waterfalls. Drink fresh water from streams and rivers. Norway keeps a kid on his or her toes. The hikes are not easy, but they are full of great waterfalls, amazing mountain formations, and mind-blowing viewpoints." ∎

# Helsinki

## *A Child's Magic Island*

The people of Finland, with their balance of decorum and whimsy, delight in children. In fact, their national epic poem is the stuff of stories and childhood fantasy that has informed many aspects of Finnish life. The *Kalevala,* a masterpiece of world literature, shares many themes with the *Lord of the Rings* and the *Harry Potter* series. It brims with stories of romance, kidnapping, and mystery: The Sampo, a magical talisman, shamans, raids on enemies, weddings, bear killings, and adventures in distant lands. And Väinämöinen, a great sorcerer who knew more—and more powerful—runes and spells (which could be undone if sung backward) than common folk.

Art nouveau– and modernist-flavored, sea breeze–enhanced capital Helsinki (where you can shop for moose, reindeer, and bear salami) has deep, dark, agonizingly long winter nights etched with the shimmering northern lights, and sublimely long summer days under a midnight sun (midsummer is the time to go, when Helsinki gets 17 hours of sun daily).

> ### FAST FACTS
>
> ■ In olden times during Finland's midsummer solstice superstitious girls would **sleep with a coin under their head,** believing that the first man they would see the next day would one day be their husband.
>
> ■ To this day, Finnish lore contends that mischievous creatures like the *menninkäinen* **(goblins)** and the *keiju* **(fairies)** inhabit the depths of the forests that cover Finland.

With kids, one way to get a taste of the country is to head to Seurasaari Island, only 2.5 miles from Helsinki's center and a wonderland of culture, history, and childhood delight.

"Seurasaari is a fairy-tale island based on reality," says Miika Lauriala, chairman of Friends of Seurasaari Association. "It is a mixture of history, nature, sea, land, and rocky shores. It is seagulls screaming, ducks and swans with their chicks, tame squirrels climbing up your trousers in search of peanuts in your pocket." Imagine that some Scandinavian storybook giant scooped up some 85-plus expressive buildings from every corner of Finland and lovingly scattered them on this island to be savored in all seasons.

Explains Lauriala, "We have farmhouses, warehouses, horse stables, a church, a manor house, and village-like surroundings. You can walk through 400 years of Finnish architecture assembled in one location and imagine what life was like back in the past." The backdrop is the epic *Kalevala*. "At Seurasaari, stories about gnomes and trolls go into motion," she says. "A guide tells a fairy tale and it becomes real in these old buildings. The gnomes and animals seem to come alive in front of your eyes."

Here, the walk is the thing. Start at the bridge with its exquisite wood carvings. Buy an ice cream or barbecue a sausage at the Festival Grounds. And look around. Let the kids set the pace, and if it is warm enough you might even swim or picnic on the beach. Maybe they'll notice the bats, one of the largest concentrations in southern Finland.

"They live in the houses and start flying by thousands around the island at dusk," says Lauriala. A history walk reveals Finland's past—old farm tools and a huge boat that took people to church on Sundays in lake districts with few roads.

## BUY WORTHY

**Glass birds** shaped in Finland are traditionally romantic gifts to bring back to loved ones. Also, **figures of the animals** that live in the woods of Finland, like deer and elk, are reminders of its Nordic natural beauty.

The most arresting part of the Saurasaari open-air museum is Kahiluoto Manor. "It still has the old-fashioned atmosphere created by these self-made villages and their inhabitants," says Lauriala. "One can feel these people and children like ghosts."

Mid-December's Christmas Path walk is a way to experience a culture that truly celebrates cold. "You taste traditional Finnish Christmas *riisipuuro*, a warm rice porridge," says Lauriala. "You can sing Christmas carols, listen to fairy tales, watch plays, or play with Santa's little helpers. You can also give your Christmas wish list to Santa Claus and his wife." Or visit on Shrovetide in late February and join the locals for a horse-drawn sleigh ride.

Spookier on Seurasaari is Easter. On Holy Saturday, huge bonfires roar high. According to Finnish tradition, evil spirits, witches, and trolls are particularly busy on that day, and bonfires are believed to scare them away. ■

## Know Before You Go

**BOOKS FOR PARENTS**............
■ *The Kalevala: The Epic Poem of Finland* **by Elias Lonnrot (1835)** Experience the rich literary accomplishments of Finland by reading a translation of its epic national poem, the *Kalevala,* which played a major role in the development of Finland's national identity after the country gained independence from Russia.

**BOOKS FOR KIDS**............
■ *Tales from a Finnish Tupa* **by James Cloyd Bowman (1936, 1964)** This collection of Finnish fables helps kids of all ages to understand bits of age-old wisdom celebrated throughout the country.

**FESTIVALS**............
■ During the summer season, many proud Finnish people and curious tourists visit Seurasaari Island in June to take part in the **Midsummer Festival,** or **Juhannus.** The lighting of the Seurasaari Kokko, or midsummer night bonfire, by a newly wed couple highlights this jubilant evening.

# St. Petersburg

*Queen of the North*

For kids with an aversion to bedtime, St. Petersburg is just the place from mid-May to mid-July, when twilight can last all night. These are the so-called White Nights, when you can experience not only a majestically lovely city but one of the world's great arts festivals—with ballet, opera, Russian dance, and theater. It ends with the Scarlet Sails competition, Russia's largest event (as many as three million people, mostly students, attend). Known in Russian as Alye Parusa and inspired by Alexander Grin's popular book *Scarlet Sails,* it marks the end of the school year with pinwheeling fireworks and a massive water show that includes pirate-filled boats battling on the Neva River. The city's celebrated circus leaves town from July to September, so attend during the White Nights. In a red-domed building in which it has performed since 1877, you'll see its famous Russian bears (along with tigers and lions), net-defying jugglers, and clowns that prove humor transcends language.

Brasília, Canberra, and Washington, D.C., owe a huge debt to St. Petersburg, the first example of a modern capital built from scratch to reflect the new direction and image of its mother country. "Everything is on a vast and colossal scale," wrote an 18th-century English visitor shortly after the city was finished. "The public buildings, churches, monasteries and private palaces . . . are of an immense size, and seen as if designed for creatures of a superior height and dimensions to man."

St. Petersburg seems that way still, with proportions that are bound to stagger young travelers. The city reveals itself best when you just wander, along the canals in an open-topped boat or hydro foil. Point

"I love thee, city of Peter's making; / I love thy harmonies austere, / And the Neva's sovereign waters breaking / Along her banks of granite sheer."—*Poet Aleksandr Pushkin (1837)*

out the shimmering onion domes of the Church of the Savior on Spilled Blood, step into the Cathedral of Sts. Peter and Paul for a spooky visit to the tsars' crypts, then have a picnic in the Summer Garden, with its fountains, statues, and menagerie.

"When we walk the city, I usually tempt my daughters with a surprise," says Anna Avdeyeva, head of the English Language Center at St. Petersburg State University. "Maybe we'll stumble upon an obscure passage or square or a sculpture of some little animal." If your kids are game, they can learn to paint Russian nesting dolls—the iconic Matryoshka. If they are drawn to ballet, arrange a backstage tour of the Mariinsky Theater, home of what was once the Kirov ballet. "This city has its own nature and character," says Avdeyeva. "And this cannot be explained— you can only feel it." One way for kids to feel it is to bring along classic Russian music by the likes of Tchaikovsky's *Swan Lake,* Mussorgsky (they'll know his "Night on Bald Mountain" from *Fantasia*), and Rimsky-Korsakov's "The Flight of the Bumblebee."

Another showcase of Russia's love affair with culture is the incomparable Winter Palace, primary

### INSIDER TIP

Don't be deterred by the trademark St. Petersburg sternness—it's easily overcome. Smiling faces and greetings can go a long way; saying "Hello"—or zdravstvuyte (pronounced ZDRA-stvooy-tyeh) in Russian—is a great start.

home of the Hermitage—one of the world's oldest and largest art museums (under 17 get in free). We can hear the kids' groans now—not another museum. This one is worth at least 90 minutes a visit, but don't push it. Narrow your child's interests before diving in, concentrating on, say, ancient Egypt, medieval knights and armor, French Impressionism, or whatever engages. Avdeyeva recommends spreading your visit over several days. "One problem is that children aren't allowed to touch. And that is against their nature. So think of some activity where the kids can do something." For her kids, Avdeyeva invents games, treasure hunts, riddles, or fairy tales that complement the art they plan to view that day. After all, St. Petersburg is all about creativity and invention. Point examples out wherever you see them. ∎

---

### BOOKS FOR KIDS
■ *A Russian ABC* by Florence Cassen Mayers (1992) This bilingual book illustrates the letters of the Cyrillic alphabet with paintings and sculptures from the Hermitage, St. Petersburg's grandest museum.

■ *Angel on the Square* by Gloria Whelan (2003) The causes and effects of the Russian Revolution are sensitively addressed through the story of a young girl who becomes

## Know Before You Go

close to the imperial family in St. Petersburg as war threatens.

### BOOKS FOR PARENTS
■ *Crime and Punishment* by Fyodor Dostoyevsky (1866) A harrowing tale of guilt and redemption set in St. Petersburg.

### MUSIC
■ *Ultimate Tchaikovsky* by Various

Artists (2007) This five-CD set released by Decca features the best of Tchaikovsky, performed by an international array of superstars from the world of classical music.

### MOVIES
■ *The Captivating Star of Happiness* (1975) This beautifully filmed Russian movie depicts the struggles in the aftermath of the 1825 Decembrist uprising in St. Petersburg.

# Krakw

## *There Be Dragons*

One version of the legend of how Kraków, Poland's most fabled city, was founded says it was as the result of an epic struggle between a ruler named Krak and the fire-breathing Dragon of Wawel Hill.

The people of the city, it is said, kept the beast at bay by offering it the snack of a young maiden each month, until only the king's daughter was left. Rather than give her up, King Krak pledged her hand to anyone who could kill the dragon. A lowly cobbler's apprentice named Skuba stepped up and filled a dead lamb with tar and sulfur, leaving the carcass at the dragon's cave. The monster supposedly consumed the offering and became irresistibly thirsty. Seeking relief, it drank so much of the Vistula River that it became engorged and burst into pieces. Skuba wed the king's daughter, and a new city, named after Krak, was founded atop the dragon's lair.

More than 800 years later, Kraków has embraced the once dreaded dragon as a symbol of the city's fiery determination—and as a cool attraction for kids. Legend or not, dragons are now a part

**INSIDER TIP**

Wawel Castle was the seat of Poland's kings and queens for more than 500 years, before the capital shifted to Warsaw in 1611. Visit the royal crypts in the cathedral, where you can pay respects to luminaries like Kazimierz the Great and see oddities like the vertically challenged Wladyslaw the Elbow-High.

of everyday life in the southern Polish metropolis.

A bronze dragon statue in front of Smocza Jama (Dragon's Cave) on the side of Wawel Hill, for example, actually belches fire every few minutes. And one of the high points of the cultural calendar is June's Great Dragon Parade through the streets of the old town, during which marchers dressed like medieval knights and princesses carry dragon effigies of various shapes and sizes.

Start your family quest for Kraków's lore on Wawel Hill, where Poland's monarchs lived (and died) for hundreds of years. The royal compound, one of Europe's largest, is surrounded by thick battlements with bird's-eye views of the city all around.

"Kids probably won't be interested in the historic interiors of the State Rooms," says Mara Vorhees, mother of two and author of a guidebook to Kraków. "But this is a medieval castle, after all, where imaginations can roam." Inside the walls is a massive Gothic cathedral where many of the notables of Polish history are buried.

A collection of animal bones beside the church entrance is supposedly all that's left of the Wawel Dragon. Ask the kids what animals the remains are really from, and see who comes up with the correct answer: whale, rhino, and mammoth. The castle armory boasts an impressive collection of ancient weapons, knightly armor, and military oddities such as the avenging angel–like wings that 17th-century Polish cavalrymen strapped to their backs when they entered battle.

For families that want to continue the dragon hunt, check out the excellent municipal zoo (Krakowski Ogród Zoologiczny)—home to an oddball lizard called the sail-finned water dragon. As one of the continent's top captive-breeding facilities, the zoo features many other rare and endangered species from around the globe.

Another option is to crank things back a few million years at Dinozatorland, where dozens of animatronic dinosaurs inhabit a primeval forest on the outskirts of Kraków. The eclectic theme park also features go-karts, bumper cars, pony rides, and giant slides.

Kraków offers plenty of other family-friendly venues, like the Rynek Glowny, the largest medieval town square in Europe. "Just as adults might want to spend an hour relaxing and having a drink on the Rynek Glowny, kids will want to feed the pigeons and watch the crowds and see the bugler in the Mariacki Tower," says Vorhees.

Even the Collegium Maius—a university dating from the 15th century that counts Nicolaus Copernicus among its alumni—has interactive scientific exhibits geared toward children, not to mention a charming chiming clock with wooden figures of kings and professors in the courtyard.

Parents of older children may want to teach a real-life lesson by visiting the Kazimierz, once one of the largest Jewish ghettos in Eastern Europe, wiped out in World War II. Jewish synagogues, cemeteries, and other landmarks have been faithfully restored to honor residents murdered as part of the Holocaust and to reflect on the area's early history. ∎

---

**BOOKS FOR KIDS**........................
■ *The Trumpeter of Krakow* by Eric P. Kelly and Janina Domanska (1992) Take a journey to 15th-century Poland and Renaissance Kraków with Newbery Medal–winning illustrations.

■ *The Dragon of Krakow and Other Polish Stories* by Richard Monte and Paul Hess (2008) This illustrated

## Know Before You Go

volume brings classic Polish folktales to life for all ages.

**BOOKS FOR PARENTS**.....................
■ *A History of Krakow for Everyone* by Jan M. Malecki (2008) This work blends history, anecdotes, witty quotes, and colorful

characters to provide readers with a sense of what makes the ancient city tick.

■ *The Complete Maus: A Survivor's Tale* by Art Spiegelman (1996) The author explores his parents' ordeal in the Kraków ghetto and the Auschwitz concentration camp in a graphic novel with mice as characters.

# Vien♪a
## *Fairy-Tale Stallions*

I n a city that embraces new ideas and forward thinking—Vienna was the home of Sigmund Freud and philosopher Ludwig Wittgenstein, after all—the majestic white Lipizzans remain a window into Vienna's old-world charm. Performing in the magnificent Hofburg Palace, where walls are adorned with portraits of kings, the stallions transport audiences—especially children—to an enchanted time of princes and princesses.

"Children just adore animals, but besides that general attraction to all living creatures, the beautiful white stallions in Vienna have their own special appeal," says local Julia Damianova, who took her friend's eight-year-old daughter to see the horses perform. The girl was "amazed by the dancing horses, which she found to be so smart

because of the complex steps they can perform and the way they all move together. They look like they have just stepped out of a fairy tale. As in *Sleeping Beauty* or *Snow White,* every fairy tale involves the prince or princess riding a horse toward the happy end of the story."

Much like the Viennese Waltz, traditional coffeehouses, and baroque architecture, the Lipizzans are reminders of the leading role—from politics to philosophy to music—Austria's capital city played in the world during the height of the Austro-Hungarian Empire.

The horses are so revered, in fact, that Emperor Franz Josef insisted on riding one during the ceremony when he was crowned king of Hungary in

1867. He even demanded weekly updates on the progress of each animal as it grew and was trained.

From birth, the Lipizzans are pampered. As foals, they live in a herd at the Piber Stud Farm in Styria, Austria, in the meadows high in the mountains about two hours southwest of Vienna. There, they eat fresh grass and build stamina and lung capacity in the Alpine terrain.

When the foals are four years old, they leave the Piber farm and are paired with a student rider, and both begin their training at the Spanish Riding School at the Hofburg Palace, the oldest and one of the most prestigious riding institutions in the world.

The history of the school dates back to the 16th century, when Archduke Charles II of Inner Austria founded the Court Stud Lipiza and imported Spanish horses. In 1735, Emperor Charles VI commissioned construction of the grand riding hall that still exists today. The academy "continues to cultivate classical equitation in the Renaissance tradition of the Haute École [literally translated as 'high school,' but referring to difficult equine jumps known as 'airs above the ground']," says the school's Susanne Langer.

The training is intense—it takes about two years just to teach a Lipizzan to walk properly. During their almost decade-long training, the horse perfects other moves like the *piaffe,* where it trots in place, or the passage—a powerful, elevated trot. Colonel Alois Podhajsky, the late director of the Spanish Riding School, once described the movement: "The horse throws the diagonal pair of feet upward with the greatest of energy and pauses a moment longer than when trotting. This awakens the impression that he sways free of all earthly weight." The horse and its rider are trained to move in perfect unison, and the effect is as if the stallion is dancing.

The Lipizzans are most recognized by their stark white coats; however, they're not born this way. Most Lipizzans are black at birth and turn white by ten years old. Sometimes, a stallion does not change hue, but in Vienna, that is good luck—for the horses and for children yet to see them perform.

"There is a saying that if there is a bay [brown] Lipizzaner stallion in Vienna, then the Spanish Riding School will continue to exist," says Langer. "They are our lucky charms, so to speak. And currently, we have two bays—so that is a *very* good sign." ∎

---

**BOOKS FOR KIDS**..........................
■ *Who Was Wolfgang Amadeus Mozart?* by Yona Zeldis McDonough (2003) Kids will be fascinated by the life of Austria's most beloved composer, who wrote his first pieces before he was six years old.

**BOOKS FOR PARENTS**......................
■ *A Death in Vienna* by Frank Tallis (2007) Get a peek into turn-of-the-century Vienna as sleuths

Know Before You Go
———

Max Liebermann and Oskar Rheinhardt tackle crime in the first book in a series of gripping mystery novels.

■ *Wittgenstein's Vienna* by Allan Janik and Stephen Edelston Toulmin (1996) Discover the people and movements that shaped the world of turn-of-the-20th-century

Vienna, from the dissolution of the Austro-Hungarian Empire to Sigmund Freud to the philosopher Ludwig Wittgenstein.

**MOVIES**....................................
■ *The Sound of Music* (1965) With songs like "My Favorite Things" and "Sixteen Going on Seventeen," one of the most popular musicals of all time opens audiences' eyes to pre–World War II Austria.

# Austria's Tyrolean ⛰lps

*Into the High Country*

**F**ew of us reach adulthood without seeing the *Sound of Music,* whose classic film poster of Julie Andrews flinging arms wide in front of a towering Alpine peak has become a Hollywood collector's item. That peak is near Schellenberg, but much of the film was shot in Los Angeles. So while the cinematic version of the rugged Tyrolean Alps might be a bit faux, the real deal is as iconic and breathtaking as any landscape on Earth. "The great Alps," writer and historian Hilaire Belloc once said, "link one in some way to one's immortality." The entire Alps—80,000 square miles—form a great arc that curves through six countries: France, Switzerland, Germany, Italy, Austria, and Slovenia. The Tyrolean Alps are located in the sliver of Austria between southern Germany and northern Italy, and their regional center of Innsbruck, smack-dab in the middle of the Austrian state of Tyrol, is an arresting place to introduce kids to European culture and nature.

**INSIDER TIP**

Depending on the length of your stay, you can purchase an Innsbruck Card, which provides access to 21 sightseeing attractions, free travel on public transportation, and other benefits.

Here you'll find baroque church towers, carved-wooden medieval buildings, and peaks that tower more than 12,000 feet. In winter, the area is blanketed in snow, and the mountains become a mecca for family skiing, snowboarding, sledding, and other cold-weather activities. The Winter Olympics have been staged here twice (1964 and 1976), and many of Austria's top winter athletes were born in and around Innsbruck. With more than 30 ski areas—including legendary spots like Seefeld, St. Anton, and Kitzbühel—Tyrol boasts one of highest concentrations of snow sports in Europe. Seefeld's Alpbachtal Resort is one of Austria's top family destinations, with a children's ski school, a separate ski/snowboard area for kids, free skiing during the low season for anyone under 15, and the opportunity to watch first-class ski-jumpers from the modern observation deck at Bergisel.

For Sandy Breuer, who grew up in Innsbruck, the city's storybook Christmas Market, which runs through most of December, summons up the quintessential Alpine village tapestry. "We go to the market after 5 p.m., when everything is lit up. Lots of little stalls sell Christmas decorations, handmade children's toys, hot punch and roasted almonds—my favorite stall was where we could make our own cookies. A nativity scene unfolds under a huge Christmas tree. They play carols from the balcony of the little Golden Roof [a royal townhouse covered in 2,657 gold-plated tiles]."

Explore Innsbruck on foot. Start along Herzog-Friedrich-Strasse, a pedestrian street in the heart of Innsbruck's Alte Stadt (Old Town), flanked by sidewalk cafés and a medley of Gothic, Renaissance, and baroque architecture. Overlooking the street is the 15th-century City Tower (the Stadtturm), which kids can climb for a bird's-eye view of medieval Innsbruck. But little ones be warned: It's a steep 148-step climb.

Innsbruck is the home of Swarovski crystal;

on the outskirts of the city, families can tour the Swarovski Crystal Worlds factory and art gallery. That may seem a little ho-hum for kids, but they'll get a glittering lesson in classic craftsmanship. And the place has the young in mind: Hidden inside a building shaped like a reclining green giant, a waterfall gushing from his open mouth, the 14 "Chambers of Wonder" feature dazzling glass works and attractions such as the interactive "Tour of the Giant"—here families become researchers and explorers ready to unlock the mysteries of the "Crystal Worlds."

Or if you're nervous letting the little ones loose near breakables, take them to the Grassmayr Bell Factory in nearby Tyrol. Here 14 generations of the Grassmayr family have been casting bells since the late 1500s. The kids can try their hands ringing bells

# Yum!

■ **Gasthaus Anich** Just a few blocks from downtown, this pub is always thronged with locals. Families can quickly fill up on generous portions of *schweinebraten* (pork roast) or *Wiener schnitzel* (breaded veal).

■ **Katzung** This cozy coffee shop located in the heart of Innsbruck's city center is the perfect place to sit and unwind after a day of sightseeing. Kids will love its large choice of homemade Austrian desserts like *tropfenkuchen* and *apfelstrudel*.

■ **Restaurant Goldenes Dachl** After viewing Innsbruck's 500-year-old landmark Goldenes Dachl (Golden Roof), eat outside at this homey restaurant right next door.

large and small without worrying about breakage.

Spend two days in Innsbruck and then head into the wild. "Green against white, alpine meadows dotted with an exuberence of wildflowers in close proximity to snow peaks and glaciers—these startling combinations are what make the Alps special," says Maria R. Leiberman, author of *Walking Switzerland—The Swiss Way.* "You can't see it anywhere else. I have been awed by other mountains, but my heart sings in the Alps." What will mesmerize kids—winter or summer—are the views from the mountain railway (actually a supersteep funicular railway and an enclosed car suspended from steel cables) up to Hafelekar, perched at 7,400 feet above sea level. From the top you can see snowcapped peaks and Innsbruck at your feet—or you can trek across the mountaintop to other vertigo-inducing points.

On the way up or down, though, stop at one of the world's most unusual zoos: the Alpenzoo. High-altitude animals inhabit large, natural enclosures—from brown bears and tuft-eared lynx to rarely seen creatures such as the European bison and giant lammergeier vulture. "My sister and I loved going to the Alpenzoo," says Breuer. "They have animals that live only in the Alps. You can see them year-round and watch how they adapt to the seasons—the ptarmigan gets white feathers in winter and the snow rabbit gets a white coat." Sandy's sister, Bella, is drawn to the otters: "Fast as anything, slipping in and out of the water—turning, twisting, and diving. And every night at about six the wolves start to howl. Scary."

Also nearby is the Karwendel Alpine Nature Park, which runs from the top of the railway to the Austrian-German border, through primeval forests,

---

## FAST FACTS

■ Innsbruck's history dates from the **Roman Empire.** In 15 B.C., the future emperor Tiberius **built a road through the Alps** from Italy to the Inn valley. The Romans later built a fort, Veldidena, in what is now the city's Wilten district.

■ At nearly 2,000 feet, the **Alpenzoo** is the highest zoo in Europe. One hundred and fifty alpine animal species, like the mountain-climbing chamois, call this place home.

---

wild rivers, and Alpine valleys right out of *Heidi.* The highest reaches of the Alps can get snow at any time of year, though generally not before October or after June, when the wildflowers start blooming. This park features hundreds of miles of hiking and biking trails, and scores of mountain huts where backcountry visitors can overnight. Wilder still is the Hohe Tauern National Park in eastern Tyrol. Austria's largest and oldest national park protects a huge chunk of the Alps, including the nation's highest peak (12,461-foot Grossglockner) and the 1,247-foot Krimml Waterfall, Austria's highest and fifth in the world. During the summer months, park rangers lead guided treks, many of them accessible for kids as young as six. The hike menu includes a five-hour "national parks detective" kids program that revolves around figuring out the mysteries of nature.

There's also a unique family excursion to the Obersulzbach Valley to learn about traditional highland agricultural methods and Alpine farm animals. And if you're lucky, as you tramp in open meadows, you'll hear the signature sound of the Alps—cowbells clanging as a farmer urges his small herd down a dirt path. ■

# Ljubljana to Bĺed

## *Europe's Simple Surprise*

Slovenia is plenty beautiful, but what is so illuminating for children is that it is *not* some tailored-for-tourists destination. Instead, visiting this doughnut hole of Europe gives kids the opportunity to see a place that, in many ways, has been frozen in time. It is the sheer simplicity of life here and the accessibility of a country about the size of Massachusetts that attract families.

"Slovenia is hardly bigger than an Australian sheep farm, with two million people," observes Rok Kraternik, a food expert and father of two.

Once the domain of the Habsburgs and part of the Holy Roman Empire, Slovenia is bordered by Austria, Hungary, Croatia, and Italy and includes just a sliver of Adriatic coastline. In part a storyland of castles and monasteries, most of the country is a landscape of limestone caves, forests—58 percent of the nation—rumpled peaks, and a valley featured in Ernest Hemingway's *A Farewell to Arms* (1929). The region's flora and fauna are among the richest in the world; more than 500 almost-extinct brown bears, for example, live in

- - - - - - - - - - - - - - - - - - - - - - - - - - - -
### INSIDER TIP

Slovenia's Ljubljana is known for more than its status as the nation's capital. This crowded city boasts a history full of mythical adventure. According to Slovene lore, during the return from his quest to attain the Golden Fleece, Jason killed a dragon, the beast that would eventually symbolize this city. This dragon is represented on Ljubljana's coat of arms, flag, and famous Dragon Bridge.
- - - - - - - - - - - - - - - - - - - - - - - - - - - -

the nation's fir and beech forests. The country's salt is coveted by high-end eateries from Manhattan to Tokyo.

Formerly part of Yugoslavia, a nation the world map no longer includes, Slovenia is just emerging from decades under socialist power. Unlike some Soviet-bloc countries dominated by mondo-cities like Berlin, Warsaw, and Zagreb, Slovenia is mostly rural and you still get a bit of old-world innocence. You must respect a country that has packed so much into such modest borders. You can ski a glacier in the morning, take an afternoon swim on the coastline, and just drive the small, winding roads that lead you into a simpler time.

"Slovenia is an honest, small place," says Kraternik. "My secret thing with the kids is canoeing across Lake Bohinj to a secluded beach, with no access by foot, to spend a day in complete serenity. Another one would be to bike near Prekmurje, where there are no hills, and visit farms and the friendly people. See a *kozolec,* or hayrack, where farmers dry grass for cows. In Maribor, we have a special wooden machine whose noise turns birds away from the vineyards to protect the world's oldest grape. Kids will also love the Museum of Apiculture [beekeeping] in Radovljica. An hour from Ljubljana in Hrastovlje is the best fresco painting in this part of the world, showing the so-called death path, where everybody is taken to the final judgment, in a nice, picturesque way."

Kraternik also recommends kids see the Predjama Castle, built within a cave mouth. The residents of the original castle are said to have survived a siege by smuggling food through a secret passage. As if in a scene straight from *Monty Python and the Holy Grail,* the digestibles included cherries used to pelt the fortress attackers.

On a trip through Slovenia, you can tour medieval castles in Bled; walk through Pleterje, a 15th-century Carthusian monastery whose residents still take a vow of silence; tour capital Ljubljana's fog-shrouded market and cobblestone streets; and explore Postojna Cave, an underground limestone labyrinth of eerie silence and chill beauty. "It is one of our pearls," says Kraternik. "Where a small

## FAST FACTS

■ Slovenia is the **third most forested country in Europe**. Although Slovenia's total surface area is less than **7,750 square miles,** slightly more than half that is forest.

■ Most residents try to **climb 9,396-foot Mount Triglav at least once** in their lifetimes. It is a matter of national pride.

■ Slovenia's **Soča River** served as the background for scenes from Disney's *The Chronicles of Narnia: Prince Caspian* (2008). This river is also known as **the Emerald Beauty** because of its stunning green tint.

■ With more than **500 reconditioned castles,** fortresses, and historical estates, Slovenia offers an abundance of whimsical locations that bring fairy tales to life. Many have been converted into **hotels,** so families can experience them firsthand.

■ Ringing the bell—known as the wishing bell—at the top of 99 stairs in the **Church of Queen Mary** on Bled Island is a way to indulge in an old Slovene tradition, while admiring the view of **snowcapped Alps and a pristine Alpine lake.**

train brings kids to a magnificent natural phenomena, way below the surface."

For lodging, sleep in Alpine retreats, one guarded by a pair of immense Newfoundland dogs, another graced by five ebony Lipizzaner horses, a breed made famous in Vienna, but born in Slovenia. Stay in a hotel on Lake Bled, near the retreat of former Yugoslav dictator Marshal Tito, and you can row to the nation's only island. "Take your kids out on a *pletna,* a hand-paddled dinghy," advises Kraternik. "Slovenia is not interested in being something complicated. The world has enough of that." ■

# A𝐈hens

*The Acropolis and Beyond*

**T**he best part of being in Athens is the ability to explore across centuries," says Eleni Vainas, a Greek-American poet, animator, writer, and longtime resident of the capital of Greece. "Walking around Athens is a living history lesson. It's a great city for kids. Modern is juxtaposed with ancient, and art is featured throughout the city in one way or another—particularly in ways that touch people on an everyday basis."

Any child who has taken basic world history classes knows about Athens and its indelible contribution to Western civilization. But studying a place and its heritage is far different from actually being there, especially if you are on a flat-topped hill called the Acropolis, gazing up at one of the most perfect structures ever built by man—the Parthenon.

Where indeed would we be without the ancient Greeks, their legacy of philosophy and democracy, their obsession with figuring out how the Earth and

**INSIDER TIP**

Keep in mind that the Greeks dine late. If you're trying to feed the family in a relaxed and timely manner, take advantage of the quiet early evening hours. If you're looking for a more lively experience, head out to a restaurant, taverna, or *psistaria* around 9 or 9:30 p.m., when things really get cranking.

heavens function, their groundbreaking strides in mathematics and medicine? They gave us the Olympics and strange names for college fraternity and sorority houses. Their dramas and comedies literally set the stage for modern entertainment. From *athlete* and *television* to *pirate* and *octopus,* so many of the words that we speak each day have their origins in ancient Greek.

Greek civilization didn't start in Athens, but it reached its greatest height here in the fifth century B.C. under legendary figures like Pericles, Sophocles, and Socrates. Kids who clamber across the Acropolis and enter its new museum—which displays, among many other things, statues of a three-bodied bearded monster and the goddess Nike leaning over to tie her sandals—gain a tangible connection with a bygone world that gave us so much of our own civilization.

The Parthenon alone is worth the trip. Dedicated to the goddess Athena, the temple arose between 447 and 338 B.C. The roof may be gone and the Elgin Marbles in London, but nothing can detract from the building's graceful, geometric lines. Focal point of the Acropolis hill, the Parthenon was later turned into a Byzantine church, a crusader cathedral, an Ottoman mosque, and a warehouse to store gunpowder for the Venetian army, before it was resurrected as a global icon after Greece gained its independence from the Ottoman Empire.

The shimmering white structure is one of 20 atop or attached to the sides of the Acropolis, including two open-air theaters on the southern flank. In a flashback to those ancient times, families can attend performances at the hillside Odeon of Herodes Atticus during the annual Athens Hellenic Festival and other special events (Sting and Elton John have both performed there).

"The Acropolis is, of course, a must-see," says Sherry C. Fox, who knows the Greek capital as both a mother and a director of the American School of Classical Studies at Athens. But she warns parents to be prepared: "There is not much shade,

## FAST FACTS

■ With the hilltop only accessible from the west, the **strategically defensible Acropolis** has been inhabited since Neolithic times. Parts of a Mycenaean fortification wall from the 13th century B.C. can still be seen among the later monuments.

■ The first olive tree in Athens is said to have **sprouted at the Acropolis** when the goddess Athena touched the ground with her spear. An olive tree has grown in the same spot there for centuries.

■ The Olympic Games, **named after Greece's highest mountain, Mount Olympus,** originated in 776 B.C. According to tradition, the Olympian gods were the first competitors.

■ The marathon is named for the story of an **Athenian warrior** who ran in full armor from Marathon to Athens—about 25 miles—to bring news that the invading Persians had been defeated. He uttered, "Rejoice, we are victorious," before falling dead.

so children should wear hats. You should carry water with you as well. There is a lot of walking, so parents should have a stroller for small children." Fox recommends exploring the Acropolis in spring and fall, when temperatures are milder and the crowds thinner.

The space around the Acropolis was transformed into a huge pedestrian area for the 2004 Summer Olympics. Part of this sprawling archaeological park is the new Acropolis Museum, where huge collections of sculptures and other artifacts discovered in the area are housed inside what is basically a giant glass box. While touring the exhibits, point out to your kids how they can gaze up through the enormous windows to the Parthenon perched on the hilltop above.

Museum staffer Danae Zaoussi says that families can also dive into a new program called "A Day at the Museum," which consists of a range of activities. "These include Family Backpacks, which can be borrowed from the museum's information desk," says Zaoussi. "One of the activities inside the bag begins with an invitation for families to search for the 12 different representations of the goddess Athena among the exhibits of the permanent collection."

# CONNECTIONS

**Athens Info Guide**
*www.athensinfoguide.com/wts.htm*
This is an extensive tourist guide to all things Athens. This includes a focus on sights such as the Agora, which was Athens's commercial and civic center. Learn about the jumble of ancient buildings, inscriptions, and fragments of sculpture there, and imagine the frenetic buzz of political, theatrical, and athletic activity that enlivened its grounds centuries ago.

**ODYSSEUS: Hellenic Ministry of Culture and Tourism**
*www.odysseus.culture.gr/index_en.html*
The Hellenic Ministry of Culture provides a quick introduction to Greek culture, including an interactive culture map, a time line of the history of Greece, and an extensive archive of photographs.

**HELLAS:NET**
*http://monolith.dnsalias.org/~marsares/*
Billed as an "exploration of ancient Greece," this website covers the rise of the polis (the city-state), the splendor of the classical period, and the culminating Golden Age.

Athens is about a lot more than just the Acropolis, though. A vast metropolis of more than three million people, the city contains dozens of neighborhoods with their own special flavors, as well as a large seaport (Piraeus). Take the kids on the funicular railway to the top of Lycabettus Hill for a great panorama of the city. "There is good ice cream to be had in Athens too," says Fox, especially at Pagotomania in the Psiri district, not far from the Acropolis. The mountains of gelato in the display window include myriad flavors both exotic and familiar.

On the north side of the Acropolis is an old neighborhood called the Plaka, a maze of narrow streets and steep stairways that developed during the Middle Ages and was the Turkish quarter during the many centuries of Ottoman rule. Nowadays, it is the city's most colorful area, filled with traditional taverna restaurants and little shops, as well as the Hellenic Children's Museum, with its interactive exhibits on science, art, technology, and language. If you get tired of walking, you can also explore the Plaka and its archaeological park by horse-drawn carriage or a miniature train called the Sunshine Express.

Explore inland to Attica, the region of Greece that includes Athens. "Paiania Cave [with its stalactites] is great fun on Hymettos Mountain," says Fox. "And there is a wonderful zoo in Spata." Kids who like animals will also want to visit the Archelon Sea Turtle Rescue Center in Glyfada—housed in old railroad freight cars—and the Hellenic Wildlife Hospital in Aegina, where kids can adopt orphaned or injured animals (otters, eagles, foxes, falcons, and so on) that are later reintroduced into the wild. ■

# Amalfi Coast

## *In Sight of the Sea*

**T**he Amalfi Coast is the playground of the social elite and well heeled, but don't let that throw you. The Italians love kids, and this area puts everyone at close quarters.

"My family has been here for generations," says Antonio Sersale, owner of Le Sirenuse Hotel. "I played here as a child. My kids grew up in Positano. All you need to do is reach out to the locals and ask: 'Show me what your kids do.' "

John Steinbeck called the Amalfi Coast a "dream place that isn't quite real when you are there and . . . beckoningly real after you have gone."

Start your dream trip along the coast in Naples after spending an afternoon at nearby Pompeii—most kids will be captivated by this tableau of daily life frozen forever in the lava flow of Mount Vesuvius. Check out Naples's aquarium (the oldest in Europe, with 200 different species of fish and marine plants) and the Museo Nazionale Ferroviario (National Railway Museum), which enthralls children with its old engines, cars, and railway equipment.

### INSIDER TIP

Take a boat to the Faraglioni, three towering rocks just off Capri's shore, and look for the *lucertola azzurra,* or blue lizard. Known for scales as blue as the Capri sea, the lizards are only found here.

Have sublime pizza at the hole-in-the-wall Umberto (live minstrels play on Sundays), then take the two-hour curving drive south down the Amalfi Coast to the cliff-hanging town of Positano, a crush of pastel-hued buildings that tumble down hills overlooking the Gulf of Salerno, part of the Tyrrhenian Sea.

Go down to Positano's big beach, Spiaggia Grande, or the smaller Spiaggia del Fornillo beach. Enjoy some time sunbathing, then point your kids to the artists bent toward their easels and canvases doing pure *en plein air* (French for "in the open air," referring to painting outdoors). Ask your children what they see in the paintings and how these pictures speak to them.

Then take a 40-minute boat ride from Positano to the island of Capri. "With no cars on the island, Capri really lends itself to exploration by foot," says Ann Saudelli, who has lived in Italy since she was six. "Kids may at first balk, but ply them with house-made gelato, *granitas* [semifrozen desserts made from sugar, water, and flavorings], and pizza *alla Caprese*—Capri style, with slices of fresh mozzarella and basil—and not only will they discover the joy of walking, they'll get a kick out of the island's changing elevations, and they'll be nicely tired at bedtime for all the right reasons."

As you explore the island, skip the tony shops in favor of countless woodland trails. Or ride the chairlift to the top of Monte Solaro, the highest place on the island, with striking views of sea and land.

Take the hike down—and kids will be *grateful* they're going up—to experience the Scala Fenicia, a series of 900 steps carved into rock. Cross vineyards and gardens created by the island's first Greek colonizers (whose women carried wares along the route on their heads).

Kids can also hide-and-seek their way through Villa Jovis, the ruins of a villa owned by the Roman emperor Tiberius, who ruled the area from A.D. 14 to A.D. 37. The ruins are on top of Monte Tiberio, the second highest spot on the island. "I'd go there for the jaw-dropping cliff-top views of the Bay of Naples and the island of Ischia," says Saudelli. "They get a 'wow' from everyone."

Then there's the water, so clear you can see ancient statues on the ocean floor. The beaches on the island are rocky and tough on the feet, but locals take the winding path via Krupp from the area of the Charterhouse of San Giacomo and the Gardens of Augustus to the bay of Marina Piccola, a chic area with one of the most child-friendly beaches on the island. The water is tranquil and the bathing areas well protected.

Another option is to take a boat to explore Capri's coast, which is riddled with sea caves. "I like seeing everything from the water," says Matteo Saudelli, Ann's son.

The most famous caves are the Blue and Green Grottoes. "Really, truly blue," Matteo says. "And cruise the narrow channel between the Faraglioni rock formations, which are named Stella, Mezzo, and Scopolo. To swim in the ocean—this is the perfect way to spend a summer day." ■

# Yum!

■ **Da Vincenzo** To satisfy that sweet tooth, take the family to this spot in Positano. They have original dishes like strawberry mousse, as well as the more common tiramisu. But this place is not just about dessert; seafood is the main cuisine here.

■ **Lo Guarracino** Not necessarily known for its food, which is mostly seafood with pizza and steak, this place is famous for its views. It is positioned on a path connecting the two beaches in Positano. You can choose to sit in the garden, or the kids might enjoy watching the cooks from their table. It is popular, so make reservations.

■ **D'Alessios** One of the oldest restaurants in Capri, this family-run eatery continues to serve top-rated Mediterranean cuisine from a prime location overlooking Fuorlovado Street. It is expensive, but you may be able to rub elbows with visiting celebrities.

# Tuscany
## A Place in the Sun

"When we visit Tuscany, we try to live like the Italians," says Rachael Wettach, a native New Zealander who spent six months in Italy with her husband and two children in a rented farmhouse, "staying up late into the evening and sleeping in the afternoon, which seems to create a feeling of relaxation for the whole family. I think our children simply *love* what Italy does to their parents. We all eat more healthily, sleep a lot, drink a lot of Tuscan red wine (not the children, of course), breathe in fresh air, and *laugh* more."

Tuscany is proof that everything really does come back in fashion. During the Middle Ages, this Italian province was one of the world's power centers, home base of the Medici family and stomping ground of Michelangelo and Leonardo da Vinci. By the end of the Renaissance, however, the region had fallen on hard times, a long and slow decline that didn't change until around 20 years ago when Tuscany

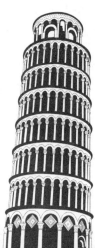

•••••••••••••••••••••••••••••••••••
### INSIDER TIP
Before you leave Florence, don't forget to rub the snout of the bronze Il Porcellino (piglet) in the Loggia del Mercato Nuovo near the Piazza della Signoria. According to tradition, doing so ensures a return trip to Florence.
•••••••••••••••••••••••••••••••••••

suddenly became *the* place for English-speaking families craving laid-back Italian adventure.

"Laid-back" and "adventure" may seem like a contradiction in terms, but Tuscany really is a place where you can take life very fast or incredibly slow, often in the same day. There's nothing that gets your blood rushing like the spectacle of the Palio di Siena, a summer festival during which riders clad in medieval garb race bareback through the streets of the old Tuscan city. Likewise, there's nothing that quite soothes the soul like watching the sunset from the patio of your own Tuscan villa or slurping gelato in a cobblestone piazza as the world passes you by.

Given its popularity, Tuscany's real estate rates have skyrocketed in recent years. But there are still bargains to be had. And if there is one place in Europe where a family with kids should consider renting a house for a couple of weeks (or even months), this is it. From anywhere in central Tuscany, all of the great sights—Florence, Siena, Pisa, and so on—are no more than a few hours' drive.

For parents (and kids) working their way through the wonders of the world, Tuscany presents a long and daunting list: the Leaning Tower in Pisa and the iconic Duomo cathedral, Ponte Vecchio bridge, and Uffizi art museum in Florence. The Italian Renaissance in all its glory. But like a great painting from that age, the genius of Tuscany as a family destination is often in the details.

Count the stairs as you slowly walk up Piazzale Michelangelo in Florence. Get lost in the backstreets of the medieval walled town of San Gimignano, famed for its stone towers. Browse a market for fresh mozzarella, prosciutto, and tomatoes and then picnic under the giant of Appennino statue in the gardens of Parco di Pratolino at the Villa Demidoff in the countryside near Florence. Search for edible mushrooms and truffles in a Tuscan forest. Take the kids olive picking if you're there in October or November.

"With children, Tuscany is best experienced at a slow pace," advises Wettach, who now lives in England, but often returns to central Italy with her family. "And without denying the benefit of visiting the 'David' or the Duomo, children may simply want to run and play in the sunshine and eat ice cream. Tuscany is about life. It's about friends and family and good food. To be honest, we never visit the tourist attractions—we try to live as normally as possible, simply drinking in the atmosphere we love so much." ∎

BOOKS FOR PARENTS..............

■ *In Tuscany* by Frances Mayes **(2000)** Mayes offers her own informal examination of the charming Tuscan lifestyle. The evocative photographs throughout the book complement her delightful descriptions of Tuscan living.

■ *A Culinary Traveller in Tuscany: Exploring and Eating Off the Beaten Track* by Beth Elon **(2009)** Elon's inventive travel-culinary fusion satisfies her readers' taste buds as well as their appetite for discovery. Her book surveys small Tuscan towns to uncover authentic local recipes.

BOOKS FOR KIDS...........

■ *Pippo the Fool* by Tracey E. Fern **(2011)** This fictional tale based on the life of one of Renaissance Florence's most famous architects,

# Know Before You Go

Filippo Brunelleschi, provides children with an amusing account of the construction of Basilica di Santa Maria del Fiore.

■ *The Authentic Story of Pinocchio of Tuscany* by Carlo Collodi **(2002)** This edition of the children's classic is the only one to be approved by the Carlo Collodi National Foundation in Tuscany. Collodi's endearing story and its artwork simply introduce children to the treasures of Italy's artistic culture.

FESTIVALS...........

■ **Luminara di San Ranieri** Every June 16, Pisa honors its patron saint with an incredible display of candlelight, bonfires, and fireworks. The celebration illuminates the city's bridges, balconies, and buildings as well as the Arno River with close to 80,000 *lumini* (small glass lamps burning oil or wax), a stunning scene your child will not soon forget.

■ **Scoppio del Carro** On Easter Sunday, travel back in time while Florentines observe the Explosion of the Cart. This fiery celebration dates back to the First Crusade and commemorates a brave Florentine soldier who, according to tradition, was the first man to ascend the walls of Jerusalem. During the celebration, four white oxen pull a cart to the Piazza del Duomo and, after Easter Mass, an imitation dove symbolizing good luck sets off a dazzling display of fireworks from within the cart.

# Venice

## *Place of Light and Water*

The big debate is not *whether* you should take your children to Venice in northern Italy, it's *when* the family should travel there.

Somewhere in the neighborhood of 18 to 20 million people each year pour into a city whose permanent population has shrunk to fewer than 60,000. Summers are incredibly crowded, literally elbow to elbow on the Rialto Bridge, with hour-long lines to enter landmarks like St. Mark's Basilica and the Doge's Palace. That said, many kids seem to relish the excitement that critical mass brings, the hustle-bustle in the squares and along the waterfront. Winter offers a different feel—the rarity of having Venice largely to yourself and the pre-Lent Carnival with its elaborate masks.

"What's the big deal about Venice?" your kids may ask. In the words of *Great Expectations* author Charles Dickens: "Nothing in the world that you have ever heard of Venice, is equal to the magnificent and stupendous reality . . . The gorgeous and wonderful reality of Venice is beyond the fancy of the wildest dreamer." There really is something

magical about this city of canals, the interplay of light and water, gondolas slipping past Renaissance facades, and a warren of alleys and narrow streets that always lead somewhere interesting.

"When I take my kids to Venice, the first thing we do, after taking the boat down the Grand Canal and climbing up something, is get lost," says Madeline Jhawar, a travel consultant and former art gallery guide who lived in Italy for five years. "We pop into bakeries for snacks. We pop into churches or little shops. Then when we're done being lost, I ask them to keep their eyes open for Venice's famous yellow signs that point to San Marco, Accademia, or Rialto."

No matter what season you are there, don't miss getting out on the water. A private gondola ride is unforgettable, but can also be expensive. On the other hand, the *vaporetto* (water bus) between the train station and St. Mark's Square is a bargain.

Enjoy a leisurely meal in a piazza café, if not in St. Mark's then one of the dozens of other cobblestone squares scattered throughout the city. Although it may be tempting to order pizza or pasta, dine like the Venetians on a selection of *cicchetti* (small bites) that might include petite sandwiches and different types of cheese, olives, and grilled vegetables, polenta or rice, and small servings of seafood or meats.

Take a boat to Lido island and Venice's beachfront, where you can rent bikes and cruise a shoreline path that runs for miles along the Adriatic. Another fascinating day trip is to the island of Murano, where glassmaking became an industry in the early second century. Take note of the lighthouse whose beam shines straight out into the Adriatic to guide ships into the lagoon at San Nicolò.

Or take the kids to Tragicomica, a factory that creates handmade Carnival masks and costumes. Get up early and visit the *pescheria* (fish market) on the Rialto Bridge. "Tell the kids the island is shaped like a fish and that Italians refer to Venice as *il pesce,* or 'the fish,' " says Jhawar. "Show them the map and ask whether they can see that fish shape."

She also recommends using the city to practice math: "My kids like to count bridges—there are over 400 in Venice. And lions! Venice's symbol is the winged lion, and kids can keep their eyes open for lions around the city." ■

---

BOOKS FOR PARENTS.................
■ *The Venice Experiment: A Year of Trial and Error Living Abroad* by **Barry Frangipane and Ben Robbins (2011)** Charmed by the city on previous visits, the author and his wife pack up their lives in the United States and move to Venice. This humorous memoir recounts their year of trying to live like Venetians far off the tourist track.

BOOKS FOR KIDS...........................
■ *Daughter of Venice* by **Donna Jo Napoli (2002)** Rich with historical detail, this book reveals the complex society of 16th-century Venice in the story of a 14-year-old girl who is determined to obtain an education and fully explore her city.

■ *Looking for Marco Polo* by **Alan Armstrong (2011)** A young boy

## Know Before You Go

and his mother head to Venice to help find his anthropologist father, who vanished on an expedition retracing Marco Polo's travels. While searching the city's canals and neighborhoods for clues, the boy learns about the 13th-century Venetian explorer's life and famous journey from Venice to China.

■ *Kids Go Europe: Treasure Hunt Venice* by **Ellen Mouchawar and Marvin Mouchawar (2006)** This book encourages kids to learn facts about Venice through famous attractions, such as the Piazza San Marco and the glassblowers of Murano. Kids are motivated to interact with the city by "treasure hunting points" they can gain by

counting winged lions, tasting espresso, and saying *"buongiorno."*

MOVIES..........................................
■ *Indiana Jones and the Last Crusade* **(1989)** The third film of the adventure series brings America's epic hero to Venice as he searches for his missing father, a Holy Grail scholar.

■ *Scooby Doo: "A Menace in Venice"* **(1978)** Episode 13 of season three follows the gang as they set out to solve the mystery of the ghostly gondolier.

■ *The Thief Lord* **(2006)** Set in Venice, this film follows two brothers as they live in an old movie theater and find a masked friend who teaches them his ways of surviving.

# Vatican City
## *Home of the Popes*

The question is straight out of Trivial Pursuit: "What's the world's smallest country?" And the answer is always the same: "Vatican City." Completely encircled by Rome, this tiny city-state is a minuscule 0.2 square mile, or, to put it another way, the Vatican would fit into New York's Central Park six times with room left over. With about 800 residents, it's also the world's least populous nation.

But size isn't everything. The spiritual and administrative home of the globe's one billion Catholics, the Vatican is a trove of treasures that will hook kids—if you know where and how to look.

"A visit well done is a memory that remains for life," says Enrico Bruschini, a longtime Vatican scholar and author of several books on the city, including *In the Footsteps of Popes* and *The Vatican Masterpieces*.

Avoid visiting at midday in high season—your kids may experience little more than a sea of rear ends. Try late in the day or early in the morning, off season if possible.

Elizabeth Lev, who consulted on the films *The Da Vinci Code* and *Angels and Demons,* highly recommends going on a Friday evening in summer—"a magical way to meet the 'Apollo Belvedere' or the 'School of Athens' in the ambience of twilight."

It also helps to do your homework first. "Talk to your kids about who the main players are in biblical history—Jesus, Abraham, Moses, and so on," advises Lev. "Introduce them to Michelangelo and Raphael and the Renaissance, as well as the gods of ancient Greece. Tell them about the pope. The more children are familiar with what they are looking at, the more likely you are to keep their interest."

Start your visit by strolling across the round St. Peter's Square. Straight ahead is the imposing facade of St. Peter's Basilica, an instantly recognizable

global icon. A window on the upper right-hand side is where the pope arrives to bless devotees gathered in the giant square. For some exercise, scale the 320 steps to the basilica's roof, where you can peer down on St. Peter's Square.

Unfortunately, visitors can't reach the Vatican Museums and Sistine Chapel directly from the square; you must walk for 10 to 15 minutes around to a separate entrance on Viale Vaticano on the city's north side. The collections, from papal carriages to aboriginal artifacts, are arranged in some 1,400 rooms, and are impossible to see in a day. Select a few must-sees with your kids ahead of time.

"My children have been visiting the Vatican Museums since they were quite young," says Lev. "We often stop to say hello to old friends like

## FAST FACTS

■ Vatican City **covers 108.7 acres** on a site known to ancient Romans as Mons Vaticanus.

■ This tiny state within the city of Rome **operates its own bank, post office, and pharmacy.**

■ From the time the Piedmontese conquered the Papal States in the 1870s until the Concordia was signed in 1929, the **pope did not leave the Vatican.**

■ The **Castel Sant'Angelo,** once used as a mausoleum, a fortress, a prison, a papal refuge, and a barracks, was the setting Puccini used in his opera *Tosca* for the suicide scene.

■ Vatican City is the only World Heritage site that is **an entire state;** UNESCO added it to the list in 1984.

## INSIDER TIP

The ticket line outside the Vatican Museums each morning often stretches for blocks on end. To avoid a lengthy wait, purchase advance tickets online through the official Vatican Museums website at *http://mv.vatican.va/3_EN/pages/MV_Home.html.*

'Laocoön' or Raphael, but we also like to see the surprises in the picture gallery when they change the paintings around. My younger daughter likes animals, so she always enjoys the Roman animal sculptures in the Pio Cristiano Museum, as well as the wondrous painting of the Garden of Eden by Wenzel Peter."

"Children love the strange, curious, and mysterious things," adds Bruschini, who recommends the Egyptian Museum with its celebrated mummy collection. "Inside you can meet a lady who lived over 3,000 years ago—the mummy of a young priestess. Explain to children that she was young by pointing out the pretty face carved on the lid of the sarcophagus, and show them her blond hair colored with the henna, as Egyptian women still do today. It is a way to make children understand that art began thousands of years ago." Another choice is the Treasury Museum where the robes of the popes are on display.

After the collections you reach the incomparable Sistine Chapel, with its Michelangelo ceiling. Painted between 1508 and 1512, the recently cleaned ceiling panels portray stories from the Bible, with the creation of the world—God and Adam touching fingertips—at the center. Bruschini calls it "masterpiece number one, the most beautiful thing in the world." ■

# Rhine Valley

## Glory of Old

In the Rhine Valley a child can sleep in a real castle. Originally constructed in the tenth century, Schloss Schönburg, for example, squats on a cliff with commanding views of the Rhine River. The castle/hotel gives kids a glimpse of life in the Middle Ages: rooms with hulking four-poster beds, roaring fires, dining halls hung with old tapestries, everything enclosed within thick stone walls and turrets. "This is an authentic, bona fide, genuine castle that protected Oberwesel during medieval times," says manager Barbara Hüttl, whose family has owned Schönburg since the 1950s.

The world's fascination with the Rhine Valley started much earlier though. The vivid descriptions of the German river by the young English poet Lord Byron set off one of the world's first tourist booms. "Ye glorious Gothic scenes! How much ye strike all phantasies, not even excepting mine,"

• • • • • • • • • • • • • • • • • • • • • • • • • • •

**INSIDER TIP**

On the last Sunday in June, the Mittelalterlich Phantasie Spectaculum revives the medieval era in the Middle Rhine with handicrafts, jesters, and knights' swordplay. The festivities extend to many hilltop castles, where kids can learn how to wield toy broadswords and axes.

• • • • • • • • • • • • • • • • • • • • • • • • • • •

wrote Byron after traveling up the Rhine in 1816. This attention brought a flood of writers, musicians, painters, and poets who had to see the wondrous, romantic river for themselves.

"Mark Twain and Herman Melville, Lord Byron and William Turner, so many people traveled through the Rhine Valley at that time," says Hartmut Hager, a retired German Army and NATO officer who now guides families around the historic riverside city of Koblenz. "Mozart and Thomas

"The faint air cools in the gloaming, / And peaceful flows the Rhine, / The thirsty summits are drinking / The sunset's flooding wine"— *"Lorelei" by Heinrich Heine (1823); translated by Mark Twain*

Jefferson also came here to see our ruined castles and churches." As did horror writer Mary Shelley, who presumably got much of her inspiration for *Frankenstein* from the brooding castles along the Rhine.

What stirred the imagination of people 200 years ago is exactly what fascinates kids today: romantic castles perched on rocky outcrops above the river, reminders of an age and way of life when Europe was all about knights on majestic steeds, acts of chivalry, fighting for a noble cause (or beloved damsel), rather than for profit.

The 40-mile stretch of the Rhine between Bingen and Koblenz has more castles than just about anywhere else in Europe, so many that UNESCO declared it a World Heritage site in 2002.

There are several ways for families to explore the region—hiking and biking trails meander through vineyards and woodland and along riverbanks and cliff tops. And, of course you should take to the water on one of the many riverboats that ply the Rhine. Children normally head straight for the open top deck with its unobstructed views of the river, villages, and cliffs. Tell them to watch for such famous landmarks as the Cat Castle (Burg Katz); the Mouse Castle

(Burg Maus), a toll station; the shiplike Pfalzgrafenstein Castle in mid-river; and towering Lorelei Rock, named for a siren who supposedly lured ships to wreck on the spot.

River trips take a full day, but families can break up the journey by staying overnight at medieval towns along the route. Still surrounded by its ancient ramparts, Oberwesel, for example, seems little changed in 1,000 years. Kids can scamper along the fortified town wall and climb into one of the old defense towers. The town's narrow cobblestone streets and giant Gothic churches also set the bygone mood, as do local festivals like the Night of a Thousand Fires, a fall fireworks show; the Night of Wine-Witch in the spring; and a massive biennial medieval pageant. Or perhaps stop over at Boppard and take the chairlift to the Four Lakes View. Later climb aboard the steep little railroad that travels west from Boppard to the high Hunsrük plateau.

If that's not enough to give kids a taste of the Middle Ages, take them to the Medieval Torture Museum in the riverside town of Rüdesheim. Among many gruesome artifacts are whipping posts and head screws, heretic forks and wooden stretching racks, guillotines, gallows, and metal executioner masks. ■

---

**BOOKS FOR PARENTS & KIDS**......
■ *The Rhine* by Roland Recht (2001) A beautifully illustrated review of the Rhine landscape, with a scholarly treatment of the art, architecture, and history shaping the region.

■ *The Roman Empire and Its Germanic Peoples* by Herwig Wolfram

## Know Before You Go

and Thomas Dunlap (2005) Learn about five centuries of Germanic migrations and Roman rule.

■ *A Tramp Abroad* by Mark Twain (1880) The legendary American author details his travels through

Germany, Switzerland, and Italy in a humorous account that is equal parts travelogue, cultural commentary, and tall tale.

■ *Legends of the Rhine* by Joanne Asala (2000) A compilation of the famous folktales that have charmed German children and adults for centuries.

# Berlin

## *Europe's Free Spirit*

I t's difficult to imagine what this city was like in the early 1960s, when the 87-mile-long Berlin Wall was still intact and bristling with barbed wire and gun emplacements. So desperate were they to cross to the West, East Berliners tried such arcane tactics as tunneling, hot-air ballooning, ultralights, and hiding in hollowed-out car panels. Many were shot for their efforts. Today, the wall has essentially been shattered into tiny bits, now scattered as souvenirs around the world.

You can navigate its former route by guided Segway, walking, or "video bus" tours. Or hike or bike the Berlin Wall Trail, marked by signs and special cobblestones that trace the wall's former path. Ask the kids to lead the way with a street map or handheld GPS-based *MauerGuide.* Only three small sections of the concrete wall remain, now safeguarded as national historic treasures. "It's ironic," says local painter and historian Martin von Ostrowski, "that a wall that divided us for 28 years is now protected by a fence in places."

A remnant on Bernauer Strasse is seen from a viewing tower that also shows old

## GET INVOLVED
. . . . . . . . . . . . . . . . . . . . . . . . . . . .
■ **WORKING FARM:** Billed as "Germany's only working farm with subway access," the Dömane Dahlem open-air museum has great programs on growing, harvesting, and preparing food. Tour the organic farm and check out the tool collection chronicling the region's agricultural history.

black-and-white movies of people trying to escape East Berlin. The East Side Gallery showcases the work of more than 100 international artists commissioned to cover the wall in marvelous graffiti.

Another one of the few standing remains is between Potsdamer Platz (where Europe's first traffic lights were installed in 1924) and Checkpoint Charlie, once the key crossing point between East and West used by foreign diplomats and military. A museum is nearby and kids will be able to travel back to a long lost era through fascinating memorabilia, escape apparatus, and films of the divided city in paroxysms of celebration. And they will get an important lesson here—the fall of the wall is a symbol of how man's lust for freedom can topple authoritarianism.

When the wall came down in 1990, East Berlin was a dour warren of bombed-out buildings, courtyards filled with rusty cars and makeshift sculptures, budding basement cafés, and shabby apartments. Now East and West are virtually indistinguishable, though cross a street in Berlin and you'll see a quaint echo of Communist yesterday: the now cherished little green and red men called Ampelmännchen who signal walk/don't walk (you'll see them on T-shirts and souvenirs everywhere).

"Many who live in the East have a selective memory, a deep nostalgia for the good old DDR [East Germany]," says journalist Cornelia Höhling, a native East Berliner. "This includes the Ampel men and the old Trabi cars. Everything else is disappearing quickly."

You can explore historic East Berlin in that Trabi, the cute car manufactured during Communist days. "It has a two-stroke engine like a lawn mower," says Trabi-Safari manager Simone Matern. "There was a shortage of steel in those days, so the outer shell is made from cotton resin." Led by a driver/guide, you pilot the Trabi on a tour that passes the site of Hitler's bunker, the Holocaust Memorial, the reconstructed Reichstag, and Karl-Marx-Allee, with its imposing socialist realist architecture.

Since the meltdown of the Iron Curtain, the German capital has evolved into Europe's most exciting "new" city—new in the sense that the bleak, brooding, and broken city that emerged from World War II is a slick, immense (nine times bigger than Paris), urbane place indeed. "Berlin has developed wonderfully," says von Ostrowski. "I like it much more now than during the division. You can be anything you want in Berlin. It's like nothing else in Europe—really a free spirit."

And kids will respond to that. A lot of that spirit is on the street and in the parks (Berliners

# Yum!

■ Just about any *imbiss* (snack stand) in Berlin serves up the city specialty—lightly spiced sausage bathed in a tangy sauce. Bratwurst (grilled sausage with ketchup or mustard) is also a street-side favorite.

■ *Boulette* is a kind of meatball, usually fried and served in a halved bun. Pickled eggs, gherkins, and a shot of mustard are common accompaniments for this hearty and flavorsome snack.

■ You haven't had apple pie until you've tried it the Berlin way. *Apfelstrudel,* loaded with thick apple chunks and dripping in creamy vanilla sauce, is an indulgence you just can't miss.

love to celebrate). Start at the Tiergarten, 600 acres of gardens, grassy fields, hidden bridges, and overgrown paths. Let your kids climb the stairs of the Victory Column, crowned by a golden angel, then rent a paddleboat or grab a snack at the Café am Neuen See.

Leave the park through the Brandenburg Gate, which for so long epitomized the divided city—and Europe. Now this old Prussian victory arch is an impromptu carnival, a magnet for street performers and protestors, strolling vendors, and camera-clad tourists. Children will beg to have a photo snapped with professional posers clad as Soviet soldiers, Darth Vader, or Berlin's brown bear mascot.

Then head up tree-lined Unter den Linden into what was once the heart of royal Berlin. The leafy avenue, one of Europe's greatest, is flanked by 18th-century neoclassical buildings and the hulking Russian Embassy (wonder how many spies the kids think have passed through there?).

Unter den Linden eventually arrives at the River Spree, which in summer attracts sunbathers to its urban beach. Here you should explore Museum Island, sometimes called the Prussian Acropolis. A UNESCO World Heritage site, it has perhaps the best cluster of small museums in Europe. There is something to appeal to every child: the Pergamon Museum with its priceless collection of ancient Greek and Babylonian artifacts (including the incredible Ishtar Gate); the Old National Gallery and its vaunted Impressionist art collection; the New Museum with its ancient Egyptian artifacts, including the iconic bust of Queen Nefertiti.

Then take it easy. Picnic in the grassy square

in front of the island's hulking Domkirche Cathedral or in riverside Monbijou Park at the east end of the Friedrichsbrücke footbridge. Or hop a 45- to 60-minute boat tour on the River Spree through Berlin's historic city center. And if you have any energy left, check out the zoo; it's Germany's oldest and Europe's biggest, and with 19,000 animals, it has more than any zoo in the world. ∎

# CONNECTIONS

**Visit Berlin**
*www.visitberlin.de/en*
Berlin's official website has a section on visiting the city with kids, where it recommends family-friendly museums, parks, cafés, and theaters such as the Atze children's music theater.

**Wall Museum**
*www.mauermuseum.de*
Originally a place from which to observe the border crossing and help people trying to escape across the Berlin Wall, this museum next to Checkpoint Charlie opened in 1962. Exhibits detail the history of the wall and nonviolent struggles for human rights around the world.

**Trabi-Safari**
*www.trabi-safari.de*
Book a tour around the city in the iconic car of East Germany. Kids will get a kick out of the giraffe-, leopard-, and zebra-patterned options in the company's fleet, or go with the classic pale blue model from 1989.

**Berlin Zoo**
*www.zoo-berlin.de*
Find tickets and visiting information to Berlin's popular zoo, aquarium, and Tierpark here. Check the feeding times for the polar bears, lions, and great apes, always a hit with kids.

# Waterloo

## *Where Napoleon Surrendered*

Some kids may know "Waterloo" as the Abba song that closed the Broadway musical *Mamma Mia!* But Waterloo is a war story. And a trip to the real-life Waterloo will help children understand that the song's lyric—"At Waterloo, Napoleon did surrender"—refers to a place in Belgium and an epic battle that forever changed Europe and the world. And they'll learn that Napoleon, at five feet six, showed that small folks have a long reach—but they don't always get what they want.

About a half hour south of Brussels, Waterloo, the only fully preserved battlefield in Europe, offers a Continental version of Gettysburg. First,

a bit of background: In 1814, French emperor Napoleon Bonaparte abdicated his crown and was exiled to the Italian island of Elba. He escaped, made his way back to France, and took power again. No way, said the British (under the Duke of Wellington) and the Prussians (led by Gebhard Leberecht von Blücher), who were poised to invade France.

---

**BOOKS FOR PARENTS & KIDS**......
■ *Cat Paws through History: Ko-Ko the Cat Meets Napoleon Bonaparte* by Isabel H. Stepanian (2011) Learn about the great Napoleon Bonaparte's legacy through the eyes of Ko-Ko. This spirited feline encounters the famous leader while traveling the world with his human parents.

## Know Before You Go

■ *The Exploits of Brigadier Gerard* by Arthur Conan Doyle (1896) These comic short stories follow Etienne Gerard, a vain and glory-obsessed cavalryman in the French Army during the Napoleonic Wars.

■ *Four Days in June: A Battle of Honor and Glory* by Iain Gale (2007) Experience the Waterloo campaign from the view of British, French, and Prussian soldiers.

**MOVIES**................
■ *Waterloo* (2007) This historical film is at its best in a lavish depiction of the fateful battle.

"I used to say of him [Napoleon] that his presence on the field made the difference of forty thousand men."—*Arthur Wellesley, the first Duke of Wellington (1831), who led the victorious Anglo-allied forces at the Battle of Waterloo*

Napoleon took the initiative and led his army to confront the allies near the tiny Belgian village of Waterloo on June 18, 1815. Some 200,000 troops fought, 72,000 were killed or wounded, and the English language gained the classic expression to "meet your Waterloo" (ultimate end) as Napoleon certainly did.

"If Napoleon had won at Waterloo, the catch-phrase to the history of the world would be different," says military history expert Caleb Carr. "There were just a lot of impressive guys on both sides. Start with Napoleon, one of history's greatest figures." Emperor of France in the early 1800s, the founder of the Napoleonic code (have your kids look it up) was a legendary military strategist. "You also had the Duke of Wellington and von Blücher, an amazing character who was 72 years old and charging around the battlefield."

Join the battle at the hamlet of Lion's Mound, where a visitors center offers a free treasure hunt book for children (and two giant-screen movies chronicle the conflict). Across the road is the Waterloo Wax Museum, and in a huge, round building a giant fresco (the Panorama) that's as long as a football field and brings the conflict vividly alive.

From there is a bird's-eye view of the battlefield and its main memorial, the Lion's Mound, a 131-foot-high, man-made cone of earth so named for the 28-ton iron lion that crowns it. Hop aboard an open-sided bus for a multilingual narrated journey across the battlefield's slopes and ridges where Wellington set up his position. The tour continues to the Hougoumont Farm, the site of some of the bloodiest fighting.

On July and August weekends, the battlefield reverberates with cavalry, cannon fire, and troops in Napoleonic-era uniforms. Every June 18, thousands of reenactors participate in a restaging of the battle. "Waterloo has taken on the status of a great battle," says Carr, "but it really was something that transcended military history. The battle drew to a close a 23-year war that started in 1792. Its aftermath defined many of the nations of Europe as we know them today, and it was almost like a crowning of the British Empire. The world was never the same again." ∎

## BUY WORTHY

■ **Neuhaus Chocolates** invented the world-famous **Belgian praline,** a bite-size chocolate filled with ingredients such as hazelnuts and fresh cream, in 1912. Head to their their Waterloo shop at 276 Chaussée de Bruxelles.

■ Brussels is famous for its statue of **Le Mannekin Pis,** a little naked boy urinating into a fountain. Be sure to check him out and see what costume he is dressed in at the moment. **For a souvenir, kids can find these little statues for sale all over the city.**

# Brittany

## *Europe's Great Shore*

The town of St.-Malo looms out of the mist, off the rugged coast of Brittany, a place steeped in the mystery and tradition of Celtic times. Just three hours by train from Paris, it was once a staging ground for pirates intent on raiding ships in the English Channel. See the replica of the legendary 19th-century corsair *Le Renard* under sail. Listen to a pied piper sound a haunting bombard (what someone once called "an oboe on steroids") or a *biniou bras* (a bagpipe). Dive into a *fest noz,* a town dance and party—a favorite of Jane Anderson, a mother of two. "They have cotton candy and old-fashioned games of chance, like hooking presents in a fishing boat with a rod. Fresh food includes mussels

and fries, steak, and cups of Breton cider. And then the Celtic country dancing begins. Everyone holds hands and dances in a circle, with children swept up in the fun." And if you're lucky you'll hear tall tales of mermaids and giants and pixies.

Go in the spring or fall when many festivals unfold on the rustic peninsula that runs from St.-Malo to the city of St.-Nazaire, where the Loire River tumbles into the Atlantic. The Festival de Cornouaille, a nine-day "grand rendezvous" of Breton culture staged every July in the medieval town of Quimper, is the largest of the celebrations.

A place apart, Brittany treasures its separateness from France—it has more in common with

---

**BOOKS FOR KIDS**......................
■ *Folk Tales of Brittany* **by Elsie Masson (2009)** First published in 1929, these tales were gathered from Breton legends and the Barzaz Breiz folk songs. Vivid pen-and-ink drawings illustrate stories such as "The Castle of Comorre" (set in the ancient town of Vannes, former seat

## Know Before You Go

of the Dukes of Brittany) and "The Country Bumpkin and the Hobgoblin."

**BOOKS FOR PARENTS**......................
■ *A Gift from Brittany* **by Marjorie Price (2008)** In this moving

memoir, a young American artist moves to rural Brittany in the 1960s and makes lasting friendships with her local neighbors.

■ *Colloquial Breton* **by Herve Ar Bihan (2003)** This easy-to-use beginner's guide deconstructs Breton, the Celtic tongue of Brittany.

those across the English Channel than with its fellow French. During the sixth century, Celtic tribes from the British Isles settled the peninsula. And for a thousand years, Bretons switched allegiances between France and England several times, still preserving their language, food, music, and other customs.

In Brittany "families get to explore nature in the raw," says Anderson. "There are 1,740 miles of coastline, with fabulous beaches and sailing schools, while stretching from the coast inland is the lovely and sometimes mystical Armorique Regional Nature Park, with its wolf museum geared to kids and storytelling in the woods." The tales unfold in the tiny village of Botmeur deep in the park on so-called Ribambelles et Ritournelles walks—full of song and story hosted by Katell, who animates her songs and stories with finger puppets, and guitar-playing troubadour Fred. No matter the language—Breton, French, English—it all works to involve children in something foreign.

The Armorique Regional Nature Park is the largest of a half dozen parks that protect the coast and islands. The Brière Regional Nature Park is a giant marshland best explored in a flat-bottomed *chaland* boat. Cap Fréhel Nature Reserve, near St.-Malo, features large seabird colonies (including puffins), 200-foot cliffs overlooking the Atlantic, and a 17th-century stone lighthouse.

Scattered off the coast of Brittany are tiny islands, some uninhabited

and others settled, but seemingly little changed in hundreds of years. "One of our favorite places," says Anderson, "is Belle-Île-en-Mer off the Morbihan coast. It's a great place to learn to surf. We also visited Île de Groix and Parcabout Chien Noir, where kids can release their inner monkey and literally swing from the trees." Parcabout is an "acrobatics park" featuring nearly seven and a half acres of nets, inspired by those on sailing ships, strung up to nine yards high among the trees—a massive spider web for kids to scramble about. Your family can spend the night sleeping in nets among the branches.

Wrap up your trip with a short journey 30 miles up the Britanny coast (buses run regularly) to Mont-St.-Michel, a medieval abbey with the aura of a fairy-tale castle that occupies an island a half-mile walk along a causeway. Help children reimagine what it must have been like here before cars and crowds by overnighting at one of several inns and watching the almost spooky advance of high tides that leave you orphaned from the mainland. ∎

# Paris
## *Medieval to Modern*

**P**aris may be one of the most richly vivid cities in the world," says writer Jim Morgan, author of *Chasing Matisse*. "The place is like one great piece of art. Every quarter, every street, every character seems painterly." Most older children are familiar with the iconic symbols of the city—the Eiffel Tower, Notre-Dame, the "Mona Lisa." But it's the small scenes, the little moments that give this city its artistic moments. Help connect your children with its artistic luminosity before you go. Introduce them to some paintings of the greats who lived and worked here: Picasso, Cézanne, van Gogh, Monet, Chagall (some suggestions: *Monet and the Impressionists for Kids* or Usbourne's *Famous Paintings*, 30 illustrated cards with explanatory text). Show them classic Paris scenes—Monet's "The Boathouse on the Seine," Marc Chagall's "Paris Through the Window," Van Gogh's "Sidewalk Café at Night." This gives the makings of an art scavenger hunt they can pursue when actually in Paris.

Once there, don't overdo the sightseeing. Begin with a trip on a *bateau-mouche*, a glass-enclosed or

---

**INSIDER TIP**

The Parisian Metro system offers more than 130 miles of train tracks, zigzagging through 300 stations and interlocking tracks beneath and above the city. Families can buy booklets *(carnets)* of up to ten tickets for use on the Metro mix of trains, buses, or trams. Have a buddy system in place before descending into the labyrinthine railway stations, though, as they are perennially crammed with frenetic subway patrons, artists, and musicians.

---

open-top boat that plies the Seine and gives you a graceful overview of the city. "Sightseeing without walking," says Linda Healey, an editor at the *International Herald Tribune* newspaper, who raised her daughter in Paris. Tours take about an hour and depart from several places along the river.

You'll be tempted, but don't gorge on sightseeing (save that for the food). This city rewards the concept of living like the locals (consider renting an apartment, especially if staying longer than a week). Linger in small cafés over hot chocolate and French bread and jam. Watch Parisian life go by; have the kids count the number of dogs they see—Parisians love their dogs. Less is more. "Doing three museums in a day is a huge mistake," says Doni Belau, blogger and creator of the Girls Guide to Paris website. "Plan one cultural thing per day and one fun thing the kids choose themselves. Have it be interactive and all about them." Rather than trying to see everything displayed in the Louvre, for example, narrow your visit to periods or genres that most interest your children—like the Egyptian mummies in the Sully Wing. You might want to see the "Mona Lisa," but the crowds are usually huge and pint-size kids will have problems catching a glimpse. Be polite and gently maneuver your child forward and you'll probably end up right in front of the masterpiece (an advantage of traveling with children).

Then follow with a surprise. Pop into Au Nain Bleu, the city's oldest (1836) and largest toy store. A great treat in the ninth arrondissement is la Mère de Famille, an old-fashioned sweet shop

(founded in 1761) with more than 1,200 types of candy.

When you do sightsee, try starting on the Île de la Cité—the island in the middle of the Seine. Remember: Think stroll, not power tour. Notre-Dame Cathedral dominates the island. Let the kids light votive candles and climb up into the towers for a glimpse of the gargoyles and a Quasimodo-level view of Paris. Go medieval inside the Conciergerie, the notorious prison where Marie Antoinette and so many other notables were held (and often tortured) before losing their heads to the guillotine. If you're there on a Sunday, visit the Marché aux Oiseaux, where birds and pets are sold inside a classic pavilion.

On another day see the Eiffel Tower—which offers a 42-mile panoramic view of city and environs on a clear day. Pose intriguing questions—"Why do you think so many Parisians hated the Eiffel Tower when it was first built?"—that make history more relevant and give them something to think about. On the first floor you can pick up a booklet that poses questions

**BOOKS FOR PARENTS**
■ *Paris to the Moon* by Adam Gopnik (2001) What would it be like to raise your family in Paris? Read an American writer's perspective on living and working here from 1995 to 2000.

**THEATER**
■ *Les Misérables* (1862) Widely acclaimed as one of the greatest novels of the 19th century, the musical version of Victor Hugo's masterpiece tells the story of former convict Jean Valjean as he explores the laws

## Know Before You Go

of justice, morality, and grace across the backdrop of French history.

■ *Phantom of the Opera* (1910) The legendary novel by French writer Gaston Leroux has been adapted to numerous literary and dramatic works, including this musical. The underground pond referenced in the story lies beneath Paris's famed Opéra Garnier, constructed in the 1860s.

**MOVIES**
■ *Midnight in Paris* (2011) Woody Allen's 42nd film was shot in Paris except for a few sequences in Giverny and at the Château de Versailles.

■ *Ratatouille* (2007) This delightful Disney animated comedy is set in one of Paris's finest restaurants. In pursuit of his lifelong dream to become a French chef, a determined young rat spurs a hilarious chain of events that turns the town upside down.

kids can answer as they follow tour guide Gus along a trail of yellow footsteps. Another essential stop is the futuristic Centre Pompidou, a building that looks like it's been turned inside out. Home to the National Museum of Modern Art, it includes a section called the Galérie des Enfants, with exhibits and activities designed specially for kids. Out front is the best place in Paris to catch musicians, acrobats, fire-eaters, and other street performers.

Let your child's age rule. "For small kids, rent a wooden sailboat at the Luxembourg Garden; they use a stick to push it from one side of the large pond to the other, like generations of Parisian children before them," advises Healey. "Also in the Luxembourg area: pony rides and a pay-to-enter playground with lots of stuff to climb on. For a truly French experience, take small kids to the marionettes show, a Parisian tradition."

Paris is perfect for specialty tours. You can spend a day exploring beneath the city, clambering through the Catacombs—subterranean crypts with thousands of bones—and the Parisian sewers that have been turned into an underground museum (without the smell or rats). If you have a budding gourmand, consider cooking classes. And while you're roaming, says Healey, be sure to "observe the ritual of French *goûter* [snack time] at 4:30 p.m. with Nutella on a baguette or a fruit tart from a bakery."

Doni Belau recommends tours based on movies or books that kids can see or read before the trip—for younger children, *The Hunchback of Notre-Dame, Madeleine,* and *Ratatouille,* and for older ones, Sofia Coppola's film *Marie Antoinette* or *Amélie* with its myriad Montmartre locations. "One time we read *Linnea in Monet's Garden*—about a little girl who visits Paris with her grandfather and discovers the artist—and did a progressive book tour," says Belau.

Now it's time to relax. Think about something as simple as a picnic in one of the city's magnificent green spaces—the Tuileries beside the Louvre, the sprawling Bois de Boulogne, the Jardin des Plantes (home to a zoo), or the offbeat Buttes-Chaumont with its artificial lakes, waterfalls, and mountains. "Make a big deal about going shopping for the picnic and have the kids pick out what they want to eat," says Belau. Our suggestion: Visit small shops for fresh French bread, cheese, salami and other meats, local fruit, and mineral water (*avec* or *sans gaz*) for the kids, local *du vin* for you. Adds Belau: "That's France—creating a day around food—talking about it, planning it, buying everything, and finally eating." ■

# CONNECTIONS

**City of Paris Portal**
*www.paris.fr/english*
This site keeps a comprehensive up-to-date list of happenings about town. It also provides links for booking hotel rooms and city tours.

**Paris Convention and Visitors Bureau**
*http://en.parisinfo.com*
This website offers a rich menu of musical and theatrical events, museums and tours, scenic outdoor strolls, and more ideas to build a packed itinerary. Purchase museum passes and event tickets here.

**Catacombs' Musée Carnavalet**
*www.catacombes.paris.fr/en/home*
Travel underground more than 2,000 years back in time. Visit the website of the Catacombs' Musée Carnavalet for activities geared to parents and children.

# Barcelona
## *The Greatness of Gaudí*

**M**any artists have brought alive the cities in which they live through their genius: Michelangelo (Rome), Toulouse-Lautrec (Paris), Rembrandt (Amsterdam). But no one has had as great an influence on a place as the incomparable Antoni Gaudí. If Dr. Seuss had designed a city, it would look like the gaudy Gaudí architecture of Barcelona, Spain. He changed the face of his beloved home.

Kids love Gaudí's flamboyant, colorful, over-the-top style. They want to touch, feel, and imitate his eccentricity. His genius amplifies the childlike joy of Barcelona. Watch them discover an artist who lived a century ago and refused to allow others to tell him what art should be. So unique is his style that seven of his structures in and around the city are collectively a UNESCO World Heritage site ("Works of Antoni Gaudí").

Born in the Spanish countryside in 1852, Gaudí moved to the Catalan metropolis at 16 to study art. Over the next 50 years, he created buildings so utterly unique—"eccentricity raised to the level of monumental architecture," says architectural critic Paul Goldberger. His free-flowing style presaged the psychedelic works of the 1960s. And so did his personal lifestyle. (Kids: Gaudí was a vegetarian when it was extremely unusual; an ardent recycler who created an art form—*trencadís*—from broken tile shards; a deeply spiritual man; and a nature lover).

"He was inspired by nature," says Rachel Rodríguez, author of *Building on Nature: The Life of Antoni Gaudí.* "Growing up in the countryside outside Barcelona helped foster and reinforce his love

### INSIDER TIP

A proper Spanish greeting imparts two *besos* (kisses) or light touches cheek to cheek, with one on each side. This applies to friends and strangers alike, as well as men and women and boys and girls. Don't be bashful about making the move; Catalans are renowned for their passion and spirit.

of the natural world. You'll see ceilings like swirling waves, pillars like bones, and even a dragon on a rooftop. A fun way to tour his buildings or park is to identify as many shapes or objects from nature as you can in his works. His references to nature give his buildings their timeless appeal."

Gaudí's masterwork is the Templo de la Sagrada Familia, a cathedral that towers over central Barcelona. Begun in 1882 it is due to be completed sometime in the next 25 years, more than 100 years after Gaudí's death. To young eyes, the church appears like a giant, elaborate sand castle. Combining aspects of Gothic, modernism, and art

## CONNECTIONS

**Casa Batlló Gaudí Barcelona**
*www.casabatllo.es*
Gaudí's unmistakable work, and his telltale whimsicality, animates Passeig de Gràcia. Passersby can't miss Casa Batlló's famed facade, emulating the effect of a stone thrown into a pool of flowering water lilies, from its site in the city center.

**Tibidabo Amusement Park**
*www.tibidabo.cat/en/homepage*
More than 25 rides and attractions await at the top of Mount Tibidabo, the highest point on the Collserola Ridge at 1,680 feet above sea level. The park is more than 100 years old and provides some of the most spectacular views of Barcelona.

**Barcelona Turisme**
*www.barcelonaturisme.com*
Barcelona's tourism website features practical information on where to eat, where to shop, and what to see.

nouveau, it is a fantasy of spires, columns, and soaring stained-glass windows. Ask your child to discover nature in the design: columns that resemble the trunks of giant sequoia trees, stone turtles, snakes and chameleons, and 36 different bird species. "It's unlike any other church on Earth in terms of architecture, symbolism, sheer size, concept, and most important—we get to see the process of construction," says Jordan Susselman, an American who runs a tour company in Barcelona. "You can spend days at Sagrada and not uncover all of its mysteries and symbolic elements. I find new things all of the time."

Another Gaudí landmark and a terrific place for a bike ride is 30-acre Parc Güell, a former housing project on a hillside overlooking Barcelona. Once envisioned as a garden city for the well-to-do, today it is a child's fantasyland composed of mosaic benches, checkerboard walls, and dragon fountains that could be mistaken for Whoville or some other Seussean creation. (Gaudí lived in one of its two show homes during the last decade of his life.)

A great view of Barcelona is from the roof of Casa Milà, designed as a private home. The rooftop is straight out of director Tim Burton's 2010 epic *Alice in Wonderland*—a phantasmagorical blend of air vents resembling African masks and medieval knights, and odd-shaped chimneys called *espanta bruixes* (witch scarers). "Walking the rooftop at Casa Milà feels like being on a ship in big ocean waves," says Rodríguez. "And picture the storm troopers from *Star Wars*. The decorated chimneys atop Casa Milà apparently inspired George Lucas to create the film's white-masked warriors."

And when you have your fill of Gaudí (hard to do), treat the kids at the Chocolate Museum, which has nifty chocolate sculptures and a store that will please their sweet tooth. On weekends there are chocolate-making classes for kids age three and up (book well in advance at *www.pastisseria.com/en/PortadaMuseu)*.

Then head for what's been called the world's greatest pedestrian promenade: broad, tree-lined Las Ramblas, an animated avenue of mimes, musicians, and street performers. Start from the Plaça de Catalunya and walk toward the harbor, past the Canaletes Fountain and—a kids' favorite—stands selling baby turtles, ducklings, chicks, and other birds. Visit La Boqueria, a food market that is a colorful, fragrant feast for eyes and stomach (and has cooking classes for children upstairs on Saturdays). This might be a good place to teach your children a few words of Spanish. Point at a fruit and ask the seller what it's called.

Leaving the market, continue down the pedestrian walk past buskers and those robotic, costumed mimes that got their international start on Las Ramblas. If it's Sunday, detour to the nearby Catedral de Barcelona, where locals perform the sadana, a lively circle dance forbidden during Francesco Franco's rule. Then continue on Las Ramblas to the Mediterranean waterfront, where you can lounge on the

## FAST FACTS

■ Las Ramblas, **the frenetic pedestrian boulevard winding from the city center to the port,** was originally a dry riverbed. In both Spanish and Catalan, *rambla* refers to the water flowing through the channel that was walled in on both sides in the mid-13th century.

■ Catalonians pride themselves on the one-of-a-kind sporting tradition known as **castell-building—the formation of festive human towers.** In a remarkable acrobatic feat, *castellers* assemble such castles as high as 35 feet.

■ Barcelona's patron **St. George (St. Jordi)** is honored at a feast and festival in April and September, at which time mechanical fire-breathing dragons roam the city's streets.

■ Barcelona's seaside port, once heavily industrialized, was transformed for the **1992 Olympic Games;** it began with visitor-friendly restaurants, cafés, and bars.

sand at palm-fringed Barceloneta beach or visit the Museu Marítim de Barcelona (where the kids will walk through a full-size model of the 1859 *Ictieo I* submarine on their way into the musem). The area, once squalid industrial land, was transformed for the 1992 Olympics into a lively district of restaurants and striking architecture. Lunch in a tapas restaurant and enjoy the spectacle. Tapas, uniquely Spanish, are finger foods of every imaginable kind. Typically you order eight or more small dishes—so children can enjoy a tasty adventure without committing to any one option. Meanwhile, you can appreciate why Cervantes said of Barcelona in *Don Quixote, Part II* that it is "the treasure house of courtesy, the refuge of strangers." ■

# St. Ives & Penzance

## *Where Pirates Ruled*

From Lizard Point to Land's End, Cornwall, Britain's southernmost landfall, is the end of England and made to spark kids' imagination. It's a place of mystery and magic, of larger-than-life characters and landscapes that seem plucked from medieval legend.

At Tintagel, for example, remain the ruins of what is said to be Camelot, home of King Arthur and his knights. "Some historians might tell you King Arthur was a myth," says photographer Jim Richardson, who is a Cornishman at heart with countless visits to his credit. "But I remember hearing the tale while walking the castle ruins straight

from the town crier of a nearby city, and when I heard it from him, I knew he believed it, and so I believed. It's such a story of honor and glory, so wrapped up in mists and mysteries, so full of juicy legends, that it really ought to be true. And so going out to a headland, with the wind in your face and the waves crashing at your feet, is all you need to recall the time of chivalry, knights, and the wonders of lost causes."

The Cornish were muckrakers and renegades— its sailors defeated the Spanish Armada and its smugglers sneaked in brandy from Brittany. The region is littered with Celtic crosses and prehistoric relics— the Merry Maidens Stone Circle is said to be lasses turned to stone for dancing on a Sunday. Around a hundred prehistoric monuments can be found within

---

**INSIDER TIP**

Costumed pirates invariably show up at the Golowan Festival held annually at the end of June. Parades, feasts, and fireworks blend traditional customs with modern attractions.

---

100 square miles on haunting Bodmin Moor. So put the family in a rental, and drive the impossibly narrow roads that seem like tunnels of flowers, as Richardson calls them, because of colorful summer gardens. "Glendurgan has a maze to die for," he says, recommending places to see, "and the Lost Gardens of Heligan are worth getting lost in. Then there is the Eden Project, with its huge domes enclosing whole ecosystems, including the world's largest rain forest 'in captivity,' with steamy jungles and waterfalls."

Along the way, stop for a Cornish pasty (one recipe: beef, onion, potato, and turnip in thick pastry), then head for Penzance, inspiration for Gilbert and Sullivan's operatic *Pirates of Penzance* and the most westerly town on the Cornish Riviera—where subtropical plants bloom above the beach. It is here that Cornish wreckers lured hapless ships to the rocky coast—perhaps thousands—with false lights on stormy nights; entire towns would turn out to share in the spoils.

"What you must do," says Richardson, "is take your kids straight out to St. Michael's Mount. It rises from the sea like a fairy-tale castle, so they'll beg to go there. From the broad, sweeping beach, the little village at the base of the mount is only a few hundred yards away. As the tide recedes, a magical causeway is revealed and you can walk right across. Pass the wee harbor and go up the hill to the castle, once a monastery, where the St. Aubyn family has lived ever since 1647. From the top of the castle, you'll see all the way down the coast south to the Lizard Peninsula and west to the village of Mousehole, a grand sight on a fair day. But don't linger too long. The tide will return and you might find yourself wading back across the causeway as St. Michael's Mount becomes an island once again."

There is always more coast to explore. "If you are lucky the evening will bring out the pilot gig crews," says Richardson, "rowing their long boats around the island, practicing their craft from the times when they raced out to sailing ships coming into the English Channel. Explore the afternoon away on one of the little beaches along the south coast, building sand castles (with moats, of course), and wait for the tide to return in the evening, sending you back up the cliffs, or behind the breakwater of the harbor, and into the village for a dinner of fish-and-chips. There is just so much coast." ■

## Know Before You Go

**BOOKS FOR KIDS**
■ *The Pirate Tales of Lantern Jack* by Peter Steele (2008-2011) This series of books for kids follows Lantern Jack and his crew of Cornish pirates in their quest of the unknown.

■ *Treasure Island* by Robert Louis Stevenson (1883) Filled with adventure, mystery, and suspense, this classic tale follows Jim Hawkins through his journey on the high seas to find hidden treasure.

**MOVIES**
■ *Pirates of the Caribbean: On Stranger Tides* (2011) Watch Johnny Depp and his pirate crew in scenes filmed in St. Ives, Cornwall, for this popular Disney franchise.

**MUSIC**
■ *The Pirates of St. Piran: Three Sheets to the Wind* (2010) Listen to a CD of traditional pirate music sung by the locals of Cornwall.

**LINGO**
■ **Arrr** The annual "Talk Like a Pirate Day" is September 19. Child and parent pirates alike can learn phrases and songs at *www.talk likeapirate.com/junior pirates.html.*

# Stonehenge
## *An Enduring Mystery*

**T**he huddled circle of 150 immense stones, the most famous of 900 stone circles in Great Britain, beckons from its lonely perch on the windswept chalk downland of Salisbury Plains in central England. You walk past a few of the ancient barrows (burial sites), then approach the monolith as the ancient Britons would have. "You can find the original route into the site via a central avenue and imagine you are a Neolithic person walking to great ceremonies and rituals," says Timothy Darvill, a Bournemouth University archaeologist and author of *Stonehenge: The Biography of a Landscape*. "Think noise, people, fires, smells, animals, and so on."

Stonehenge is an enigma. A total mystery that fascinates kids—in fact, all of us. A 12th-century legend claims Merlin the wizard created Stonehenge from rocks hewn by giants. In the 17th century some considered it an elaborate fake—one "artificially made of pure sand, and by some glewie [glue] and unctuous matter knit and incorporated together," wrote William Camden in 1610. In Victorian times, a theory floated that ghosts of its ancient builders would magically appear if you recited the Lord's Prayer backward during a night at the site.

For all our knowledge and technology, we've never discovered who made it. The Druids? The Greeks? Or, as some once suggested, the Atlanteans? Nor do we know why and how it was constructed. Does it have some astronomical significance? Was it a sacrificial site? A sacred gathering place? Evidence of more than 60 creation burial sites here suggests that Stonehenge was the largest Neolithic burial ground in the British Isles. This, however, does not suggest that it was only an ancient graveyard.

> "Pile of Stone-henge! So proud to hint yet keep / Thy secrets, thou that lov'st to stand and hear. / The plain resounding to the whirlwind's sweep, / Inmate of lonesome Nature's endless year"—*From "Guilt and Sorrow, or Incidents upon Salisbury Plain" by William Wordsworth (1793–94)*

All we really know is that Stonehenge was constructed (taking some 30 million hours of labor) sometime between 3000 B.C. and 1600 B.C. And that the stones are arranged to align with the rising midsummer sun and the setting midwinter sun. "These must have been important turning points in the annual cycle of people's lives," says Darvill, "and presumably triggered great festivals and rituals that drew people from many miles away."

The site consists of round earthworks and a ditch surrounding the outer and inner stone circles made from two types of rock. Big sarsen stones were quarried from Marlborough Downs and provide the framework of the structure, while the smaller bluestones were brought 240 miles from Wales (they turn bluish when wet). Darvill is among those who believe the builders of Stonehenge considered the bluestones magical. "That is why they were brought from such a great distance," he says. "And periodically moved and broken up—so pieces could be taken away as lucky charms or talismans."

Even as late as the 13th century, the site was thought to have magical properties. Layamon, a British poet who wrote *Brut*, the first English work to mention the legends of King Arthur and the Knights of the Round Table, wrote: "The stones are

## FAST FACTS

■ Speculation for the reason Stonehenge was built ranges from **astronomical observation to human sacrifice.**

■ Stonehenge is **not a henge** in the strict sense, because its bank and hedge are reversed.

■ Stage one of the construction of Stonehenge consists of **56 "Aubrey holes,"** which are named after John Aubrey, who discovered them.

■ The largest of the sarsen stones weighs up to **50 tons.**

great / And magic power they have / Men that are sick / Fare to that stone / And they wash that stone / And with that water bathe away their sickness."

So many people now visit that access is restricted. You either follow a trail around the circle's periphery or you sign up to enter inner Stonehenge on guided tours before and after regular hours. "The best way for younger kids to explore the place," advises Darvill, "is to leaf through a copy of *The Amazing Pop-Up Stonehenge* at the visitors center before going out to the stones." After your visit, ask your kids who they think built Stonehenge—and why? ■

### BOOKS FOR PARENTS & KIDS
■ *If Stones Could Speak: Unlocking the Secrets of Stonehenge* **by Marc Aronson (2010)** National Geographic tackles the mystery behind the archaeological wonder in a read for children of all ages.

■ *Stonehenge: A History in Photographs* **by Julian Richards (2004)** Enjoy a striking array of images

## Know Before You Go

flavored with anecdotal passages from professional archaeologist and Stonehenge expert Richards.

### BOOKS FOR PARENTS
■ *The History of the Kings of Britain* **by Geoffrey of Monmouth (2011)** This medieval text tells the story

of King Arthur and Merlin, who some thought magically transported stones to Stonehenge.

### DOCUMENTARY
■ *Secrets of Stonehenge* (2010) Follow a team of archaeologists as they unearth ancient graves and Welsh bluestones around Stonehenge, offering clues to its construction and purpose.

# London
## *The Tower That Captivates*

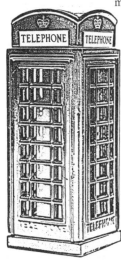

**M**ost visitors don't realize that the Tower of London is a 24/7 operation, with a community of 47 families within the walls who have perfectly normal lives. As a Yeoman Warder or 'Beefeater' I actually live here. It's my favorite thing," says John Keohane, whose fellow Yeoman Warders have guarded the tower for more than 500 years.

Because it mixes past and present-day life, the most compelling attraction for kids in London, a city of attractions, is the brooding tower, redolent of history and rich with stories of ghosts and beheadings, torture and murder.

Built on the north bank of the River Thames by William the Conqueror beginning in 1078, it was Europe's first fortress and one of the most famous fortified buildings in the world.

### INSIDER TIP
Before heading off to visit the Tower of London, try to catch the first ride of the day (10 a.m.) on the London Eye for an overview of the city, including the Tower in the far distance on a clear day.

Now an 18-acre complex encircled by walls and a moat, it has served variously as an armory, treasury, royal residence, prison, menagerie, home of the Royal Mint, and public records office. "It was the largest building in London at the time it was built," says Keohane. "It's made of Caen stone brought from France. All other buildings in London were mainly made of wood.

"Children are in awe when walking between its walls," he continues, "and they really appreciate being shown where history actually happened—like the murder of the two princes, who disappeared in 1483." The story goes that 12-year-old Edward had been confined to the tower with his younger brother, Richard. Historians believe they were murdered in what is now called the Bloody Tower by the Duke of Gloucester, allowing his ascension to the throne as King Richard III a month later; what are thought to be the brothers' bones were discovered in 1674.

"The most common question kids ask is, 'Where are the dungeons?'" says Keohane. "Children have this Hollywood image of dark, dank rooms below ground. In reality the tower was a prison, not a jail. Prisoners lived normal lives under what we would today call 'house arrest.'"

The place does have its dark side. The tower has never had a permanent torture chamber, although the White Tower once housed a rack. Seven people were beheaded here (including Queen Anne Boleyn in 1536). Older kids will love these gruesome facts: Victims are conscious for eight seconds after the blow until lack of oxygen kicks in; executioners often had to take several whacks at the head; and the head was hoisted, not to allow the crowd to view it, but to enable the dying victim to see the crowd and body.

Prisoners included the heir to the Scottish throne, later King James I of Scotland, the eventual Queen Elizabeth I, and Guy Fawkes, who was tortured in 1605 into confessing to the Gunpowder Plot. During World Wars I and II, several men were shot here for espionage.

Not surprisingly, the tower is said to be haunted. Boleyn allegedly wanders around the White Tower carrying her head under her arm. Other ghosts include Henry VI, Lady Jane Grey, and the little princes. As you walk the grounds, look for the immense black ravens that have frequented the tower area since the 1600s. If they ever leave, legend says, the tower will fall, and along with it the kingdom.

Indoors, the star attraction is the dazzling Crown Jewels, Britain's most precious treasure. Kept here since the reign of Henry III, the jewels, plate, and symbols of royalty such as the crown, scepter, and orb are now in the Waterloo Barracks.

Kids flock to Henry VIII's massive 1540 armor displayed on the entrance floor in the White Tower. "Henry's armor is a basic body with extra pieces to literally *bolt* on for different uses—from sport to war," says Bridget Clifford, keeper of the Royal Armouries. "It had to fit the individual, so here in the 21st century we can actually see Henry's bulky

**BOOKS FOR KIDS**
■ *Tower of London: England's Ghostly Castle* by Gail Blasser Riley (2006) An eerie read, this book brings the legends and myths of the tower to life.

■ *The Ravenmaster's Secret: Escape From the Tower of London* by Elvira Woodruff (2005) A slightly harder read and one for older children, the story follows a boy who works in the tower but faces a challenge when he

## Know Before You Go

makes friends with a prisoner and must help her escape before she is executed for being a Scottish rebel.

■ *Sebastian at the Tower of London* by Margaret Hall, Dawn L. Jones, and David Wenzel (2002) Younger kids will enjoy reading about teddy bear Sebastian taking it upon himself to save the ravens at the tower, while

learning a valuable lesson about freedom.

**MOVIES FOR KIDS**
■ *The Tower* (2007) For a visual tour of the Tower of London, watch an eight-part series that features reenactments and expert interviews, and explores forgotten secrets. Kids will get a better understanding of its rich history and an appreciation of this English landmark.

outline—more than six feet tall and apparently a fine figure of a chap, with broad shoulders and shapely legs. It's only when you see the sideways view of the armor that you realize there is a lot of Henry's *bottom* hidden behind. This is one of the last surviving harnesses of the king, and the gold decoration on the borders is said to be based on designs by Hans Holbein, the court artist who created the iconic power portrait of Henry that usually illustrates him."

Clifford also suggests pointing kids to the armor of Henry Stuart, who was just 15 when the suit was given to him by Sir Francis Vere. "It is richly decorated with scenes from the life of Alexander the Great," he says. "Look closely and you'll find exotic elephants lurking in the design—a reminder that the tower had a menagerie here until the 19th century."

Animals housed at the tower included, at times, kangaroos, ostriches, the king's polar bear (which went fishing in the Thames), and three leopards from the Holy Roman Emperor. "And famously an elephant from the King of France in 1255," says Clifford. "Sadly, it died after two years and was buried on site."

Check out the stone royal coat of arms dating from the time of William and Mary—the unicorn has a twisted horn and cloven hooves, but the lion is really a pug dog in a wig. "And look for the 14th-century lion's head corbels on the vaulting underneath the Bloody Tower," says Clifford. "It used to be called the Garden Tower, but Bloody's much more fun. The lion's head is another reminder of the menagerie that lived here."

"Allow at least two hours to see the tower," Keohane suggests. "Preferably four, if you can afford the time. The tower is a lot larger than people expect."

If you stay late, watch the Ceremony of the Keys, a tradition that has unfolded here every night for at least 700 years. At 9:53 p.m., the tower's Chief Yeoman Warder, in long red coat and Tudor bonnet, emerges from the Byward Tower with a candle lantern and the Queen's Keys, and joins a military escort. Together, they lock the main gates of the tower, while all of the guards salute the keys.

After you tour the tower, guide your children toward some of the other sights to see in London. Westminster Abbey, for example, is the burial site of 17 English and Scottish monarchs, and where royal weddings and coronations have been held since William I's in 1066. It's full of tombs and memorial slabs—more than 3,300 people are buried here. Poet's Corner alone commemorates Chaucer, Shakespeare, Tennyson, Dickens, Emily Brontë, and many others.

A monthly sleepover at the Natural History Museum enables kids to encounter meerkats and millipedes, and snooze under a life-size diplodocus skeleton. King's Cross Station is the home of Harry Potter's platform 9³/₄ (actually filmed on the real platform 4). And what child wouldn't love Mrs. Kibble's Olde Sweet Shoppe, with two outlets that serve 180 types of candy, mostly hard and old-fashioned, such as sherbet dip, sugar mice, and the best-selling rhubarb and custard? ∎

## INSIDER TIP

Take the kids to the London Dungeon (*www .the-dungeons.co.uk/london/en/index.htm*). This location will scare them to their bones, with attractions such as the Ride to Hell, which takes them through the Tower of London's Traitor's Gate.

# Edinburgh
## *Castles, Kilts, and Ghosts*

**F**ew cities in the world have such a dramatic, iconic silhouette—of church spires and lofty, brooding, ancient Edinburgh Castle. Built on the "plug" of a long-extinct volcano, it lords over the city—settled in 9 B.C.—that sprawls at its feet. "So strongly grounded, bounded and founded, that by force of man it can never be confounded," wrote John Taylor of it in 1630. It seems more fantasy than real, fitting if you consider Harry Potter creator J. K. Rowling calls Edinburgh home.

Children will find the castle's menacing profile and dark history irresistible. (In 1830, a child's bones were discovered in a wall in the Royal Palace; beneath the floor of King James's birth chamber is a pit-prison whose occupants remain a mystery; in 1720, 21 pirates were held in the castle dungeons, most to be later "hanged by the neck upon the gibbet" on Leith Sands).

To visit the castle, walk from the city center up the Royal Mile (actually it's 107 feet more than a true mile) to the eastern flank of the castle hill, where people have been living for 7,000 years. You

## BUY WORTHY

Next door to the **Edinburgh Castle Esplanade** is the Edinburgh Old Town Weaving Company. Visit the working mill to see power looms in action and head to the shops on the building's five stories to buy from its **colorful showcase** of cloth goods.

can scramble across the ramparts and visit the Royal Palace and the National War Museum with its arms, medals, and uniforms. But what really engages kids is their brush with living history. Actors in period garb offer daily talks and demonstrations, and portray such historical characters as Mary Queen of Scots, the ninth Earl of Argyll, Lady Euphemia, a Highland clansman, Cromwellian soldiers, and colonial prisoners of war kept in the castle during the American Revolution.

The best time to visit the castle is in August. For three weeks, on the esplanade parade ground, it hosts the Royal Edinburgh Military Tattoo, a stirring spectacle that will dazzle kids. The nightly extravaganza features military bands and drill teams from the British armed forces and from around the world. It is all skirling bagpipes, swaying kilts, and booming drums—a blend of music, marching, fireworks, and a sound-and-light show. Featuring more than 1,000 participants, its climactic conclusion of massed pipes and drums march onto the field to join a gathering of military bands for renditions of the national anthem and "Auld Lang Syne." A flag is lowered with buglers sounding the "Last Post" or the "Sunset" call of the Royal Marines. Then

## CONNECTIONS

**Royal Edinburgh Military Tattoo**
*www.edintattoo.co.uk*
Hundreds of thousands of spectators
turn out each August to view the Royal Edinburgh Military Tattoo, and space is limited.
Purchase tickets online at the event's website,
which also describes the Scottish regiments
(including the Black Watch and the Royal
Scots Dragoon Guards) that take part
in the festival.

**Edinburgh Castle**
*www.edinburghcastle.gov.uk*
The castle's official website provides a
time line of the fortress's history through
the centuries and offers tips on how to
beat the crowds. It also notes castle highlights
such as the Mons Meg, one of the world's
oldest medieval siege guns, and the Stone of
Destiny, the coronation seat of all
British sovereigns.

**Edinburgh and the Lothians**
*www.edinburgh.org*
Edinburgh's area guide details the culture
of the Lothians region and includes a
special family section for activities
with kids.

from the ramparts high atop Half Moon Battery a lone piper caught in floodlights sounds a mournful lament before all the performers troop down the Royal Mile into town to the sounds of songs like "Scotland the Brave."

The Tattoo coincides with the Edinburgh Fringe Festival, which includes more than 2,000 productions at hundreds of venues throughout the city. Many performances are appropriate or designed specifically for young visitors. The Edinburgh International Book Festival, for example, always features prestigious authors of teen and preteen titles who give talks and sign books in the leafy Charlotte Square Gardens.

The Edinburgh Fringe also includes a Kid-Zone in the Pleasance Courtyard, "with one of the best programs of children's shows anywhere on the Fringe," says Claudia Monteiro, a festival organizer and co-author of *The Locals' Guide to Edinburgh*. "From ukulele workshops to arts and crafts. And there's the infamous Mischief Makers Protest Camp, where kids with stuff to say are encouraged to express themselves through creative installations."

Billed as the largest arts festival on Earth, the 50-year-old Fringe consumes the city so entirely that you are thrown into a maelstrom of entertainment drawn from every continent. The Fringe is open to any performer who is willing to come and has a venue to host them. Expect a culturally eclectic blend of theatrics, street performance, mime, and virtually anything else someone can dream up. "You can walk around without a plan and experience all sorts of things," says teenager Matthew

McDonald Peterson. "Cool street music, comedy from all over."

The festival has changed his son's worldview, says his father, Keith Peterson. "Before going to Edinburgh, Matt's entire take on music and the arts was narrow, shaped by television and the Internet. But suddenly he was exposed to things he didn't know existed—all live rather than on a screen."

Can't visit in summer? "Edinburgh is a year-round festival city," says Monteiro, who also recommends the two-week International Science Festival in April. "From bubble workshops to dancing custard and the science of chocolate, no project is too large or too small for kids." One of the recent guests for this festival was ASIMO, the world's first humanoid robot. What kid wouldn't love to interact with this creature or this year's gem?

Among Edinburgh's other annual shindigs are the children's theatre festival (May), the Scottish International Storytelling Festival (October), and the Beltane Fire Festival (April), which revives an ancient Celtic rite with dancing, drumming, and fire-wielding performers on Carlton Hill. Or end the year with Edinburgh's famous four-day Hogmanay celebration.

Part of the adventure of visiting Edinburgh is the food. Head to The Elephant House on George IV Bridge— where J. K. Rowling wrote

## FAST FACTS

■ **Alexander Graham Bell,** inventor of the telephone and a founding member of the National Geographic Society, was born in Edinburgh in 1847.

■ The birthplace of writer and Edinburgh native **John Muir** is just outside of the city at the **John Muir House and Country Park.**

■ Edinburgh's population of **nearly 450,000** swells to **more than one million** during its famous arts festivals in August.

■ The **word "caddie"** originated from the men who were hired to carry pails of water up the tenement flats in the Old Town of Edinburgh. Golf caddies are thought to stem from Mary Queen of Scots, who called the **students who carried her clubs "cadets."**

the conclusion of the Harry Potter books in longhand (it's also frequented by authors Ian Rankin and Alexander McCall Smith). Its eclectic menu includes Scottish favorites like haggis (the national dish made with sheep's intestines), neeps (turnips), and tatties (mashed potatoes). While adults can try nouvelle Scottish (saddle of Perthshire venison, Aberdeen Angus steak with slow-braised cheek) at Victoria Street's Grain Store, kids will respond to the fact that the 220-year-old building is supposedly haunted. "Very haunted," says co-owner Paul MacPhail. "Among our ghosts are three mischievous children who have been known to throw cutlery about. In one corner there's said to be a ghostly arm that tries to pull you into the wall. And instead of the headless horseman, we've got a legless horseman who's sometimes seen riding up Victoria Street." ■

# Loch Ness
## *Highland Glory*

**W**hether you consider it a wild-goose chase or bona fide science, Loch Ness is proof that myth and legend can ignite a child's interest in a given place every bit as much as reality. Reports of a water "monster" living in the elongated Scottish lake stretch all the way back to the sixth century. But it wasn't until 1934, when a local doctor snapped a now famous photo of the illusive creature, that the Loch Ness monster became a worldwide phenomenon. Most adults consider the aquatic dinosaur a hoax. In the minds of many children, however, "Nessie" is just as real as her fossilized kinfolk.

"One binding thing about all the people who come to Loch Ness, and all of us with an abiding interest in Nessie, is that we would all very much like for there to be something there," says Adrian Shine, regarded as the leading expert on the Scottish monster—and a stellar example of how youthful imagination can spill over into adult life. Obsessed by Nessie as a child and young adult, Shine built a homemade submersible in his parent's backyard and spent the summers of 1974 and '75 scrunched

• • • • • • • • • • • • • • • • • • • • • • • • • • • • •
### INSIDER TIP

English is the official language of Scotland, though many Gaelic words are commonly used. "Loch," for example, is the Gaelic word for "lake," and "lochan" describes a small lake or a pond.
• • • • • • • • • • • • • • • • • • • • • • • • • • • • •

inside the underwater sphere, hoping a plesiosaur might swim past. That never happened, but Shine has made a lifelong career of talking about Loch Ness to several generations of eager children.

Start your own family Loch Ness expedition with a helicopter flight above the lake and surrounding countryside, a quick way for kids to come to terms with the sprawling local geography. "We're always flying members of the royal family when they're up here," says chopper pilot John McKenzie as he lifts off from Inverness Airport, "and rock stars, who come to play the RockNess music festival or get married in one of our local castles."

Shortly after takeoff, McKenzie spots a pod of dolphins in a long saltwater bay called the Firth of Moray, and then banks south over old Inverness.

Loch Ness is dead ahead, 20 miles long, 1 mile wide, and more than 700 feet deep—Scotland's largest lake. From high above, it's easy for kids to see how the water sits in the bottom of a deep valley called the Great Glen Fault, created more than 400 million years ago by the Earth's geological forces. The valley walls are covered in thick forest rising to rocky outcrops and heather-covered plateaus.

Back on terra firma, head for Drumnadrochit, about halfway down the lake's western shore. In addition to touristy gift shops and several Nessie statues where kids can pose for photos with the legendary reptile, the small village boasts kid-centric attractions that focus on Nessie and the lake, including Shine's own Loch Ness Center and Exhibition. "We try to use the monster story as a vehicle to open up appreciation of the lake in general," says Shine, who is, with his ever present tweed coat and gray beard, a familiar figure around the village. "There's a lot more going on in Loch Ness than people realize, from small living things to huge underwater waves."

Kids can't wait to get out on the lake. From Drumnadrochit Wharf, hop aboard the motorboat *Deepscan* for a personalized tour of Loch Ness. Skipper John Minshull has assisted in many of the Nessie hunts over the past 30 years, as well as regular scientific explorations. When you ask which of the expeditions stands out the most, Minshull says, "Finding the *Crusader*." Loch Ness was the scene of a 1952 attempt by daredevil John Cobb to set a world water speed record of 200 miles an hour in a jet boat. "The boat disintegrated during the first run, Cobb was killed, and *Crusader* went to the bottom," Minshull explains. In 2002, the Scottish skipper and his team discovered the wreck.

Have the *Deepscan* drop you and the kids at the dock below Urquhart Castle, another Loch Ness landmark, the ruins of the 13th-century bastion tower on a bluff above the lake, with sprawling lawns between the walls where kids can run off their excess energy. Over the centuries, Urquhart was the scene of many battles and sieges, mostly among Highland clans fighting one another. Kids will be especially intrigued by the giant trebuchet—a reproduction of a medieval catapult that can hurl a 250-pound stone a distance of nearly two football fields. ■

---

**BOOKS FOR KIDS**..............
■ *The Story of Loch Ness* by Katharine Stewart (2007) This delightful study balances fact and folklore to convey the biological and cultural formation of the lake.

**MOVIES FOR KIDS**..................
■ *The Ballad of Nessie* (2011) This lighthearted take on the monster and how she came to be in the bonny blue Highlands was produced by Disney.

## Know Before You Go

■ *Brave* (2012) Pixar heads to the mystical Scottish Highlands for this animated film, in which Princess Merida jeopardizes her kingdom by pursuing archery.

**MOVIES FOR PARENTS**..................
■ *Braveheart* (1995) This drama directed by and starring Mel Gibson as Sir William Wallace is about a 13th-century leader who unites the Scots to overthrow English rule.

**MUSIC FOR KIDS**..............
■ **The Scottish Fiddle Orchestra** One of Scotland's foremost traditional music organizations, formed out of one of the Fiddlers' Rallies still held throughout the country today, this group has released several listenable albums.

# New Trim To Grange

## *Landscape of the Ancients*

A short walk from the brooding castle in the town of Trim, Ireland, is an overgrown field surrounded by council houses. After two short years of excavation, the ruins of the Dominican Black Friary (a home for religious men and women) is beginning to emerge—it will be more than a decade before the work is complete.

"This is where we like children to get dirty," says geologist Steve Mandal. "Townspeople, students, young children—they are all welcome here to help us discover this religious landmark."

Here, your family will get a unique chance to help uncover a piece of the past, creating present-day memories. You are given a crash course in excavation techniques and actually get to work the ground. "We give you a trowel and a place to dig," says archaeologist Finola O'Carroll. "We teach you how to dig, plan, and record. You may be in the dirt making a map to the inch of what you have found."

In a nearby trailer are plastic baggies with small discoveries—shards of glass, an 11th-century copper penny, bits of sandstone stoneware. Painstaking maps reveal the still buried outlines of the friary, which was destroyed when Henry VIII was king and was subsequently dismantled by those wanting to use the rock to build homes.

While parents and older kids get busy digging for long-lost treasures, young children retreat to a kids camp—a mock site where they use the same techniques as the adults to discover buried relics and learn the art of archaeology. "This is the essence of experiential learning. It's the hands-on stuff," says O'Carroll. "Children learn by doing. And they ask the most amazing questions. One child challenged me about the rightness of moving a skeleton to accommodate a road. Good question. They want to handle things. You can't understand how heavy a stone axe is until you hold it. We let them. Or they get to run in chain mail—that teaches them quickly how heavy that is."

The site's archaeologists want the locals to invest in their history. "We have a responsibility to engage and involve everyone," O'Carroll says. "If you can get a community to invest in its heritage, you win. If you can help Trim cherish its past, tourists will, too."

Leave time on your trip, of course, to see Trim Castle, the largest Anglo-Norman castle in Ireland. Finished 30 years after it was begun in 1173 by Hugh de Lacy and his son Walter, the structure had a starring role in the movie *Braveheart*. It was one of Ireland's great defensive redoubts—so formidable a place that a mere 20 armored knights, stationed in the keep (the central stronghold), could hold hundreds of troops at bay. Backed by a marsh and encircled by a moat, the castle protected the bustling medieval village that was, at its height, one of Ireland's most powerful towns, perhaps several thousand strong and a commercial magnet for European merchants and a religious seat of power.

Unfortunately you can't tour the castle solo—access to the keep is by guided tour only for safety reasons. Your guide will tell you that inhabitants of the castle would "paint" the walls with human waste. You will learn that the stairways were designed to allow right-handed defenders to

# NEST

- **Trim Castle Hotel**
*Trim*
Overlooking Trim, this is the place to stay while visiting the castle and the nearby Hill of Tara, home to gods and goddesses, druids and warriors, and Ireland's high kings.
www.trimcastlehotel.com

- **Knightsbrook Hotel**
*Trim*
This family-run hotel on the River Boyne offers spacious family rooms and children's swimming lessons at the hotel pool. The Little Knights Kids Club entertains kids ages 5 through 12 with movie nights and arts and crafts.
www.knightsbrook.com

- **Castle Arch Hotel**
*Trim*
Featuring elegant rooms and only a short walk from Trim Castle, this hotel offers child care for those parents who want a little time to themselves.
www.castlearchhotel.com

ascend while keeping their sword hand free to engage trailing enemies (left-handers never got the chance to fight; they were thought to be in league with the devil). You will be told that the stained glass used in the windows was so valued in the 13th century that lords would wrap it in cloth and take it with them when they moved.

After the tour, walk around the castle and through the town of Trim itself. "You are walking the medieval landscape," says O'Carroll. Today's streets follow the original tracks of the town faithfully, past tumbledown priories and abbeys. "Imagine this place as a European powerhouse." ■

EUROPE

ASIA

Mediterranean Sea

Istanbul

TURKEY

CYPRUS

MOROCCO
Marrakech

ISRAEL
Jerusalem
JORDAN
Petra

Pyramids
of Giza

EGYPT

Red Sea

AFRICA

Indian
Ocean

Serengeti

Stone Town

TANZANIA

Atlantic
Ocean

ZAMBIA

Victoria
Falls

ZIMBABWE

NAMIBIA

Namib
Desert

**Map Key**

◻ Selected point of interest

0 ——— 1,000 miles

0 ——— 1,500 kilometers

# Africa
# & Middle East

# Marrakech

## *Deep in the Suqs*

**F**ew kids can resist a scavenger hunt. So to explore the suq (the Arab word for a bazaar) in Marrakech, actor and writer Andrew McCarthy turned the experience into a game for his nine-year-old son, Sam. They made their suq tour a search for the best example of a chest Sam had coveted.

"It was the ultimate treasure hunt for him," says McCarthy. In the marketplace, stall owners will bargain you to your knees and follow you for yards if they think they can close a deal. Much of what's sold are cheap knockoffs and tourist trinkets. "But the suq is also filled with tons of old, legit artifacts that were of real interest to Sam. Camel bones with 'contracts' written on them. Long swords fascinated him. Children seem to have an innate understanding of the authentic in a way we adults underestimate.

He was drawn to the culturally legit stuff."

When you arrive in Marrakech, start your journey in the main square of Djemaa el-Fna, center of the medieval medina (the old Arab or non-European quarter of a North African town). Here kids will see the monkey man, cobra charmers, acrobats, storytellers, henna vendors, and henna-haired artists. Beware: Attempt to take pictures, no matter how surreptitiously, and you will face a demand for money.

The medina itself is a labyrinth of jewelry, cafés, silverware, furniture, pottery, and spice suqs. The courtyards of *riad* (traditional Moroccan houses or palaces with interior gardens or courtyards) are filled with redolent jasmine and orange trees, shaded by

> "A colorful parade like flames in the dark night / leads the way to my fantasy. / Through the darkness until I feel the light's caress / I'm on my way to the streets of Marrakech."
> — *"Marrakech" by the group Incognito (1999)*

palms, and tinkling with fountains. From somewhere comes the music of *sinters* and *qarkarbebs*—Moroccan versions of guitars and castanets. Food stalls serve kebabs, fried fish, hot bread, couscous, slow-cooked lamb, and *harira* (chickpea and lentil) soup.

For the next step of your journey, plunge deep into the suq, like the McCarthys.

"Kids are so used to discovering things. Every corner was filled with strange and exotic items. What made sense to him overwhelmed me. Colors, sounds, objects needed explanation. Touching and handling things were encouraged. Every interaction made him question: 'What's this drum made of?

Goats' intestines, really? Why is that man buried in a hole up to his waist?' His curiosity was welcomed. It made interaction with locals easy and playful. I've never met people who delight in kids more than Moroccans. They all seem to be half-hustler/half-child themselves. So they were quick to play. My child wasn't used to exploit me to buy; he was given gifts nearly everywhere we stopped, with nothing expected in return. Everyone asked his name. Kids are treated as stars here."

The suq is a dizzying bazaar of mazelike passages and cacophonous stalls. It is raw with day-to-day life that most kids born to leafy suburbs will find unfamiliar, but that offers you a chance to discuss cultural differences with your child.

"My son loved people actually creating things—dying fabric different colors, men whittling wood who always gave him small trinkets after they were made," says McCarthy. "He was fascinated by the side alleys where people lived. He accepted the poverty without judgment. He interacted with kids his age with natural empathy and respect in a way I had never seen or taught him. I marveled at him spreading his wings."

Eventually, Sam found his treasured chest. "And two years later," McCarthy reports, "it is still his most valued possession." ■

## INSIDER TIP

Five times a day, there will be a call to prayer from the Koutoubia Mosque. This is an important time for the people of the city. Many drop what they are doing to go pray, so advise your kids to be aware and respectful of their religion.

# Namib Desert

## *Ever Changing Dunes*

"The Namib Desert is rugged, diverse, barren, beautiful, and a fascinating place to take your kids. In such a completely remote environment, it's just you and the earth," says Julian Harrison, African safari guidebook author and president of Premier Tours, who took his American kids to Namibia when they were 7, 9, and 11. "For my family, it was very much a bonding experience. Without other distractions you can spend time communicating and exploring the landscape together."

And there's lots to explore in these 1,200 miles of desert along the South Atlantic coast of Africa, not only because of the ecosystem's sheer size, but also because the dunes rarely present the same face twice. Wind changes the dunes' edges and erases tracks like waves on a beach—the shifting force is enough to cause entire dunes to migrate dozens of feet each year. A

> ### FAST FACT
>
> ■ In some spots here, **strange dark circular patches pepper the dunes.** Scientists haven't uncovered these so-called **fairy circles'** origins or purpose; theories include animal dust baths, poison leaked from plants, traces of meteor showers, and underground gas vent leaks. Your family can adopt and name a fairy circle near **Wolwedans Lodge,** with fees supporting the NamibRand Nature Reserve.

competition to see who can jump the farthest down a dune face can be an exhilarating family experience, the traces of which are wiped clean the next day.

The daytime heat draws moisture-laden air inland from chilly coastal waters. The effect produces a blanketing fog that is often the only source of water for this parched environment. Although the Namib Desert doesn't have the abundance of plants and animals found on other parts of the continent, it does feature a collection of unusual ones—gnarled trees, lichens, fog-catching beetles, and fleet-footed sand lizards have had time to evolve to survive on the sand. Desert-adapted elephants, bat-eared foxes,

## INSIDER TIP

Want to go without a tour company and find accommodations on your own? The most popular gateways to the Namib Desert are Sesriem and Sossusvlei, a short trip from picture-perfect red dunes. For a more remote experience, however, stay on the private tract of desert south of there in the NamibRand Nature Reserve or venture 50 miles north of Sesriem to the less frequented Solitaire—both areas are accessible by road with a rented vehicle.

hyenas, ostriches, oryx, and Africa's largest population of black rhinos eke out an existence roaming the dunes and their periphery.

The key to successful travel with children in the Namib Desert is not to zoom through. More than the landscape, it's the small things that kids will appreciate: "Stop and look for tracks, bugs, flowers—you'll see more things than most people who rush past. It looks so empty, but it's such an alive place," says Gary Webber, a guide who has worked with several tour agencies to bring families to Namibia—he's now starting his own company that targets families with young children traveling to the region (see *www.weboftours.co.za*).

While the animals adapt, you don't have

to—most camps catering to families are outfitted with canvas tents that are more like buildings, with beds, hot and cold running water, bathrooms, ceiling fans, and glass sliding doors. Wolwedans Dune Camp, for example, is surrounded by the Namib-Rand Nature Reserve in the Sossusvlei area; the reserve includes nine former farms, the owners of which agreed to preserve their land for wildlife.

For those who really want to immerse themselves in a remote desert, however, Serra Cafema camp, along the Kunene River near Namibia's border with Angola, is little more than seven thatched canvas huts amid more than 300,000 acres ripe for exploration; it is serviced by several tour companies.

When out exploring in the dunes there, you might spot members of the nomadic Himba tribe who build temporary huts with mud or dung, moving with the seasons. "You see their homes in the distance, little specks in the middle of this vast, vast desert—it's this little node of civilization," says Harrison. Visiting these communities, "the kids were awestruck. We made a point to talk to them about the similarities and differences between the Himba way of life and ours. For my children, it was eye-opening." ∎

**BOOKS FOR ADULTS**............
■ *The Sheltering Desert* by Henno Martin (2002) This is the autobiographical tale of two German scientists and a dog fleeing World War II by heading deep into the Namib Desert, surviving on the land for two and a half years.

**BOOKS FOR EVERYONE**............
■ *The Namib: Secrets of a Desert Uncovered* by Mary Seely and

## Know Before You Go

John Pallet (2008) Read descriptions of the landscape, how it is maintained by the sea and winds, and the animals and plants that depend on the desert for survival.

**MOVIE**............
■ *Babies* (2010) A funny and fascinating documentary about

how young children are reared in four different parts of the world, including Namibia, by the Himba people.

**MUSIC**............
■ *My First Time* by Unathi (2005) Listen to modern African sounds by Namibian-born Unathi, who gives hints of R&B, Afro-Jazz, soul, and house music. Recommended by National Geographic Music.

# Victoria Falls
## *Tumbling Masterpiece*

Before 1905, when explorers, natives, missionaries, and colorful, larger-than-life adventurers prefigured Indiana Jones, the few Europeans who visited Victoria Falls—a 145-million-gallon-a-minute aquatic ferocity on the border of Zambia and Zimbabwe—crossed it by dugout canoe or a barge towed by steel cable. But Cecil Rhodes, mining magnate and shaper of Africa, envisioned a Cape-to-Cairo railway—so the first bridge across the Zambezi River was laid here, at his instructions, right where spray from the falls would douse passing trains. The route never made it to Cairo, but the bridge was finished and the first living creature that crossed it was, symbolically, a leopard.

Today, that bridge overlooks a spot where families can experience some of the rush of the deluge by white-water gorge rafting (kids must be at least 15 years old to paddle in). Nearby, *aiyeee* screamers launch off a 315-foot-high bungee jump (for those age 14 or older). You can also walk the river and angle for yellowfish, African pike, or tigerfish, a ferocious freshwater fighter that weighs up to 33 pounds. Most parents will want to arrange a guided tour.

"Prepare your kids to be wowed, and to ask lots of questions," says Ludwig Munyuki, a guide with Wilderness Safaris (*www.wilderness-safaris.com*).

## CONNECTIONS

**Zambia Tourism**
*www.zambiatourism.com/travel/places/
victoria.htm*
Here you'll learn about tours and adventure packages for families as well as basic information on the Victoria Falls area.

**Travel Guide to Victoria Falls**
*www.victoriafalls-guide.net*
The Zimbabwean couple who run this website will answer questions and provide a guide to local traditions and culture.

Questions are what all guides want from kids—and what transforms a trip from watching to participating. These are the big five: Why should I care about this place? Why do you love it? What is the biggest surprise here? What should I take home from here? What is your favorite story about this place?

You approach the falls through a swirl of drenching mist and multiple rainbows. The locals call this landmark Mosi-oa-Tunya, the "smoke that thunders." Explorer and missionary David Livingstone, the first European to view the cataract, named it Victoria Falls in 1855, after the then British queen. No matter what you call it, the world's largest waterfall (5,604 feet wide, 354 feet high) is a colossus—a plunging, foaming mist machine that rattles the earth. The haze, which can be seen from 19 miles away, spawns such plants as ebony, pod mahogany, ivory, wild date palm, and snaking creepers and lianas.

"The scenic grandeur of it all takes one's breath away," says Russell Gammon, a third-generation Zimbabwean and 20-year veteran wilderness guide living in the town of Victoria Falls. Baboons and vervet monkeys bound around the falls' perimeter. Elephants, buffalo, giraffes, zebras, and antelope inhabit nearby forests. Get lucky and an occasional lion or leopard will surface. Hippopotamuses and crocodiles wallow in the waters above the falls, and elephants cross the river in the dry season.

Experiencing one of the seven natural wonders of the world is not the only reason to visit here with your kids. Use the occasion to share a deep lesson in world history: Africa was a great white playground for colonial powers that cowed locals, stripped the land of untold mineral wealth, and savaged wildlife.

"It is important to teach children that Africa is not all five-star lodges and wildlife; many less fortunate people live here as well," says Gammon. Visit either Monde or Mukuni villages for a sense of authentic local life. Gammon suggests stopping at Ebenezer orphanage: "It cares for and educates orphans of the HIV and AIDS pandemic. Sometimes we organize a soccer match between visitors and the children. This is a powerful experience for families. Outsiders should see how people in Africa go about their daily lives." ∎

# Yum!

■ **Mama Africa Eating House** Enjoy live musicians and dancers who invite audience participation—kids love interacting with the locals. Dishes include **beef, lamb, or** **chicken stew** served in individual cast-iron pots at the table.

■ **Boma Restaurant** This Victoria Falls spot features locals performing songs and dance in traditional costumes, while diners enjoy such local delicacies as **cheese bread** and (for the adventurous appetite) **crocodile tail.**

# Stone Town
## *Passageways to History*

Off the coast of Tanzania, Stone Town is a jumble of crumbling coral stone buildings smashed against the southwest shoreline of Zanzibar. Erected haphazardly over the centuries without thought for urban planning, the buildings—once opulent Omani palaces, Persian baths, modern mosques, Catholic churches, and homes with carved wooden doors—form a maze against which maps are useless. The best strategy for visiting with kids: *Get lost.*

"Rather than take a formal tour of Stone Town, with kids it's better to just explore and get deliciously lost. No matter what, you will come out on the market side or at the seaside in the end," says Rachel Hamada, who lives with her family in Zanzibar and is a founding editor of the local *Mambo Magazine.*

Narrow passageways snake through the town, saturated as much with history as the hum of *piki pikis* (mopeds and scooters) and thrum of modern Zanzibari life. Once you're lost, stop for a bottled drink or fresh unpeeled fruit from a street vendor before visiting some of the market stores to see what

---

### FAST FACTS

■ The **brass spikes** covering some 17th- to 20th-centuries traditional carved doors are a feature brought from India, where they were used to stop **battering elephants** from breaking down doors.

■ Arab traders noted many pachyderms on Zanzibar, from the 900s to 1295 when Marco Polo arrived, but by the 1600s **no elephants** remained on the island.

---

you'll find. "Some of the antique and curio shops are vast Aladdin's caves of trinkets and oddities from around the world that will capture the imagination and, possibly, even allowances of the children who venture inside," Hamada says.

Although whimsical and exciting, a trip to Stone Town is also an opportunity to discuss its more serious role in the slave trade—in the 19th century alone, around a million lives were traded through Zanzibar. "We took this opportunity to talk with my older daughter about African-American history and slavery," says Michael Kagan, who visited the area with his two kids (ages 5 years and 14 months). "Although other places, like Ghana, were more connected to the American trade, Zanzibar helped to give us a sense of the global issue." Downtown, Kelele Square is the original market site of the slave trade in Zanzibar before it was moved across town in the 1860s.

"We saw a church that was formerly a slave market. There was a very moving statue out front and we went below to the cells where the slaves were held. I know by the questions that my daughter was asking that it made a powerful impact on her," says Kagan.

If that topic is too serious, explore Zanzibar's other claim to fame: leafy spice plantations, still in operation just outside of town. Tours of the plantations are a sensory journey where children can learn about the traditional herbal remedies, try on "natural lipstick" from the bright red lipstick plant, peel cinnamon strips from the trees, and smell vanilla pods fresh from their vines. "Kids can be visceral so a spice farm is a great place to see the origins of things they've only seen in little McCormick jars—the stuff that we cook with," Kagan says.

**INSIDER TIP**

Taste the fruits of your labor after the whole family enjoys a Swahili cooking lesson, such as that offered by KV Tours (*www.kvtours.net*). Follow a local family from the market to the kitchen as you help prepare a meal that might include plantains, seafood, and pilau.

The Jozani Forest, the last large stretch of forest that once blanketed the whole island, is 20 miles southeast of Stone Town and home to red colobus monkeys. Dolphin cruises, dhow (a traditional Arab sailing vessel) rides, and snorkeling safaris can also be arranged from Stone Town—the underwater life is every bit as vibrant as life on land. And, of course, there's the beach. But, says Kagan, even a day at the beach is an experience in Zanzibar: "Most of the beach is public. Fisherman haul their nets filled with live fish right up onto the beach, even next to five-star resorts. We saw people fixing their dhows using traditional methods, smoking the boat to seal it. My kids found those things the most fascinating and we spent hours just watching." ∎

**BOOKS FOR KIDS**
■ *Is It Far to Zanzibar?* **by Nikki Grimes (2000)** This book gives a lighthearted glimpse of how life is in Tanzania and Zanzibar through poetry: "Go to Zanzibar to see a nutmeg bush, a cashew tree; cloves and ginger growing wild, chili peppers hot and mild; cinnamon and garlic plants blossoming among the ants; Traders come from near and far for all that grows in Zanzibar." Perfect book for young readers.

## Know Before You Go

**GAMES**
■ *Bao* This mancala-like game, a regional favorite, is so popular that the word *bao* means "board game" in Swahili. Played on a wooden board with a series of hollowed holes, players move pebbles, shells, or seeds to advance the game. Although there are varying levels of complexity, basic bao can be learned easily, and a game set makes a

great souvenir and a way to pass time on the flight home.

**MUSIC**
■ *Music from Tanzania and Zanzibar, Volume 2* **by Various Artists (1998)** *Ngoma*, traditional drumming music popular throughout East Africa, plays a prominent role in this soothing collection of singles—relaxing, rhythmic music to serve as a sound track for idyllic Zanzibar beach days.

# Serengeti

## *Wildlife Extravaganza*

For parent and child, visiting the Serengeti is the ultimate safari experience—in what some call the world's last great wilderness.

This vast expanse of grassland savanna is chock-full of wildlife big (elephants, rhinos, giraffes, lions) and small (bat-eared foxes, porcupines, and birds) playing out the circle of life as they have for more than a million years.

"The diversity of wildlife is one of the things that just makes this place so magical," says Amie O'Shaughnessy, a travel writer and blogger who took her son Devon, eight, to the region in early 2011. "It really drives home for kids the idea that everything has its place, that everything is related to one another. All living things have this relationship and there you get to see that in action."

Today, the chance for children to see such a full and healthy natural ecosystem is rare. "We've never seen as many animals in one place as in the Serengeti. It's like a zoo

### INSIDER TIP

To have the full Serengeti experience, visit all the different ecosystems in the park. By changing locations every day and staying at least four nights, you can see a range of habitats and animals. Spend at least one night camping in a tent to experience the bush in the dark.

without fences—on steroids," report Dereck and Beverly Joubert, wildlife photographers, conservationists, and documentary filmmakers who have dedicated their lives and careers to preserving the African wilderness.

The invisible boundary of the Serengeti National Park encircles some 5,700 square miles, but this is merely a human designation. To the animals, the Serengeti stretches in all directions as far as the ecosystem itself does—some 10,000 square miles, bigger than the state of Vermont.

One lesson visiting the area teaches is that wildlife needs space to survive. A stunning sight for families to witness, for example, is the largest migration of land mammals on Earth—the relocation of 1.2 million wildebeests and 800,000 zebras.

"Sitting in among them, watching them swarm like ants on a discarded piece of bread at a macro scale, driven forward by a biological drive to feed while running from the tawny shapes of lions and cheetahs chasing them," the Jouberts observe, "is like having a crash course in third-year biology or earth sciences. It's the one place in the world that gives you a front-row seat in understanding nature in Africa."

The migration takes place year-round as the animals keep searching for food and water, while in constant danger. During the rainy season, from January to March, wildebeests congregate to birth their calves as predators lurk in the short-grass plains. In the fall, the menagerie returns south and the wildebeests cross the Mara River in Kenya facing crocodiles, lions, and hyenas. In the Serengeti, a family can witness the visceral nature of life, birth, and death in the same day.

"Seeing wildlife like the wildebeest migration brings you closer as a family," O'Shaughnessy believes. "You're taking care of each other and you

share this experience—moments of terror punctuated by moments of joy."

Be aware, however, that the scenery is unlikely to feature the concentrated action of the National Geographic Channel. Talk to kids about what they might or might not see.

"Children need tools to encourage engagement because you could drive around for hours not finding anything—it's not the zoo. For my son, birds became a highlight because he had a checklist of species to spot, and he got excited when he saw a new one. Give your kids their own cameras and binoculars so they can experience the place in their own way," O'Shaughnessy says.

When kids are truly engaged, they're watching and aware, the Jouberts explain: "Children begin to understand that elephants eat trees, they don't destroy them, and vultures and hyenas exist for a

# OBJECTS OF WONDER

An unusual resident of the Serengeti is the fearless **honey badger.** Black with a white stripe down its back and about the size of a large house cat, this creature regularly enters active beehives to eat larvae, but will also feast on scorpions, venomous snakes, and even crocodiles.

reason, even though they aren't destined to win any beauty contests."

Although parents may be able to spend 12 straight hours looking out the window, kids often can't. Enrich your itinerary by including a visit to a local village—there are several options to experience rural Tanzanian or tribal life around the Ngorongoro Crater area.

"Meeting and engaging with the Maasai Mara people was a really moving part of the trip for all of us. Their way of life is so vastly different from ours," O'Shaughnessy recalls. "When a young child has a chance to question someone who is utterly different from them, that leaves a lasting impact. My son realized that this is the real deal—this isn't a dress-up guy; this is who he is and what he does everyday."

# CONNECTIONS

**360 Degrees Longitude**
*www.360degreeslongitude.com*
This website expands upon the book by the same name about a family that travels the world, with a favorite stop in the Serengeti.

**TanzaniaParks.com**
*www.tanzaniaparks.com/serengeti.html*
The official website of Tanzania's national parks provides resources for families traveling to the region.

**Serengeti Watch**
*www.savetheserengeti.org*
This is the site of a nonprofit organization dedicated to preserving the Serengeti ecosystem, including funding, legal defense, advocacy for preservation projects, and action against ecological threats, such as a proposed highway predicted to harm migrating wildebeests.

By incorporating the human element, children begin to get an even broader picture of the area. It's impossible to ignore humans' role in the ecosystem—the way the choices of the locals have an impact on the animals.

Michael Pius, a Tanzanian and the executive secretary of the Tour Guides Association, took his children to see the Serengeti. "My son asked me, 'Why are all these people, who don't speak our language, so interested in our area—don't they have it in their countries?' I taught him the basics of the Serengeti and its importance as one of our country's World Heritage sites. My children have started to realize this is a unique treasure with which we are endowed."

Time, the environment, and human intervention constantly change the Serengeti. Elephants, for example, did not live in the park until 30 years ago, when human populations expanding outward from the park pushed the elephants in. In the late 1980s, feral village dogs entered the park, spreading rabies to the park's African wild dogs, which then became extinct in 1991. Poachers continue to hunt rhinos for their horns—used, among other things, to make Yemeni ceremonial daggers and sold on the black market for high prices—and elephants are slaughtered illegally for their tusks and meat.

"We need to be aware that this ecosystem is bigger and older than all of us. It will go on forever—except if we mess it up. And we are very close to that," the Jouberts caution. "Humans are relentless; we should not change that part of us. Instead, though, we should turn it into a relentless drive to protect the magic places on Earth, like the Serengeti." ■

# Pyram*i*ds of Giza

*Marvel of the Ancients*

About 600 years ago, the Great Pyramid of Khufu at Giza was more dazzling than today's weathered stone behemoth. It actually was covered with casing stones that served as giant mirrors that supposedly reflected light so powerfully it could be seen from the moon (we're not sure who was around to see this firsthand). Said ancient writer Strabo: "It seemed like a building let down from heaven, untouched by human hands."

The scale of it and its neighboring structures still seems beyond the scope of human accomplishment. Which is part of their wonder. "Luke's first statement on seeing the pyramids was, 'I didn't think they'd be that big,' " says Annette Wingrave, a Welsh community councillor of her seven-year-old grandson's first encounter. "His smile told us he will remember that moment for the

## FAST FACTS

■ Ancient Egyptians **aligned the four sides** of the Great Pyramid almost perfectly with the four cardinal points, a remarkable engineering feat given that they had no knowledge of the magnetic compass.

■ Unlike the pyramids, which were assembled block by block, the Sphinx was a massive sculpture **carved straight from existing bedrock.**

rest of his life." Kids soon grasp that there's more to the site than just the pyramids and mummies. "Many kids have a good knowledge of the pyramids before they get here," says Wael Fahim, a guide at the Giza Pyramids for the last 11 years. "But there is so much to know." The pyramids are a part of an ancient Egyptian necropolis that dates back almost to the beginning of the pharaonic period, around 3000 B.C. They rise from the sun-blasted rock and sand of the Giza Plateau at the southwestern edge of greater Cairo, as if standing guard against a city seeking to encroach into the desert beyond.

Along with the famous 4th dynasty pyramids of Khufu, Khafre, and Menkaure, and the Great Sphinx, the site contains several satellite pyramids, numerous *mastaba* (benches) and rock-cut tombs, and a museum housing the solar boat used to transport the pharaoh's spirit across the heavens.

A good guide can give kids context to what they've learned about ancient Egypt in school, to appreciate the complexity of the archaeology that has gone into revealing just how sophisticated Egyptian engineering and inventiveness was. "Children can learn who the pharaohs were, why they created the pyramids, the techniques of building, and so on," says Fahim "I make it as dramatic as possible, turn it into a story." They'll learn that the first pyramid—built by the pharoah Khufu—took about 23 years to complete and consists of 2,300,000 blocks, some weighing as much as 16 tons. That pyramids would often have hidden trapdoors to keep out robbers. That it took over 100,000 people to build a pyramid.

There's also opportunity for a bit of an Indiana Jones experience. Kids can scramble down a pyramid's steep passageway (supervised, of course) and follow it until it opens onto a burial chamber. "They want to see the sarcophagus," says Fahim. There's something compelling about gazing on the wizened face of a person—perhaps a child—who has

been dead centuries. "They always ask where the mummy goes."

Such excursions are hot, sweaty, and tiring, and your kids may find it hard work. To prevent bottlenecks, guides have no time to give explanations or answer questions inside the pyramids. The smaller mastaba tombs, Wingrave feels, give children a better chance to have questions answered because guides are allowed to enter. "During the tour of the Mastaba of Seshemnufer IV, the guide told Luke about the mortuary table where they would have carried out the mummification process. This really caught his interest: Blood and guts enthrall any child past six years of age."

Another quintessentially Egyptian adventure is riding a camel—and this is one of the most dramatic places in the world to do it. "Children like being on animals they may not have at home," says Hany, a young man who has been working the pyramids with his father since age three. "Camels are slow and

"From atop these pyramids, 40 centuries look down upon you." *—Napoleon Bonaparte to his troops before the Battle of Giza in 1798*

relaxing; you can see all three pyramids from far away and can take photos from up top." With their backward knee joints, hypnotic gait, and blood-curdling moans, camels can also be off-putting. "It depends on their age," says Fahim. "Less than six is quite difficult; above is okay. I leave it to the kids themselves—how brave they are—to see if they are interested." But don't be fooled by promises of a "free" ride: Although the ride may well be gratis, getting off the camel will likely cost. Negotiate what you think is a fair price and a specific time limit before you embark. Vendors are renowned for their wily persistence—be firm and focus on your kids' experience.

Mummies are a prime fascination here, to be sure. But a trip to the pyramids often results in accidental learning—the best kind. "My son was most fascinated by the mathematics of the place," says Guro Broen, who visited with his seven-year-old. "The numbers, the dimensions, the accuracy, and how it all fits together; this has been the source of many conversations since, often ending with a sense of humility. It's great if children can grow up with some respect for knowledge and the past, and an understanding of human limitations—despite our developments and advancements."

For freelance writer and author Kayt Sukel's young son, the value was in the human connections he made. "Chet enjoyed meeting and running around with local children. While he may not remember the finer points of Egyptian culture and history, he will remember that kids can always figure out how to play together despite language barriers, and that girls in headscarves really aren't so scary. Even a young child can sense the chaos, magic, and history of Giza." ■

# CONNECTIONS

**BBC Pyramid Builder**
*www.bbc.co.uk/history/interactive/games/
pyramid_challenge*
This interactive game is perfect for getting children to start thinking and learning about the pyramids before ever seeing them. Players are charged with building a pyramid for the pharaoh before he dies, and must make all the necessary decisions to accomplish this, including where to build the pyramid, which materials to use, what sort of workers to employ, and how to pay them, even what to feed them and how often to let them rest. The game includes educational prompts that point you toward the right decisions, although success is by no means guaranteed.

**Tour Egypt**
*www.touregypt.net*
This is a good one-stop shop for all things Egypt, with more than 16,000 pages dedicated to visiting the country. It features articles on the Giza Plateau and on each of the major pyramids plus the Sphinx, all of which have a wealth of archaeological information.

**Ask Aladdin**
*www.ask-aladdin.com*
Another comprehensive Egypt portal, this site offers educational information about the pyramids, practical tips for visiting, and a discussion forum.

**Cairo 360**
*www.cairo360.com*
A more general guide to Cairo, this is the place to go to find out which are the hippest restaurants in town, what films are playing, and the lowdown on any art exhibitions that might interest you.

# Petra

## *The Rose-Colored City*

"Children can navigate this mystic and magical site as explorers," says Aysar Akrawi, a mother and executive director of the Petra National Trust. "Have a Bedouin wrap a traditional red *atta* on the kids' heads and let them ride on horseback down the Siq, which is included in the admission fee."

Petra, once called the "rose-red city half as old as time," is Jordan's triumph—a miracle of engineering hewn two millennia ago from sandstone. It was built by the Nabataeans, ancient nomadic traders who controlled the spice-driven caravan routes that reached into faraway China. They made frankincense, myrrh, cloves, and cinnamon their common

currency and Petra a commercial crossroads for Romans, Christians, and crusaders.

The Siq is the main entrance to Petra. It is a catastrophically narrow, sinuous 3,300-foot-long path, flanked by towering 260-foot-high rose cliffs, that changes from dirt into the original Nabataean pavement unearthed by archaeologists in 1996.

As you walk, point out to kids that they are

Yum!

■ **Petra Kitchen** Kids will love this place where they can cook right alongside local Petra women. They will learn how to prepare traditional dishes and even catch glimpses of the secrets behind making them.

■ **Al Ghadeer Roof Garden** Here's the spot to watch the sun set over Petra while relaxing, tasting local fare, and listening to live music. Kids might want to try some local ice cream.

■ **Al Qantarah** Close to Petra's gates, this castlelike restaurant welcomes guests with Bedouin coffee. Ask for *mansaf* (lamb cooked in yogurt), Jordan's national dish.

not walking through a natural formation but rather a "secret" city hewn from rock by great craftsmen. The creators also engineered an ingenious system of channels (see if you can spot remnants of terra-cotta pipes on the right side of the Siq) to transport water to be stored in hidden underground cisterns. The system protected the city from flooding, capturing water during the rainy season and storing it for use when the desert was parched.

The end of the Siq opens to a dramatic view of Al Khazneh (the Treasury), a 13-story tomb carved in the cliffs, and where Harrison Ford discovers the Holy Grail in *Indiana Jones and the Last Crusade.*

Next, make the 800-step climb to the top of Al Deir (the Monastery), which honors Dusghara, the Nabataean god of heaven—appropriate given the view of the surrounding desert. Scattered throughout the site are ruins of some 500 tombs, sluiceways and drains, banquet halls, colonnaded streets, obelisks, sacrificial altars, and Nabataean wall paintings.

"Kids can wander into empty caves and tombs and enjoy breathtaking views while riding donkeys, horses, or camels," says Akrawi, warning that you must always remember that Petra is an active archaeological site. "Less than 5 percent of the city has been uncovered, and many mysteries still remain hidden beneath desert sands and stones."

Petra is a perfect place to introduce kids to traditional Bedouin life, advises Akrawi. "Go on a sunset hike through the cliffs and spend the night in a desert cave or Bedouin tent. Eat a traditional Bedouin meal of *mansef* and *zarb* with your hands, making little rice balls and flicking them into your mouth. Around a fire, play the one-stringed *rababah*

# NEST

■ **Mövenpick Nabatean Castle Hotel**
*Petra*
This hotel is located outside the entrance to Petra. Kids can enjoy the view of the ancient city and also dive into the swimming pool to cool off.
www.moevenpick-hotels.com

■ **Taybet Zaman**
*Taybeh Village*
The ancient village of Taybeh, on the verge of abandonment, was transformed into a resort that preserves a vision of 19th-century Jordan. Bougainvillea adorns the stone walls along paths leading to the old village center, which still retains its original well.
www.taybetzaman.jordantourismresorts.com

■ **Sella Hotel**
*Petra*
After using the hotel's tours to explore Petra and the surrounding area by horse or camel, relax in its traditional Turkish bath. On the roof garden, families can admire mountain views while sampling Arabic desserts like baklava.
www.sellahotel.com

■ **Bedouin Adventures**
*Wadi Rum*
Adventurous families can sleep under the stars and trek into the desert on camels at this encampment. The Bedouin owners share their tribe's poetry and folk stories over a dinner of *zarb*, a traditional dish cooked under the sand.
www.bedouinadventures.com

and sing traditional songs with new Bedouin friends."

Akrawi cites a Bedouin quote that will pique kids' interest in these remarkable desert dwellers: "The sky is my blanket, the earth is my bed, the Bedouins are strong as the desert, soft as sand, and move as the wind; forever free." ■

# Jer🕎salem
## *Where History Lives*

J erusalem was founded more than 3,000 years ago, and is a holy city for Judaism, Islam, and Christianity. The historical heart of the capital of Israel is the ancient Old City, where you and your children can connect with the ancients by leaving a message in the Western Wall.

To explore this place of living history, enter the Old City through the Jaffa Gate at the city's western end—one of eleven entrances to the area, only seven of which are open—and follow the ancient footpaths to the famous Western Wall.

Along the way, kids will love navigating the suqs (marketplaces), an enthrallingly alien experience for a first-time visitor. "One of my favorite memories of growing up in Israel are the suqs. The scents of the fresh fruit, vegetables, and cooked meats were magic," says Merav Benaia, whose father is a tour guide in Jerusalem.

The narrow streets are a chaotic circus of honking trucks, crowing roosters, and bustling crowds. The aromas of baking bread and exotic spices fill the air. Although it can sometimes be intimidating for adults, kids love the local practice of haggling

---

**BOOKS FOR PARENTS**................
■ *Jerusalem, Jerusalem: How the Ancient City Ignited Our Modern World* by James Carroll (2011) A deep read about the importance of Jerusalem in world history, this book follows the author's attempt to interpret history, theology, and popular culture in a way that offers hope that religions will "celebrate life, not death."

### Know Before You Go

**BOOKS FOR KIDS**............................
■ *Jerusalem Sky: Stars, Crosses and Crescents* by Mark Podwal (2005) This book for kids age eight and older explains why Jerusalem is important to so many people. Combined with colorful illustrations, this is a great primer on the holy city.

**MOVIE**................
■ *Kingdom of Heaven* (2005) This film is a heavily fictionalized account of a 12th-century crusader who travels to Jerusalem to aid in its defense. It may not be the greatest story ever told, but the movie-magic scenes of ancient Jerusalem offer a glimpse into what the city might have looked like in medieval times.

over the price of trinkets sold at the stalls lining the narrow alleyways.

Take a few minutes to visit the roof of the Aish HaTorah building (One Western Wall Plaza), suggests Joanna Shebson, who runs *FunInJerusalem .com*. It offers a superb view of the Western Wall, the plaza in front of it, and the Temple Mount, the most revered religious site in the Old City.

The wall has many names. In the West, it is usually called the Wailing or Western Wall, but in Jerusalem, it is simply known by its Hebrew name, the Kotel. This ordinary-looking limestone structure was one of the support walls constructed around 19 B.C. as part of the renovation of a temple by Herod the Great. The Kotel is the last remnant of that holy place, and it has been a site of pilgrimage and prayer since at least the fourth century. More than a musty place of rocks and dust, the wall today feels alive, unlike so many other relics found in the city.

Ruth Waiman, a hotel executive in Jerusalem, holds the Kotel in awe as an adult, but it was even more enchanting to her as a child. "I was told that this is the closest connection that we have to Hashem [Hebrew for "God"]. As a child, the thought of having direct contact with Hashem sent shivers through me that still persist—even though I am a not-so-religious young adult. At the Kotel, my mother would say, 'Close your eyes and imagine that everything you now wish for can come true if you really, really try.' "

Because the Kotel is an important religious site, it commands respect—so kids need to be briefed and supervised to be reverent. The best

time to experience the wall and what it means to the faithful is Friday at sunset, the beginning of the Jewish Sabbath. As the sun slips below the horizon, the square transforms into a mix of the penitent engrossed in prayer and the jubilant crowds who dance and sing the night away as they celebrate the start of the Jewish holy day. Don't be shy; let your kids join in the festivities.

To help your kids connect with the antiquity of the Kotel, have them join the tradition of writing notes and placing them in the cracks of the wall. "Ask them to write a prayer or their greatest wish," advises Jerusalem travel expert Joel Haber. "Explain that they might consider writing prayers on behalf of others, rather than themselves—such as for ill friends or relatives, or for peace in the world. Once you prep them and give them pen and paper, let them know their note will be private. Don't read it. One of the most powerful aspects of the Kotel is the ability to have a personal moment while surrounded by many others doing the same thing.

"You know, while we who are Jewish pray at the Kotel, we are not praying to the Kotel," continues Haber. "We touch the millions of people who did exactly the same thing there over the generations." ∎

# Cyprus
## *Crusader Island*

For much of the 11th and 12th centuries, the crusaders used Cyprus as a jumping-off point for their military expeditions of the Holy Land. The Knights Templar may have been fiction in *The Da Vinci Code*, but on Cyprus they were the real deal: At one point, the secretive warriors controlled the entire island. Crusader heroes such as Richard the Lionheart and Guy de Lusignan laid the foundation for a kingdom that would endure for more than 400 years.

Their castles are scattered across the land, some restored and others in ruins. But it seems to make no difference to kids fascinated by tales of knights and sword fights: Their imaginations run riot regardless.

Limassol Castle, in the middle of the island's second largest city, is a great place to start your family quest to discover the island. Inside the thick stone walls, kids will find genuine suits of armor and other relics, plus a crypt with ancient tombstones and sarcophagi.

"According to tradition," says local guide Myria Stasoulli, "this is where Richard the Lionheart married

his fiancée"—after she was shipwrecked on the island, taken captive, held for ransom, and then rescued by the dashing crusader king. "To this day it is the only English royal wedding that took place outside of England."

In retribution for kidnapping his fiancée, Richard conquered the entire island and then sold it to the Knights Templar. They established their headquarters at Kolossi Castle on the western edge of Limassol. It's a classic medieval bastion with a central keep that can be reached only via a wooden drawbridge. Perched high above the gate is an overhang from which the defenders could pour boiling oil or melted tar on attackers. Scampering up three stories to the roof, kids can glimpse the often snow-capped Mount Olympus and the Troodos Mountains in central Cyprus.

After the children have had their fill of castles, head into the Troodos, one of the cradles of ancient Christianity. Many of the mountain villages seem little changed over the millennia, strewn with cobblestone streets, ancient houses, and tavernas hung with grapevines where the kids can dig into such delicious Greek dishes as moussaka, pita bread, feta cheese, and baklava.

Many of the culinary treats from the Troodos are made with the grapes that cover the hillsides. At a small shop in the village of Koilani, Marios Hadjicharalambous creates several grape-based desserts. "This is *soutzouko*," he says, holding up a five-foot-long pastry that could easily be mistaken for a sausage string. "Almonds dipped in grape juice batter and then strung together." Marios grabs a jar from the wooden shelf behind, pours some into a spoon for tasting. "And this is *espuma*—grape juice boiled for a long time until it's almost like honey. You can add it to your milk or put it on toast or ice cream, or soft white cheese."

The Cypriot mountains also serve up plenty of history and nature. The Greek Orthodox monasteries, for example, are among the most impressive in the Christian world, especially Kykkos, with its castlelike walls, gold and silver treasure room, and life-size mosaics telling Bible stories.

As for the natural side of Cyprus, the nearby Cedar Valley is a great place to hike or picnic among the towering old-growth cedars, last of their kind in the Mediterranean. Tell the kids to look for rare and endangered mouflon (bighorn sheep).

Increasingly rare, but certainly not endangered, are the donkeys that once did all of the heavy lifting in the Troodos. Most have been abandoned in favor of motorized transport, but you can find more than 120 at the donkey sanctuary in Vouni village. Founded by British expatriate Mary Skinner, the sanctuary lets kids feed, groom, or walk the retired beasts of burden.

"The farmers no longer want to look after them," explains Skinner. "So we take them in. Our adopt-a-donkey program helps feed them. Each of them has their own character. And they're very intelligent animals—much more than horses." ∎

**BOOKS FOR PARENTS**
■ *Hostage to History: Cyprus From the Ottomans to Kissinger* by Christopher Hitchens (1997) The author examines the events leading up to the partition of Cyprus, essential background for understanding the country's role in the modern world.

## Know Before You Go

■ *Mint, Cinnamon & Blossom Water: Flavours of Cyprus, Kopiaste!* by Ivy Liacopoulou (2010) To more than 150 recipes, Liacopoulou adds her own twists to flavors unique to her homeland.

**MUSIC**
■ *Cyprus: Aphrodite's Paradise* by Various Artists (2010) As a trip sound track, choose this compilation of Cypriot folk music. The Greek and Turkish influences echo through the mix of violin, lute, and oud (a pear-shaped Middle Eastern string instrument).

# Istanbul

## *Where East Meets West*

No one could blame Istanbul for suffering from a bit of an identity crisis. It's one of the few cities in the world to straddle two continents—Europe and Asia—and it has, at various times over the last few millennia, been called Byzantium, Constantinople, and Stamboul. Moreover, it was the capital of three great empires: Roman, Byzantine, and Ottoman. This schizophrenic history makes Istanbul the perfect place to let children experience the clash of the ancient and modern worlds.

"On a ferry ride on the Bosporus—a mile-wide strait that splits Europe and Asia—children can observe the lines of the old city, the walls that run along the Sea of Marmara that the Greek Byzantine emperors built," observes David Cuthell, Jr., who grew up in Istanbul and is the executive director of the Institute of Turkish Studies. "And they'll see the modern commercial skyline behind the European buildings in the Beyoglu district. From the water, you really get a sense of the dynamics of the city."

The metropolis of more than ten million presents an intoxicating mixture of East and West. Here contemporary American pop music blasts from cafés and nightclubs, blending with the five daily Muslim calls to prayer blaring from loudspeakers mounted on the city's thousands of mosques.

# Yum!

■ **Turkish dishes** are a blend of Arabic and Mediterranean flavors incorporating lots of tomatoes, olives, and lamb. Street vendors sell piping-hot **shish kebabs** and juicy fresh fruit such as **peaches** and **oranges.**

■ Head to the Beyoglu district, around Istiklal Street, for *islak* **burgers,** mini burgers with garlicky tomato sauce.

■ The best **fresh-baked *simit*,** a ring of crisp bread sprinkled with sesame seeds, can be found at the Citir Simit Bakery.

■ The "cucumber man" in front of the Galata Tower sells **chilled and salted cucumbers,** the perfect snack.

Located on the European side, south of the Golden Horn, the name of the freshwater estuary cleaving the city, is Sultanahmet. It is the oldest quarter of the city, dating from 660 B.C., and the area that contains most of the city's historic sites.

In business for 550 years, the Grand Bazaar is a riot of color and commerce, with nearly 4,000 shops lining miles of stone and marble hallways that sell everything from carpets to clothing to jewels to souvenir scimitars. Let your children's imagination run wild as you explore the maze of corridors and alleyways.

"The vendors cry, 'Come on in, come on in,' when you pause by their shops, and offer you tea," Cuthell says. "They serve it in tiny glass cups called *fincan* and talk with you about your family and where you come from. You make friends. They especially love talking with kids."

For a less wallet-threatening adventure, take children underground to the mysterious Basilica Cistern, a sixth-century Byzantine cavern supported by 336 mismatched marble columns. The reservoir of water helped Istanbul withstand sieges throughout the centuries. Lit with a soft orange glow at the base of each pillar, it is a shadowy, secretive place, with dim echoes and shimmering watery reflections fit to fire children's imagination—challenge them to find the massive carved heads of the snake-haired Medusa, green with algae, at the bases of two of the columns.

Completed in A.D. 537 by the Byzantine emperor Justinian, the nearby Hagia Sophia was the

**INSIDER TIP**

Walk along the Bosporus in the Uskudar district, on the Asian side of the city, to find small fishing boats tied up along the docks. Fishermen will grill freshly caught fish and make you a sandwich for lunch.

greatest Christian cathedral in the world for nearly a thousand years. Mehmet the Conqueror transformed it into Istanbul's primary mosque in 1453. Now a museum, the structure awes kids and adults alike as they wander beneath its soaring dome and glittering golden mosaics that date from the tenth century.

Lying directly across a park from the Hagia Sophia is the 17th-century Blue Mosque, named for the 20,000 blue tiles covering its interior that depict the Gardens of Heaven (visitors welcome when services are not being held).

During Ramadan, the Muslim month of fasting and reflection, Turkish families gather at dusk in the park. John Higham encountered the scene when he traveled to Istanbul with his children, Jordan and Katrina, then 8 and 11. "Families were sitting on picnic blankets with plates of food heaped before them, but no one was eating," Higham recalls. "Eyes were darting to wristwatches. Suddenly, loudspeakers from the mosques announced sunset and the end of the day's fast. The area before us erupted into a scene much like a Super Bowl tailgate party. Vendors in the square sold all kinds of food, treats, and trinkets. Katrina and Jordan shared a cultural experience unlike any I could have tried to make up." ∎

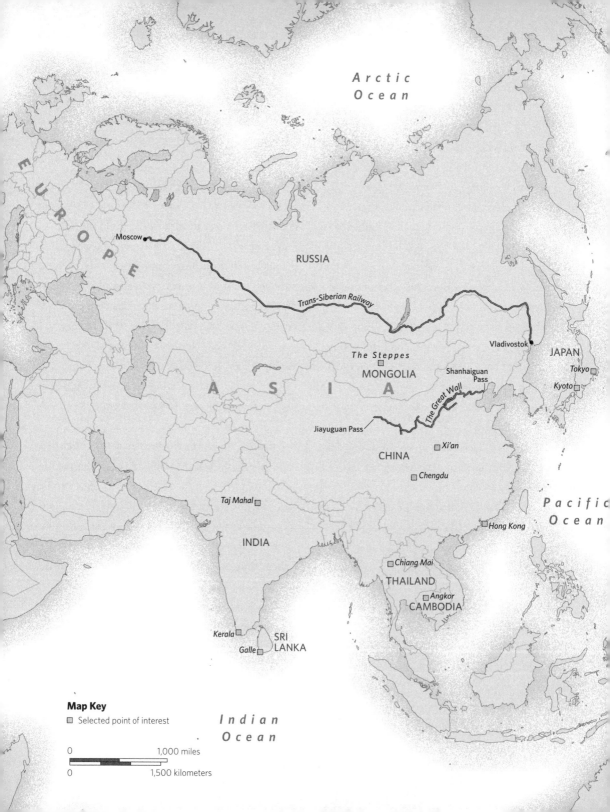

Arctic
Ocean

EUROPE

RUSSIA

Moscow

Trans-Siberian Railway

The Steppes

MONGOLIA

Shanhaiguan
Pass

Vladivostok

JAPAN

Tokyo

Kyoto

ASIA

The Great Wall

Jiayuguan Pass

Xi'an

CHINA

Chengdu

Taj Mahal

Hong Kong

INDIA

Pacific
Ocean

Chiang Mai

THAILAND

Angkor

CAMBODIA

Kerala

Galle

SRI
LANKA

**Map Key**

☐ Selected point of interest

*Indian
Ocean*

0                    1,000 miles

0                    1,500 kilometers

# Asia

# T🐟kyo
## *The World's Largest Fish Market*

Tokyo, the world's largest city, has—at 35 million souls—more people than in all of Canada. It's a full-on video game that no child can resist, especially if they are *gaijin*, or foreigners: Ice Cream City, where dozens of stands sell more than 300 flavors, from soy chicken and orchid root to sea island salt and eel; high-tech public toilets with "modesty" buttons that trigger the recorded sound of flushing water; the world's third largest subway (13 lines, 269 stations); the neon smear of flickering, pinwheeling tangerine, red, yellow, and purple signs stacked to the heavens.

Akihabara (Electronic City) is where lurid storefronts offer towering columns of DVDs, camcorders, vacuum cleaners, HDTVs, speakers, computers, tiny phones, cameras no bigger than a deck of cards. Some products are only tangentially electronic:

Japanese graphic romance novels, manga comics for boys and girls, walls of autographed animation cels, and fantasy titles like *Fullmetal Alchemist*.

But the best reason to come to Tokyo with your kids is to connect with the world's oceans, the environmental canary in the coal mine that indicates how healthy the Earth is. To show a child an amazing side of the natural world, the best bet is a 4 a.m.

---

**FAST FACTS**

■ One of the Japanese words for **"mother"** is *haha.*

■ There have been **24 recorded instances** when people have received skull fractures or have even been killed while performing the traditional Japanese greeting of bowing.

■ Due to the amount of people, **a giant heat bubble forms over Tokyo in the summer,** increasing the average temperature by ten degrees.

■ A Japanese custom is to wear slippers in the house—and hosts even have **special shoes for guests to use when they go to the restroom.**

visit to Tsukiji Market, the globe's biggest seafood bazaar. This is not a tourist attraction, though.

"Go with someone who knows the market," advises Daisuke Utagawa, Tokyo native, chef, and father of two. "The place is not made for visitors. This is somewhere every child should see, but it isn't designed for their consumption. It is a slice of life, real in every respect, a place I would take my daughter to understand how food comes to be. It will mesmerize kids and help them to understand where fish comes from, the whole chain of events that brings seafood to the plate."

And kids will be enthralled. They will see acres of real estate unlike any on Earth: enormous auction floors lined with shiny black tuna and alive with the clanging of bells and the chanting of auctioneers and 1,500 stalls selling some 450 varieties of sea creatures—*tako* (octopus), *ika* (squid), *unagi* (freshwater eel), *hamachi* (yellowtail tuna).

"You can't *not* look at the fish," says Utagawa.

"It's a stage, a jewelry store of marine life, where even chefs will see some fish species for the first time. It's like a zoo. Kids will have 200 questions: 'Why is this bubbling?' 'What is that huge knife for?' 'Why is that creature so smelly?' 'How come the fish has eyes on its back?' 'Sea urchin—you eat that?' They see ginormous tuna lying on a gurney; octopus live, dead, or boiled; fish swimming in a Styrofoam bucket, multicolored, some moving, some glistening. Everything is something to eat. Even what they think is gross: a bunch of eel in a tub, salmon roe in a sack, sea cucumber." This is the active classroom we should all seek to share with young people—a place where real work gets done.

"I tell my daughter not to waste this ocean," concludes Utagawa. "It produces these things. We must respect the resource. Yes, this is a market. But it is one that so respects what it sells. We live off the oceans. Most of the world is an ocean. And look at what the ocean gives us." ∎

## BOOKS FOR KIDS
■ *I Live in Tokyo* by Mari Takabayashi (2004) This book follows a young schoolgirl in Tokyo and highlights each month's important traditions. Filled with bright illustrations and simple phrases, this volume helps teach readers about Japan's culture.

■ **Manga** is a term for comic books created in Japan or by Japanese authors. There are many genres and some made for all ages in English.

## BOOKS FOR PARENTS
■ *Tokyo Megacity* by Donald Richie and Ben Simmons (2010) Jam-packed with pictures and essays

# Know Before You Go

about the largest city in the world, the book starts with its ancient roots and continues on a journey through the changes that make this modern metropolis what it is today.

## MOVIES
■ *Globe Trekker: Tokyo* (2005) For a virtual look at all that Tokyo has to offer, watch this documentary that pairs old traditions with the visions of the future. Viewers will find themselves on bustling streets looking at technology, having sushi for breakfast in the Tsukiji Market, and snacking on squid balls and beer.

## MOVIES FOR PARENTS
■ *Lost in Translation* (2003) Just for parents, this Bill Murray movie follows a washed-up actor as he finds himself in Tokyo with a Japanese-speaking director and a 25-year-old married Scarlett Johansson. The movie follows their relationship and gives viewers a glimpse of life in Tokyo.

## MUSIC
*Enka Damashii: Enka Best* by Various Artists (2005) This CD is a compilation of standards that are loved by many in Japan, even if they won't admit it.

# Kyoto
## *Geisha and Gardens*

**W**ander the streets of the Gion district in Kyoto, Japan, with your kids and, eventually, you'll spot a geisha—which is akin to seeing a ghost.

Gion is where kabuki is king and where geisha have lived since the 1600s. Around 7 p.m., the sun flirting with the horizon, you may be ambling along the Shirakawa Canal, crisscrossing from side to side on an occasional bridge. The lights of bars and teahouses wink on. You turn a corner, and there, like an apparition, seemingly gliding inches above the pavement, propelled by the choppy locomotion of tiny feet, is a figure with a solemn mask of white broken only by the scarlet of her lips. Her flowing robes are splashed with whirls of color. Pink and white flowers rain down from her knot of jet-black hair. In an instant, she is gone.

According to Daisuke Utagawa, a celebrated Japanese chef who knows Kyoto intimately, a geisha is an example of *wabi-sabi* (not to be confused with *wasabi,* or Japanese horseradish), one of those maddeningly elusive concepts so common to Asia. "Wabi"

suggests freshness and simplicity. "Sabi" describes a beauty that is burnished by age—the weathering of buildings, the nicks of time on furniture, the crawl of moss on stone, the scarring of old bronze. It's a Zen notion: a fleeting, imperfect, accidental beauty—unpretentious, simple, and intimate.

Says Utagawa: "It's our spirit. It's what we think is beautiful. We're not a literal people. We're emotional. We understand nuance. Wabi-sabi is akin to the inherent beauty within, something you can't put your finger on. It's like in *Where's Waldo?* It is important to really *see.* To open your senses to every detail, every glimmer, every breath of the breeze."

Two and a half hours southwest of Tokyo by bullet train, Kyoto is the perfect place to introduce children to the concept of wabi-sabi. "In my experience, kids are much more open to subtlety than we think," observes Utagawa. "And if you introduce the notion of looking beyond the obvious, you'll find they'll get it very quickly. It's what's behind the appeal of the *I Spy* books. You can almost make a game of it—one that becomes fun for parent and child."

Japan's eighth largest city and the imperial capital for more than a thousand years, Kyoto escaped bombing in World War II, leaving intact myriad temples and shrines—its 18 UNESCO World Heritage properties are outnumbered only by those in Rome.

When you are in Kyoto, the ultimate wabi-sabi experience to share with your child is a visit to the moss garden, what Utagawa calls one of the greatest gardens in the world. Drive the winding back roads in the foothills of Mount Matsuo through densely packed, sun-streaked bamboo glades of green and tan bamboo—and you are there.

The garden is at Saiho-ji Temple, whose monks, wishing to preserve their ring of peace, are blessedly anti–mass tourism. You *must* book at least a month in advance. You can visit only at set times each day and you must reserve in writing—the priests running the temple wish to keep the solemn, peaceful atmosphere intact. Include your name, address in Japan, occupation, age, number of people in your group, and the date you wish to visit, along with alternative dates. Include a self-addressed envelope (stamped or with international reply coupons for the return postage) and mail it to: Saiho-ji Temple, 56 Jingatani-cho, Matsuo, Nishikyo-ku, Kyoto. (If you are already in Japan, you should send a double postcard, or *ofuku hagaki*.) The recommended "donation" to enter is 3,000 yen. "You can't

## BOOKS FOR PARENTS

■ *Kyoto: Seven Paths to the Heart of the City* by Diana Durston; photographs by Katsuhiko Mizuno (2002) In this well-illustrated walking guide to Kyoto's seven historic districts, Durston highlights notable architecture, foods, crafts, and festivals.

■ *Memoirs of a Geisha* by Arthur Golden (1997) This is the story of Sayuri, who started as a bereaved servant and went on to become Gion's most celebrated geisha in the years before World War II.

■ *Old Kyoto: The Updated Guide to Traditional Shops, Restaurants, and*

## Know Before You Go

*Inns* by Diane Durston (2005) This is a good guide for finding out-of-the-way shops, restaurants, and inns in the various neighborhoods.

### BOOKS FOR KIDS

■ *Commodore Perry in the Land of the Shogun* by Rhoda Blumberg (2003) A lively account of Commodore Matthew Perry's naval expedition to Edo-era Japan, this volume is illustrated with 19th-century Japanese prints.

■ *Japanese Children's Favorite Stories* by Florence Sakade; illustrated by Yoshio Kurosaki

(2005) This is a compilation of popular Japanese folktales accompanied by watercolor images.

■ *One Leaf Rides the Wind* by Celeste Davidson Mannis and Susan Kathleen Hartung (2005) Brought to life with beautiful illustrations, the book introduces young readers to Japanese gardens and the haiku.

■ *The Sign of the Chrysanthemum* by Katherine Paterson (1988) This book tells the story of Muna, a teenage boy who sets out on a quest to find his father and discovers himself along the way. It is set in 12th-century Japan.

just walk into the garden without first doing a little work," sums up Utagawa.

At the appointed time of your visit (please be prompt), you trade shoes for slippers and pad into a room crowded with people hunched over small, low desks. You spread out the page of 262 Japanese characters you have been given. Beside you is a small box containing a bit of water and a charcoal cube. You rub your box vigorously with the cube, generating a rich, black ink into which you dip a bamboo brush. You trace each unfamiliar character, capturing every stroke and dot. The only sounds are the twittering of birds and the wind in the eaves. At one point, the monks break into a chant. As the minutes pass, you're drawn deeper into a task that began as pure drudgery. Older joints may ache; youth feels no pain. Finally, after about 30 minutes, you finish. You write your name, address, the date, and a wish on your sheets, place them on a shrine, bow, and leave. "The purpose," says Utagawa, "is to put you in a mood to open yourself to the beauty around you."

Enter the moss garden. "This is when you want to get your kids to really focus on every little detail," says Utagawa. "Because you've just been so intent on the tiny calligraphic characters, everything seems crisper, brighter, and more fully detailed in the garden."

Imagine a moss bed acres in size, tended by white-gloved caretakers who literally sweep the carpet, shaded by great trees whose trunks reveal reflected patterns of light on water. Imagine 120 species of moss bisected by fingers of water, tendrils of roots, small streams, and sun-ribboned rock paths bordered by rope. Imagine moss with endless currents

# NEST

If you want your kids to experience a culturally authentic lodging experience in Kyoto, you should try staying in a *ryokan*—a traditional Japanese inn where you sleep on the floor. Some ryokans won't accept children—ask before making reservations.

### ■ Three Sisters Inn Annex
*Kyoto*
This 12-room ryokan located near the Heian Jingu Temple has a homey atmosphere with large, comfortable rooms. The three sisters who own this ryokan are very accommodating of families and are more than happy to help guests craft itineraries for their time in Kyoto. www4.ocn.ne.jp/~k3sisanx/32/index.html

### ■ Westin Miyako Kyoto
*Kyoto*
For those families who know their kids need all the distractions provided by a larger, all-inclusive hotel, this is a tasteful option. Known for its spectacular view of Kyoto, this renovated 300-year-old hotel offers guests the option of staying in traditional Japanese-style rooms. www.miyakohotels.ne.jp/westinkyoto/

of shifting greens. Thick moss, thin moss, humped moss. Moss clinging to rock. Moss that climbs trees. Moss on bridges. Moss coating the ramshackle boat pulled to the pond's shore. Moss reflected among the koi in the pond. Meadows of moss. Mountains of moss. Moss everywhere. This moss haven was originally planned almost 700 years ago as two gardens—one dry, one moist—but the moss, following true wabi-sabi principles, encroached on all to create a sublime and unexpected beauty. You could say that this moss garden is a paradise on Earth. ■

# The Steppes
## *Where Nomads Roam*

**T**ell kids the story of Genghis Khan and watch their eyes light up. He is the original exotic menace, the prototype for every Hollywood bad guy.

Nine hundred years ago, he laid siege to the world. Using his brutal, fierce Mongol nomad hordes, he brought much of Asia to heel, and became lord of the largest contiguous land empire in history, eventually 22 percent of the planet's terra firma. He was one bad dude, but he wasn't the first. In 209 B.C., Mongol forces so threatened China that it built its Great Wall.

"Mongolia is a place where you can feel the strong pulse of a warring and nomadic culture," observes photographer Chris Rainier, father of five-year-old Skylar. "I want to ride horses with him and stay in a *ger* (round tent) at

**INSIDER TIP**

If given a snack or meal, at least try a small bite. It is considered impolite not to taste food offered to you.

night under the vast stars of the inner Asian steppes. What a special experience for a father to share with his son."

Mongolians believe that "*Er huny jargal ezgyi heer*—Man's happiness is in empty, open space." No wonder. Tucked between China and Russia, slightly smaller than Alaska and more than twice the size of Texas, it's home to some of the globe's last true nomads. This is a world ruled by camels and movement. Kids will love it when you tell them that after dark the locals "check on their horses" (go to the bathroom), and fuel their stoves with dried camel dung. They live in gers made of white felt. They play *shagaa* by rolling dried sheep's ankle bones. And like them, your kids can ride horses on the vast rich green plains or on a two-humped camel in the Gobi desert.

Anything but dangerous, today's Mongolians are a generous, community-focused people who show us all how to live closer to the land.

"Sticking together, being a community is so important," says Jalsa Urubshurow, founder of the Three Camel Lodge, Mongolia's first community-based eco-lodge. "Stories are the tie that binds. Like this one my very Mongolian father would tell me: A mother has five children who don't get along. She gives each an arrow with instructions to break it. They do so easily. Then she gives each five to break at once. They can't. She says: 'If you stay together no one can break you. If you go alone, you are at risk.'"

Mongolia's nomadic tradition centers on hospitality (don't sit too close to the door—it means you want to leave soon). These nomads roam the planet's largest unfenced grasslands, most living in tents and half moving up to four times annually.

"There are few places in the world where you see people living off the land in harmony," says Urubshurow, who has brought back the annual October Golden Eagle Festival, which preserves the tradition of hunting on horseback using eagles. "We all seek a simpler life. That's what Mongolians have. We try to help children understand that the land is your friend. The nomads have a truly complete existence. They have their own kind of richness."

The most global expression of this lifestyle is July's Naadam Festival, a deeply cultural celebration of Genghis Khan (warrior reenactments) and nomadic life (ancient costumes) that galvanizes the country and showcases the best of its great skills—competitions in archery, wrestling, and bareback horse riding (kids as young as six compete).

You can still see the underpinnings of this life firsthand. "Six-year-olds herd sheep," reports Urubshurow. "They take on responsibility so young and they work so hard. This is a lesson in maturity. Communism destroyed the work ethic. Now it's back."

### BOOKS FOR PARENTS
■ *Dateline Mongolia* by **Michael Kohn (2006)** An informative account of life in Mongolia written by journalist Kohn, this book delves into the everyday life of the nomadic people of this country. Told in fast-paced prose, it covers everything from exiled Buddhist monks to child jockeys.

### BOOKS FOR KIDS
■ *Mongolia (Vanishing Cultures Series)* by **Jan Reynolds (2007)** This work provides children with a visual study of what life is like in nomadic Mongolia. The pictures tell children's stories and give an accurate portrait of their lives.

## Know Before You Go

■ *The Young Riders of Mongolia* by **Rob Waring (2008)** Most Mongolians ride horses at a young age. Horseback riding is considered a tradition and every year there is a race to celebrate it. *The Young Riders of Mongolia* explores this event and helps kids understand why it is so important.

### MOVIES
■ *The Horse Boy* (2010) A moving documentary based on the best-selling book of the same name follows one family and its autistic son as he finds healing riding on horseback through Outer Mongolia. The film shows how something so simple can change lives.

■ *Ancient Voices, Modern World* (2010) This streaming video from the National Geographic Channel on Amazon showcases how the ancient nomadic horse culture still thrives after 2,000 years.

■ *The Cave of the Yellow Dog* (2007) This is a perfect movie for the whole family. Half documentary, half children's story, the narrative drama follows the daughter of a nomadic Mongolian family and the small dog that she finds.

Steppes govern much of Mongolia's land-scape, with mountains to the north and west and the Gobi to the south. In the best sense, it is a strikingly throwback country, the world's 19th largest and most sparsely populated, where animals outnumber humans ten to one—2.7 million people, 28 million animals. It is hard to find a land more authentic, more pure.

"I have seen all four seasons in one day," says Urubshurow. "Lake Hovsgol near the Siberian border is the cleanest freshwater lake on Earth. In the Yol Valley you can walk on ice in the middle of an 80-degree desert."

You'll start your trip, inevitably, in the capital of Ulaanbaatar, a bit of a frontier town and home to 45 percent of the population. "Even city dwellers go out to the country to connect," says Urubshurow. There's great horseback riding 50 miles northeast in Gorhi Terelj National Park, near where Genghis Khan was born. Tell your horse *chew* (go), then squeeze with your feet and tap a flank with a stick. "My son learned how to ride a horse in half a day. You watch the milking and a horse being broken, if you're lucky. Men in Mongolian culture have it easy. Women prepare the food and fetch water."

Head into the Gobi, site of the 60-mile-long Hongorïn Els sand dunes, the largest in Mongolia, and an endless vista of flatland punctuated by occasional pockets of civilization and, to fascinate kids, remnants of dinosaurs.

"You can be walking along," says Urubshurow, "and find a dinosaur jaw in the sand." Of the 12 known species of predatory dinosaurs, Mongolia has yielded 8. At nearby Tugrigiin Shiree, the

# NEST

■ **Continental Hotel**
*Ulaanbaatar*
This hotel offers modern comforts for the beginning or end of your trip. Its location in the city makes walking to downtown easy. Another perk is the free continental breakfast. *www.ubcontinentalhotel.com*

■ **Terelj International Resort and Spa Hotel**
*Gorhi Terelj National Park*
For a quiet resort outside the city, check into this hotel. It offers luxury settings in the quiet of nature. Kids can enjoy the indoor pool as well as the wilderness surrounding the hotel. *www.tereljhotel.com*

■ **Kempinski Hotel Khan Palace**
*Ulaanbaatar*
The large rooms at this place give families space to relax and catch some shut-eye before exploring the country's nomadic land. *www.kempinski.com/en/ulaanbaatar/*

■ **Three Camel Lodge**
*Bulgan Sum, Omnogovi Province*
Traditional Mongolian hospitality reigns in this *ger* camp located in the Gobi desert. There are 20 felt tents modeled on the traditional ones. *www.threecamels.com*

remains of a battling protoceratops and a velociraptor were found.

Ground zero for dino-hunting, though, is the Flaming Cliffs, named by American paleontologist Roy Chapman Andrews for its orange glow, especially vibrant at sunrise and sunset. In 1922, Andrews discovered the world's first dinosaur eggs here. The place is a treasure house of 60-million-year-old petrified dinosaur bones and eggs. ■

# The Great Wall

*Legacy of an Ancient Time*

The Great Wall impresses everyone who sees it for the first time, from children to adults, from the general tourists to scholars," says Henry Ng, the manager of the World Monuments Fund's China projects. "The vastness of the structure helps children grasp the great achievements in human history—from the Great Wall to the great pyramids—and can help inspire them to learn more about human achievements over the millennia."

Constructed over a period of 2,000 years, the stone sentry actually consists of many great walls, some dating back to the fifth century B.C. The first emperor of China, Qin Shi Huang, ordered these earlier long wall sections linked and extended with watchtowers to protect the new empire from marauding northern tribes. Succeeding emperors and dynasties continued the construction, spreading westward into the Gobi desert to guard the Silk Road. All together, the walls may have stretched more than 30,000 miles.

"Because the walls were defensive structures, you can learn about building and engineering skills

● ● ● ● ● ● ● ● ● ● ● ● ● ● ● ● ● ● ● ● ● ● ● ● ● ● ●

**INSIDER TIP**

The Great Wall was designed for protection, but don't forget the forts that were another part of China's defenses. The 16th-century Yaoziyu Fort, for example, is the best preserved of Huanghuacheng's six forts. Changyucheng Village was founded 500 years ago to guard one of the wall's most important passes.

● ● ● ● ● ● ● ● ● ● ● ● ● ● ● ● ● ● ● ● ● ● ● ● ● ● ●

throughout ancient China as well as its military history and strategies," Ng says.

"The wall raised my daughter's awareness of China's long history," says Beijing resident Pan Ningxin, who took her daughter Mengmeng, eight, to the wall at Badaling. "We talked about the function of the Great Wall when it was built, so she got some idea of the wars between nations and how dynasties change."

Early sections of the wall were built from layers of rammed earth and local materials—red palm fronds in the Gobi desert, wild poplar trunks in the Tarim Basin, reeds in Gansu. Many of these sections have eroded over the centuries; the Great

Wall as we know it largely dates from the Ming dynasty from the 14th to the 17th centuries. The Ming wall stretches nearly 4,500 miles from Shanhaiguan Pass on the Bohai Sea to Jiayuguan Pass in the Gobi.

People of the Ming dynasty layered stone and brick over packed earth, building walls 20 feet wide at the base and nearly 30 feet high that twist along the steep mountain ridges north of Beijing. Surrounded by misty green hills with watchtowers that disappear into low-hanging clouds, the wall is a place for reflection—the sense of history and the craftsmanship required to build it permeate the ancient stones.

"We wonder about the builders, the soldiers who were stationed at some of these lonely outposts, the nearby villagers who may or may not have appreciated the garrisons near them," says Jennifer Ambrose, who lives with her family north of Beijing and visits the Great Wall several times a month. "We explore around the wall, surprised to find remains of older walls that predate the Ming by centuries."

Forced laborers used pulleys to haul stone slabs nearly seven feet long and weighing a ton up the steep mountainsides. Some 10,000 watchtowers and beacon towers are located every 200 to 300 yards for quick communication. While drums were the main form of communication before 200 B.C., soldiers later used fire and smoke signals to broadcast the size of an enemy force. Each tower along the wall had a ready supply of burnable materials should the need arise. During the Ming dynasty the sounds of cannon warned of approaching danger.

Children will delight in wandering the ramparts, lined with battlements and parapets and wide enough for five horses to ride abreast. "We encourage our seven-year-old son, Myles, to explore the construction as much as he can," Ambrose says. "To look for signs of pieces that are missing, like bars on the windows, or to try to figure out from which direction invaders were expected to come based on the slots through which archers shot. Often a visit will leave us with more questions that we try to research afterward, like, Why was the Ming wall built in this direction when an earlier wall, still visible, was built so many meters in another direction?"

With more than 4,000 miles to explore, there are hundreds of places where you can visit the wall. Sites near Beijing offer the easiest access. Skip

## BOOKS FOR KIDS
■ *The Seven Chinese Brothers* by Margaret Mahy; illustrated by Mou-Sien Tseng (1992) This beautifully illustrated book tells the old Chinese folktale of seven brothers with extraordinary abilities, who band together and use their powers to challenge the emperor's mistreatment of his workers on the Great Wall.

## Know Before You Go

### BOOKS FOR PARENTS
■ *The Great Wall: From Beginning to End* by William Lindesay and Michael Yamashita (2007) The story of Lindesay's hike along the entire Ming wall, from the Yellow Sea to the desert foothills of the Qilian Mountains, is accompanied by Michael Yamashita's photos.

## MUSIC
■ *Voices of the Pipa* by Jiang Ting (2003) The elegant Chinese *pipa*, somewhat similar to a banjo, dates back 2,000 years in China's history. Ting has played the pipa since childhood and won first prize in China's national pipa competition in 1996. Here, on this album, she plays ancient and modern Chinese compositions, plus her own melodies.

the crowds at Badaling, and head for Jinshanling, two hours northeast of the capital, which offers stunning views and invigorating hikes. Children will love seeing the lights that illuminate a 1.8-mile section at night. An alternative: At Huanghuacheng, about an hour and a half north of Beijing, the wall skirts Jintang Lake and the crescent-shaped Huanghuacheng Reservoir. In summer, the mountain slopes are covered with *huanghua* (yellow wildflowers) that gave the town its name. "We most frequently go to the Huanghuacheng area because there are several access points, all rather close together, but different enough to be interesting," Ambrose says.

If you can, visit the Great Wall when it's blanketed with snow. "The snow enhances the crenellations, making the wall look more castlelike than normal," Ambrose says. "My son's imagination really gets going—when we go to Juyongguan in the snow, he pretends he's in a battle, stuffing snow into the cannon and throwing snowballs over the edge at imaginary foes."

For a quieter, less developed area ideal for young children, visit Mutianyu, a village just over an hour north of Beijing that dates from the 16th century. "This area is forested with crown pines and also full of fruit trees on the hills and in orchards—chestnut, apple, pear, and apricot," says Jim Spear, who has lived in Mutianyu for 17 years and runs The Schoolhouse lodgings *(www.theschool houseatmutianyu.com)*. "My kids roamed all over the local mountains, climbed trees, picked wildflowers, and gathered wild edibles with guidance from our neighbors. This is exactly what the local kids do when they're not busy with their studies and on vacations."

Enclosed cable cars can transport you straight from the valley to the top of the wall. "But many of our visitors like to get off the beaten track and take walks with their kids to nearby unrestored sections of the Great Wall—what we call the 'wild wall,'" Spear says. "The wild sections there are overgrown and crumbling and the ruins give one a sense of how ancient and great this civilization is." ∎

# CONNECTIONS

**Great Wall Website**
*www.greatwall-of-china.com*
This collection of essays lays out the history of the many long walls that comprise the Great Wall, analyzes the popular folktale of Meng Jiangnu, and answers commonly asked questions about the wall (such as, Is it visible from the moon? No.). Be sure to check out the Travel Guide section, which details the various sites and best times to visit the wall.

**Beijing Kids**
*www.beijing-kids.com*
This is an essential resource for families visiting Beijing. Produced by local expat families, the website provides a directory of hotels, restaurants, and educational centers in the city; tips on family-friendly events and activities in the area; and readers' personal experiences traveling to various Great Wall sites.

**"The Great Wall of China," *In Our Time***
*www.bbc.co.uk/programmes/b00s3h3w*
BBC radio host Melvyn Bragg discusses the Great Wall of China with Chinese historians in this episode of *In Our Time*. The scholars vividly describe the differences among the many sections of the Great Wall and talk in depth about its origins.

# Xi'an

## *Warriors of Stone*

The famous terra-cotta army has enthralled visitors to China since its discovery just east of Xi'an in 1974. Not as well known—and sure to catch the interest of your kids—is that the 7,000 life-size clay warriors standing in battle formation were the brainchild of a *13-year-old*.

China's eccentric first emperor, Qin Shi Huang, you see, started planning an elaborate tomb for himself after assuming the throne as a teenager. Before Qin's meteoric rise to power, China was a tangle of warring states. Qin and his powerful army conquered them all, and in 221 B.C. he unified the country under a centralized currency, language, and system of weights and measures.

He died at age 49 and was buried with the clay warriors aligned to protect him. His tomb is the largest preserved mausoleum in China. A museum is built on top of the active archaeological site, where even more statues wait to be unearthed.

"It's very impressive looking down on these soldiers and the weapons that they had, the armor that they wore," says Albert Dien, professor emeritus of Chinese at Stanford University. "And the whole story of the emperor is sure to capture the imagination of kids."

Surveying the 2,200-year-old army of life-size warriors—each with a different facial

• • • • • • • • • • • • • • • • • • • • • • • • • • • • • •

### INSIDER TIP

Send your kids to a Mandarin language camp over spring break to learn the basics. "Knowing how to say please and thank you can go a long way," says travel writer Dana Rebmann. After attending a week-long camp, her eight-year-old daughter was able to help her negotiate the price of a necklace at a local market. Laurie Higuera recommends Concordia Language Villages in Moorhead, Minnesota, which offers spring break language camps and one- and two-week camps in the summer. Visit *www.concordialanguagevillages.org*.

• • • • • • • • • • • • • • • • • • • • • • • • • • • • • •

expression—causes the minds of both parent and child to run wild.

"I was completely in awe," says Laurie Higuera, a Napa, California, mother who traveled to the site in 2010 with her nine-year-old daughter. "Out of everything we did in China, I was most surprised by seeing the terra-cotta warriors. Just the enormity of it—it was incredible. All the visitors were standing there, jaws down, staring."

Most travelers pass through the city of Xi'an to get to the warriors and there's plenty to do there. An ancient trading city on the eastern end of the Silk Road, Xi'an was China's imperial capital for 13 dynasties.

"Xi'an is a capital of great antiquity," says Dien. "If kids have any interest in digging up things or in history, it is an ideal place to visit."

Rent bikes and cruise atop China's most complete old city wall, built in A.D. 1374. Then try your hand at calligraphy at the Small Wild Goose Pagoda or head for De Fa Chang Restaurant, known for its more than 100 varieties of dumplings served in the shape of flowers and animals.

## FAST FACTS

- **Qin Shi Huang** lived in constant fear that he would be assassinated and is said to have slept in a different palace every night—**he had more than 200**—to keep his whereabouts a mystery.

- Some of the **bronze weapons** found in the pits are still razor-sharp today.

- Emperor Qin Shi Huang's tomb took **720,000 people and 38 years to complete.**

- **Small Wild Goose Pagoda** used to be 15 stories high, but an earthquake in 1556 reduced it to its current height of 13 floors.

No visit to Xi'an is complete without a stroll through the historic Muslim quarter, a warren of old alleys known for mouthwatering snacks and home to one of China's largest and best preserved mosques.

"Visiting China is not your typical family vacation," says Dana Rebmann, a travel writer whose blog, Ciao Bambino, chronicles the adventures of her family. "But you will see it resonate. The kids start piecing things together that give them a global outlook." ■

## Know Before You Go

BOOKS FOR KIDS.....................
■ *The Emperor's Silent Army: Terracotta Warriors of Ancient China* by Jane O'Connor (2002) Geared toward fourth to sixth graders, this 48-page book unravels some of the mysteries of Qin's reign even as it introduces new questions. Beautiful photographs accompany lively text that explains the history behind the terra-cotta army and offers interesting tidbits about the different ranks of the soldiers and how they were made.

BOOKS FOR PARENTS.....................
■ *I Can Read That! A Traveler's Introduction to Chinese Characters* by Julie M. Sussman (1994) A helpful book for the traveler. You can start to recognize such signs as water, hotel, and other useful characters.

■ *Terra Cotta Warriors: Guardians of China's First Emperor* by Jane

Portal (2008). This book gives readers an introduction to what has been described as the eighth wonder of the world. Kids and parents will enjoy the beautiful illustrations.

MOVIE.....................
■ *Journey in China—Travel in Xi'an* (2006) This film explores historic Xi'an, with an in-depth look at the terra-cotta army of the first emperor of China and the tombs.

# Chengdu
## Home of Giant Pandas

Giant pandas probably generate the world's longest zoo lines. And why not? Cumbersome, endearingly childlike, these roly-poly, black-and-white, seemingly cuddly creatures that locals call "big bear cats" are in short supply. Their numbers have been slashed due to low reproduction rates and habitat destruction (since the 1950s, 80 percent of their habitat has been destroyed).

Now only an estimated 1,600 giant pandas are left—on the planet—and those not in zoos lumber around the remote mountains and bamboo forests of rural China. Which is why the World Wildlife Fund has made them zoo rock stars, the poster children of endangered animals. And one of the reasons why there was such international concern when the area was savaged by an earthquake in 2008.

In the West pandas are seen only behind bars. To see them in the wild, there's only one place to go: the Chengdu Giant Panda Breeding Research Base, just six miles north of downtown Chengdu, the capital of Sichuan Province. It gives them 92 acres to thrive in something resembling their natural habitat. Founded in

1987 with just 6 pandas, it is now home to almost 100.

Before you arrive, prepare your kids: To see these animals in the wild they will walk for three to four hours. The older animals spend most of the day eating or sleeping facedown on raised platforms around the enclosures. "Kids should understand these are real animals, not toys on display for human entertainment," says Adios Adventure Travel director Jacquie Whitt. "Everything won't be perfect."

Enclosures that are home to younger pandas are more active—the animals often wrestle with each other. If you visit May through August, when most pandas are born, check out the nursery. When Sara Naumann brought her son to visit the base "he enjoyed watching pandas munch on bamboo and the adolescents playing."

"Go early in the morning," Whitt recommends. "As soon as the park opens." That's when pandas are most active (afternoons are for sleeping). Cold, drizzly weather boosts their energy—they are more sedentary in summer. Walk the center's manicured paths (signs in English offer tidbits on behavior and biology). And linger at the pond where black swans cruise and fish bob for food available from nearby vendors.

Skip the museum, but check out the Panda Kitchen, where kids will learn about what goes into—and out of—pandas. At feeding time you can see the bamboo preparation. Sample a "panda biscuit"—a cookie made for the pandas, not humans, so don't expect the kids to ask for seconds. It's better to pack your own food and drinks. "What little was available there was not very healthy," says Naumann.

Once you've spent some time with the star attractions, be sure to check out the park's other inhabitants. Red pandas, also native to China and a threatened species, look like a cross between a fox and a raccoon. They can be delightfully playful. Like their giant relatives, they are morning creatures.

## BUY WORTHY

The **gift shop** next to the main entrance sells all manner of stuffed pandas and other related merchandise. Be sure to look for the T-shirts showing pandas illustrating various **tai chi (a Chinese martial art)** poses. Keep in mind that you cannot use credit cards and there is no ATM, so you will need to bring cash.

The key to making this visit enriching for kids is to stress that they are seeing a sort of Noah's ark for pandas—a slow, challenging effort to save a species. Your family can volunteer at the base for a day (local agencies can arrange the opportunity). This gives you a chance to work closely with researchers to feed (and even bathe) pandas, clean their enclosures, collect data, and carry armfuls of bamboo. When asked to pay to have your picture taken with a panda, remember: It all goes toward saving a piece of our planet.

When the pandas lie down for their afternoon siesta, your family can reflect on what base director Zhang Zhihe once said when asked why pandas are so popular: "Because they make you smile." ∎

### BOOKS FOR PARENTS
■ *Looking for Chengdu: A Woman's Adventures in China (Anthropology of Contemporary Issues)* by **Hill Gates (1999)** As a firsthand narrative account written by an anthropologist, this is a great way to gain some insight into Chinese culture and psychology.

### BOOKS FOR KIDS
■ *Mrs. Harkness and the Panda* by **Alicia Potter; illustrated by Melissa Sweet (2012)** This is a picture book about the first explorer to introduce the panda to America.

## Know Before You Go

■ *The Year of the Panda* by **Miriam Schlein; illustrated by Kam Mak (1992)** This is a fictional account of a Chinese boy who adopts a baby panda, only to learn about habitat destruction and the attitude of the Chinese government. The book culminates in a visit to the Chengdu research base.

■ *Panda Rescue: Changing the Future for Endangered Wildlife* by **Dan Bortolotti (2003)** This is a nonfiction picture book full of stunning photos and frank explanations of the factors endangering pandas.

### MUSIC
■ *Afterquake* by **Abigail Washburn and the Shanghai Restoration Project (2009)** In 2007 a massive earthquake nearly devastated Chengdu and the surrounding areas. This CD was created to memorialize the event and support reconstruction efforts. It features performances by affected children and their parents.

# Hong K⦿ng
## *Asia's Melting Pot*

N owhere else can a child experience a city so exuberantly complex in such a geographically tiny package as Hong Kong, which packs seven million citizens into just 426 square miles, making it one of the most densely populated regions on the planet. Fiercely cosmopolitan, addicted to change, this hyperactive city encompasses villages and bustling urbanity, looming mountain ranges and ribbons of coastline. Its harbor contains 263 islands and, stunningly, parks and preserves comprise 40 percent of Hong Kong's cityscape.

Bristling with skyscrapers and crowd-frenzied streets, Hong Kong has long been a place of diversity. "It is a place you feel," author Jan Morris once wrote. "Founded by Europeans, developed by Asians, governed by Chinese, designed and run by entrepreneurs, architects, economists, and adventurers from the four corners of the world, in the streets and waterways you

may sense the turning of the Earth itself." Now a Special Administrative Region of China (since the so-called handoff from the British in 1997), Hong Kong is plenty congested, but it has the distinction of hosting a global citizenry from vastly different backgrounds who together make the place work.

Hong Kong is a city of curiosities. There's so much that will fascinate children that you can play the "Did You Know?" game endlessly. Did you know that Hong Kong may be the only city in the world named for a smell (Chinese fishermen called it Heung Gong, or "fragrant harbor")? That it is the globe's most vertical city, with more people living above the 14th floor than anywhere else? That commuters traveling from apartment buildings on the city's steep slopes to offices below are riding the longest pedestrian escalator on the planet? That the world's largest floating restaurant is moored in Hong Kong's Aberdeen Harbour? That locals eat noodles on their birthday so they may be blessed with long life? That it is illegal to spit? That Hong Kong has more skyscrapers than any other city (7,651)? That residents have so few cars that 90 percent use public

HONGKONG

**223**

transportation—the most in the world? That the most expensive home ever sold—for $101,909,312—was on the city's Victoria Peak?

And the secret to cracking Hong Kong's brash, showy confusion? An English-speaking local will be a terrific help—not so much to guide you through the sites but to help you better understand the culture and everyday street theater. "It's the small alleyways that offer the best of city life and the trails that lead over the mountain ranges that reveal the marvelous views of greenery and the South China Sea," says Mary Ellen Bailey, an elementary school art teacher at Hong Kong International School, who has lived in Hong Kong for eight years.

Bailey loves the ten-minute walk from Shikh Temple to Wan Chai Market for people-watching: "Especially on weekends, when citizens use the small sidewalk as if they own it." At the market, soak up the energy and pure exoticism of pell-mell stalls

### BUY WORTHY

At **Stanley Market**, take home an example of an ancient imperial practice by getting your **name carved on a Chinese seal.** Seals were first passed down in imperial families and court officials in ancient China as a proof of office. Today, many people still stamp these seals on official documents for identification.

hawking vegetables, fruits, and other produce your children never will have seen. Cantonese cuisine demands seasonal ingredients and natural flavors, and Hong Kongers love their food fresh. So kids will see great buckets brimming with grouper and chickens shuffling in their cages. Warn kids: These are not pets; their destination is the dinner table.

Nearby is the Blue House, a 1920s tenement building that offers a rare glimpse of old Hong Kong. Residents strongly hold to a mix of traditions, from Buddhism, Taoism, and folk religion. During the

# Yum!

■ **Lei Garden** Enjoy small plates and steamer baskets of Hong Kong's famous dim sum at this spot in Causeway Bay. Get the local favorite roast pork belly. Other *yum cha* (afternoon tea) staples include dumplings, buns, rice noodle rolls, congee, and glutinous rice in lotus leaf.

■ **Mak's Noodle** Slurp up springy wonton noodles at this place. Though the portions are smaller, the restaurant generously uses almost an entire prawn for one wonton, swimming in broth made from dried shrimp roe, powdered dried flounder, and pork bones.

■ **Hui Lau Shan** On a hot summer day, cool down with a cold soup at one of this chain's dessert stores. It's a mango lover's haven with mango in every kind of dessert possible, from pudding to drinks to *mochi* (cakes). Other popular ingredients include coconut, tapioca, and red bean.

■ **Dragon-I** If you're particularly hungry, this spot offers all-you-can-eat dim sum with kids' rates. Its outdoor area gives the kids a place to play while waiting.

■ **Tai Cheong Bakery** Bite into a soft, buttery egg tart at this bakery made famous as the favorite of Hong Kong's last British colonial leader. Best served warm, the tarts have an egg custard center cradled in a biscuit-like pastry.

Lunar New Year, for example, every dish served at traditional dinners bears a name that sounds like the Chinese words for prosperity, happiness, or longevity. On a more day-to-day basis, it's also common to visit temples or pray to certain deities for good fortune, whether it's when taking major exams, applying to colleges or potential employers, or trying to conceive.

As you move about the city, look for signs of traditional Hong Kong. The fortune-tellers with their street stands. The banners of clothing drying on windowsills. Musicians playing the traditional *erhu*, a two-stringed violin. The *dai pai dong* (big license-plate stall), open, ramshackle sidewalk restaurants. The earnest chess players hunched over boards on tables and chairs. Vendors stir-frying woks of hot chestnuts or selling sweet potatoes and duck eggs. A shoe repairman hammering away at his open-air worktable. Visit a Chinese herbal shop to show kids the alternative to Western medicine. Shops typically are crammed with bottles and jars filled with herbs, plants, and other arcane ingredients. Customers line up to be diagnosed and then wait as herbalists painstakingly mix and chop, usually rendering the "medicine" as a bitter tea that is wincingly consumed on site. And be sure to sample dim sum and dine at one of the ubiquitous Hong Kong noodle shops (make sure you use chopsticks). And if you get up by 7 a.m. you can catch a little hush in Hong Kong, and see locals doing tai chi or walking dogs. Some parks also offer free tai chi and arts classes through organizations like the Hong Kong Tourism Board.

The Goldfish Market in Mong Kok is colorfully symbolic. A local favorite, the market is a warren

## FAST FACTS

■ In Hong Kong, **taxis are not yellow.** Instead, they're color-coded by service regions: **red** for the urban area, **green** for the New Territories closer to mainland China, and **blue** for Lantau Island.

■ It might seem unusual that **cars drive on the left side of the road** in Hong Kong, but this is actually practiced in around a fourth of the world's countries and territories.

■ The Chinese **white dolphin,** first discovered in Hong Kong, are born gray, then grow lighter until they're white and flush bright pink. Scientists speculate this blush is a **regulation of temperature.**

of stalls stocked with albino tortoises, jellyfish, sea horses, tarantulas, reptiles—and one of the city's most popular pets: goldfish. Because "fish" in Chinese sounds like the word for "surplus," these specially bred carp are often kept as auspicious symbols of wealth.

There are more than 600 temples, shrines, and monasteries in the city. But temples can be dry for kids, so Daisann McLane, managing director of bespoke tour company Little Adventures in Hong Kong, recommends a trip to the 10,000 Buddhas Monastery in Sha Tin. The 400-plus steps to the monastery are flanked by countless golden statues of Buddhas: some chubby, some skinny, some with various animals, some with funny faces. Keep kids entertained and set up photo opportunities by counting and imitating the poses of the statues. Though the steps can be steep and the climb takes about a half hour, there are benches along the way.

To see the cityscape in all its glittering glory, ride the famous Star Ferry to Tsim Sha Tsui at night, when Victoria Harbour sparkles with lit skyscrapers on the island side. "Hong Kong is one of the greatest maritime cities there has ever been," says former governor Christopher Patten. "Noisy, boisterous, cluttered, and vibrant." You'll get a richly engrossing front-row seat on the ferry as it chugs past tugboats and container ships, sleek liners and battered sampans. McLane suggests spending the trip back on the lower deck to let the kids see the boat engine up close. At night, though, they'll want to be where they can see the sky—the ferry provides arresting views of the light show that starts at 8 p.m.

For a great top-down view of the city, take the tram up the intensely steep incline to iconic 1,800-foot Victoria Peak, the highest point on Hong Kong Island (see how many of the smaller islands the kids can spot). On the way down, escape the city hustle by taking the Central Green Trail, an hour-long but shady walk into Hong Kong Park. Parents and older kids can also venture onto Bowen Road, a lush 2.5-mile trail that snakes between Central and Wan Chai, or "dragon's back," a ridge of bamboo and banana thickets in Shek O.

The hidden appeal of Hong Kong is its lively island life. On Lantau, the largest of Hong Kong's archipelago of islands, kids will get a delightful case of the heebie-jeebies as they ride the glass-bottomed Ngong Ping 360 Crystal Cabin car to a giant bronze statue of Buddha. And you can swim on long Cheung Sha beach, which is overseen by yellow-clad lifeguards and elderly cleaners in wide-brimmed hats. Cheung Chau Island, a 20-minute ferry from the mainland, offers an almost Mediterranean experience. Rent bikes and lunch on squid or shrimp on a quaint quay surrounded by bobbing fishing boats (and treat your kids to the frozen fruit kebab, a delicious alternative to ice cream). Nearby is a small beach thronged by families and reassuringly protected by a shark net.

At dark, hit the city's night markets—the classic Hong Kong shopping and people-watching experience. Temple Street and Ladies' Market are places to bargain for cheap clothing, gadgets, and trinkets. Kids who love bugs and boogers can try delicacies like intestine kebabs, oyster omelets, and stinky tofu.

Hong Kong is a city of celebration. It loves its fireworks—and they are among the most spectacular in the world. The best time to see them at their grandest: Christmas Eve, Chinese New Year, the July 1 anniversary of the handover of Hong Kong to China, and the founding of modern China on October 1. Their brash, kaleidoscopic, high-flying energy is a perfect symbol of the city—the place English poet James Kirkup once said "blazes like a great flower of light with neon stamens and petals of floodlit stone." ∎

## INSIDER TIP

Most Chinese holidays are based on the lunar calendar, so dates can vary by over a month from year to year. Plan ahead if you're coming for a specific festival. On public holidays government offices close, but many shops stay open, as Hong Kongers make the most of their day off to go on shopping sprees. The exception is Chinese New Year, when almost everything is closed for up to a week.

# Angkor
## *World's Biggest Religious Monument*

"I magine a real-life Indiana Jones temple with ancient tree roots slowly creeping over stone faces lost in the steaming jungles of Asia—a place time forgot for a moment," says photographer Chris Rainier, father of five-year-old Skylar and author of a book on Angkor. "This place conjures up ancient civilizations lost in the mists of time. It gives parents an opportunity to share the story of a great civilization powerful enough to carve out of the jungle an immense collection of stone buildings and statues—but for a brief moment in history. Within 100 years, Angkor quickly fell into disrepair and was lost in the forest."

The world's largest religious monument, the Angkor Temple complex in Cambodia consists of more than 100 buildings and covers 150 square miles. Rediscovered by the French in 1860, the site is dominated by Angkor Wat, one of the world's biggest Hindu temples (also once used as a Buddhist temple) and the tomb of King Suryavarman. To enter, you cross a stone causeway over a spring-fed moat, 1,640 yards long east to west and 1,421 yards south to north. Only three of the temple's elaborately

carved *prasats* (sandstone towers) are immediately visible (once a year—March 26—the sun rises to sit directly over the middle temple at noon).

The bridge into Angkor Wat reveals seven-headed snakes, a symbol of the god of water. Inside the temple, keep an eye out for the carved symbols of the *naga*, the snake. Look for images of four-armed Vishnu (god of protection), Shiva (god of destruction), and Brahma (god of creation). The scent of incense permeates the site. Some 1,500 statues of *apsaras*—female divinities—are everywhere and exhibit 36-plus different hairstyles, but only one has teeth. (Can your kids find it? It's to the right as you enter.)

You walk past the Ramayana Tableau—a battle of monkeys and demons that will fascinate children;

there are still patches of red that were painted on sandstone in the 16th century. Have kids count the number of windows in the temple facades. Uneven numbers mean bad luck. The walls are pocked by small holes that once accommodated ropes that elephants used to haul stone to the site.

The main site is not necessarily the main attraction. "Kids shouldn't miss the Bayon Temple at sunrise before the crowds," says Rainier. Go at 6 a.m., and you are virtually alone. Climb the steep steps. Gaze at the weathered, beatific stone faces, touched by lichen, cracked and ancient. Walk across the uneven stones and watch as the sun suffuses the site.

This is a place where children can sit among the treasures of the ages. Peek in a window and you discover an ancient stone Buddha in modern dress. Among the ramshackle ruins, everything shows its age. Stone is bowed, cracked, chipped, chopped. Sagging walls are girded by scaffolding—the Cambodians are making an effort to arrest the march of time. The stone carvings depict the creatures you hear in the jungle around you—chattering monkeys, trumpeting elephants, and chirping parakeets.

Both Angkor Wat and Bayon have been excavated, but Ta Prohm Temple, where part of *Lara Croft: Tomb Raider* (2001) was filmed, remains as it was found in the 19th century. The lesson here for young travelers is that man's creations are no match for nature, which is at war with the world's great treasures.

## INSIDER TIP

Guides explain the features of the temples using the four cardinal directions. Bring a compass if you want to seriously explore the Khmer temples.

When visiting Angkor, prepare for floods of visitors, especially in winter, when it is cooler: "You can see this place but you can't really experience it," says Rainier. Every once in a while you get 30 seconds between another flush of tourists, like waiting for the silence between heartbeats. "The trick," he says, "is to avoid guided tours. Wait until those tours start, then walk against the flow, in the opposite direction. You'll leave as they come. And go as early as you can."

There is a sobering side to Angkor. The Cambodians who guard and celebrate the site are survivors of the brutal Khmer Rouge regime. Outside Ta Prohm a band plays traditional Cambodian music to raise money to help victims of land mines. (Plastic land mines last 45 years in the ground, metal 25 years, and the terrain is littered with them.)

Older kids might visit the Cambodian Landmine Museum to learn about a profound and sad period in Cambodian history. "Children should experience some of the world's darker times as well as the 'lighter' moments," Rainier says. "To travel is to see and understand both sides of the human spirit." ∎

"The temple is of such extraordinary construction that it is not possible to describe it with a pen, particularly since it is like no other building in the world. It has towers and decoration and all the refinements which the human genius can conceive of."—*Antonio da Magdalena, a Portuguese monk (1586)*

# Chiang Mai
*Where Elephants Wander*

When it comes to life-changing experiences for kids, it's hard to beat hanging out with a holy man in the ancient city of Chiang Mai in Thailand.

"Without a doubt my sons' favorite activity there was our visit to the monks at Wat Chedi Luang," says Michelle Duffy, who visited Chiang Mai with her sons, Cillian, 15, and Brendan, 10. "We spent nearly two hours meeting with these young monks. My boys found learning about their lifestyle fascinating. They were intrigued by the differences between their normal day and the regular day of a novice monk. That the monks were equally fascinated by my children, asking them questions, made the whole experience even richer."

The capital of the ancient Lanna Kingdom, Chiang Mai remains the cultural epicenter of northern Thailand, famed for its 300 temples, wandering elephants, sprawling markets, and the hill tribes that live in the green mountains north of the city.

"Chiang Mai is the place that I must go back to every time I return to Thailand," says Montatip

Krishnamra, who was born in Chiang Mai and now teaches Thai language and culture at the University of Michigan. "It's completely different from Bangkok—it still maintains a lot of the old cultures of Thailand. You'll frequently see members of the hill tribes wearing their traditional, colorful costumes adorned with silver."

"We wanted to experience a slower paced, more genuine Thailand," says Duffy. "The center of Chiang Mai is a small, walkable area with what seems like a wat (temple) on every corner."

Chiang Mai boasts almost as many wats as Bangkok, despite being only a fraction of the capital's size. Most date from the 13th to 16th centuries and display the signature Lanna architectural style with ornate woodcarvings on the temple pillars and doors. In the center of the walled old city, make sure to visit 600-year-old Wat Chedi Luang, which once housed the Emerald Buddha and where kids can meet monks.

For another spiritual encounter, take the trek about ten miles outside the city to Wat Phra That Doi Suthep, whose location on one of Thailand's highest mountains, according to legend, was chosen by a sacred white elephant. The 14th-century temple is one of the country's most famous pilgrimage sites.

"Kids can participate in the Buddhist rites here," Krishnamra says. "My college students got the lyrics of the prayers and walked around the main stupa, reading the prayers with other Thai visitors."

The city's famed Night Bazaar is held every evening near the Ping River. Members of hill tribes such as the Lisu, Akha, and Hmong sell their renowned handicrafts made from silver, leather, and hand-woven textiles. Grab a bowl of *khao soi,* a spicy, coconut-filled noodle soup that's a northern Thailand specialty, for dinner at one of the numerous street food stalls—or buy the ingredients yourself at the nighttime food market near Chiang Mai Gate.

"For older children, I highly recommend a culinary experience at a cooking school," Duffy says. "From the colors of the fruits and vegetables at the market to the flavors of the foods we cooked, it was a spectacular day of family togetherness and enjoyment—and we learned how to make traditional Thai curries from scratch. I will never forget the sight of my children pounding chilies to make a Thai red curry."

One of the best times to visit Chiang Mai is November, when the weather is not too hot and the city celebrates the Festival of Light during the full moon, Krishnamra says.

"The whole town will be there at the river," she says. "The people place candles on the bark of the banana tree—they're very simple and homemade rafts, not elaborate at all—and float them downriver. It's meant to float away all your sadness and bad luck. It's so beautiful, with the full moon and the water dotted with lights." ∎

---

**BOOKS FOR PARENTS**.................
■ *Lanna: Thailand's Northern Kingdom* by Michael Freeman (2006) The ancient Lanna Kingdom left its mark on Chiang Mai with its distinctive architecture, art, and culture, especially as demonstrated in the region's many temples.

■ *Run for the Mountains* by Gordon Young (2011) Young chronicles the true story of Chanu, a Lahu-Lisu man from northern Thailand who led an adventurous life as a farmer, hunter, bandit, smuggler, and more. The author grew up among Lahu tribes in northeast Burma and later

# Know Before You Go

helped found the Chiang Mai Zoo, and wrote Chanu's history based on their 15 years of friendship.

**MUSIC**.................
■ *Thai Elephant Orchestra* by David Soldier and Richard Lair (2001) Kids will be delighted with the sounds emanating from this unusual band—six elephants were turned loose on such instruments as drums, synthesizers, a large harmonica, and a gong.

The results are both avant-garde and surprisingly rhythmic, with spirited instrumental solos. Other tracks feature human–elephant collaborations and songs about animals performed by northern Thailand residents.

■ *Silk, Spirits and Song: Music from North Thailand* by Various Artists (2006) Ethnomusicologist Andrew Shahriari describes the social and historical context of these songs before and after each track, even detailing the different instruments used.

# Kerala
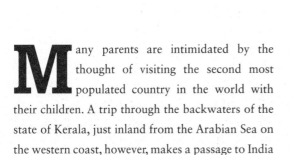

## *Backwaters Paradise*

**M**any parents are intimidated by the thought of visiting the second most populated country in the world with their children. A trip through the backwaters of the state of Kerala, just inland from the Arabian Sea on the western coast, however, makes a passage to India much more approachable.

"Kerala's backwaters are great for people who are scared to take their kids to India because of food poisoning, chaotic traffic, and grime. It's not 'India lite,' but it is much more manageable," reports Backpack to Buggy blogger Meg Keough, who took her four-year-old daughter to Kerala. "We wanted to experience all the flavors of India—the colors, the chaos, the food, the culture. Kerala takes all the best parts of these things and puts them together, while also maintaining something uniquely Keralan. You can go sightseeing without checking sights off a checklist."

A network of 560 miles of sleepy canals, rivers, lagoons, and lakes that meander through verdant palm jungle, the backwaters of Kerala have served

### INSIDER TIP

You can tell an Indian from Kerala by their traditional dress. Although people in most parts of India enjoy lively, colorful outfits, the traditional clothing of Kerala is mostly white with a red or gold border—including the men's *mundu* (wrap). Some locals say that it is so the colors will not distract from the kaleidoscopic colors of nature.

for centuries as a link from the productive spice lands of the interior to the ocean. The area thrums with workers in waterlogged rice paddies, fishermen hauling giant Chinese nets into their dugout canoes, and artisans practicing many of the same skills they have for millennia. In the cities and towns anchoring the backwaters to the coast, you'll find seafood coconut curries and abundant tropical fruits; colorfully decorated elephants guarding Hindu temples; and the minarets of mosques peeking above palm trees. The locals call it "God's country."

The real treat for families is just to observe. And the best way to do it is by boat—or better yet, by houseboat. Keralan houseboats are distinctive—

many are revamped traditional *kettuvallum*—wooden hulled boats, some over a hundred years old, used to carry cargoes of rice, cardamom, cinnamon, and ginger from the fields to the ocean port at Kochi. Kettuvallum are made without nails; instead knotted coir (woven coconut fibers) hold the wooden planks together. You can still see women weaving the fibrous strands along the water's edge.

Sithara Menon, 12, has visited Kerala with her family several times, but she recalls boating through the region's backwaters as a highlight. "You can look outside and see parts of the country that you

# CONNECTIONS

**Backpack to Buggy**
*www.backpacktobuggy.com*
Blogger Meg Keough writes about her experiences with her daughter, Mirielle, in Kerala. The site offers useful tips and advice for fellow travelers to the region.

**Kerala Tourism**
*www.keralatourism.org*
Kerala's official website full of state facts, information, suggestions, and regional contacts.

**I-to-I**
*www.i-to-i.com*
This U.K.-based volunteer outfit leads two- to four-week trips to Kerala during which travelers volunteer at the Cottolengo Special School, which helps to educate young people with special needs in the Kochi area, while learning about the local culture through homestays.

**Adventure Company**
*www.adventurecompany.co.uk*
This company leads family trips to the backwaters of Kerala.

## BUY WORTHY

**A *uru*, or big boat,** is a traditional Arabian sailing ship, built in the town of Beypore, near where Vasco da Gama first landed in the region. Actual ships aren't affordable for most travelers, so instead take home the region's most popular souvenir: a scale model built using **traditional materials and methods.**

normally wouldn't see—it's a lot of coconut trees, flowers, and villages."

Sithara's mom, Beena Menon, grew up in Kerala and thinks bringing her American kids to the region gives them a chance to experience another way of life: "We get used to the U.S., its hectic pace and conveniences, and it gives them perspective. My kids like watching the coconut man, and the fish man. They try to see how everything happens there."

A typical houseboat trip through the backwaters can last anywhere from a few hours to a few days, but the most popular route is an eight-hour voyage between Kollam and Alappuzha (Alleppey), stopping occasionally to visit tiny islands and the ashram of a famous female guru in Amritapuri.

While taking a Kerala cruise, Keough notes that villagers doing laundry and taking baths in the water fascinated her daughter. When they returned to the hotel after the trip, her daughter got in the pool, took off her clothes, and started doing laundry like they did in the waterways.

"Traveling with your kids, you notice things you wouldn't notice otherwise—you'll see it from their perspective," Keough says. "The things that they ask questions about are not what you'd expect because they have such a different view, physically, mentally, and developmentally. I think the trip to Kerala has helped my daughter realize that there is more than one way to accomplish a task. She doesn't have the same boundaries as other kids who haven't had those travel experiences."

For a more extended cruise, multiday houseboat rentals allow you to get lost in the waterways and spend nights gazing up at the vast ceiling of stars. From the deck, it's easy to imagine those same cosmic patterns and shapes guiding astrolabe-toting merchants hundreds of years ago as they traveled the spice route to Kerala.

When Christopher Columbus set out past the known horizon in 1492, he fully intended the *Niña*, the *Pinta*, and the *Santa Maria* to land on the white-sand beaches of southern India's spice coast—Kerala. Only six years later, Columbus's poor aim was Portuguese explorer Vasco da Gama's gain—he found the route to Kerala, connecting one of the world's most important spice-producing regions to Europe.

An interesting time to visit is immediately following the rainy season in late August or early September on the occasion of Onam. Local lore says a just and popular king, Mahabali, ruled over the state of Kerala when the gods became jealous and concocted a plan to lessen his power over the land. The god Vishnu came to him in the form of a small Brahmin boy, asking for a parcel of land—only as much as he could cover in three steps. Despite the warnings of his suspicious councillors, the king agreed. The boy then changed back into Vishnu, revealing his cosmic size, but Mahabali could not go back on his word. Vishnu took one step and covered the Earth, and a second that covered the heavens. Realizing there was

nothing left, the king offered Vishnu the top of his head, and the god's sweeping footstep pushed Mahabali deep underground. The king had passed the test, so Vishnu offered him one wish. The king asked to return every year to visit his people. Onam is the annual festival welcoming Mahabali back to Kerala.

During the ten days of Onam, families work together to create colorful and artful flower mats in front of their houses—welcome mats for Mahabali.

"The wildflowers are blooming all around—you gather the flowers from your yard or your neighbor's yard and make colors and patterns," says Sithara. "You can also draw patterns on the sidewalk with colored chalk and sometimes you'll put the flowers over those. I like Onam because it's fun to do the flowers."

Another highlight are the festival's snake boat races—long, slender boats with sterns shaped like cobra hoods and weighted with 25 singers and as many as 130 rowers, all competing for the Nehru Trophy. ■

# Taj Mahal

## *Monument to Love*

"The Taj Mahal shows three faces," says Nicholas Wapshott, a British writer, journalist, and father. "In the early morning, it is floating in mist, as though sitting on clouds, like a heavenly place. In the middle of the day, the heat is searing, and it's crowded. You see the Taj Mahal flat on. In the evening, or if you're lucky enough to be there during a full moon, the white-marble building glistens and shimmers. Once children see the Taj Mahal, they will constantly look at the setting of any building relative to the time of day. It will change the way they see all other buildings from then on."

A UNESCO World Heritage site and one of the new seven wonders of the world, the Taj is the icon of India. Even children cannot help but set their expectations high for a visit.

Wapshott's son Oliver, 21, learned about the Taj as a young boy. When his mom, Louise Nicholson, author and lifelong India specialist, returned to London from trips to India, she shared photos and stories with him.

---

**FAST** FACTS

■ The acoustics inside the main dome, which soars to 240 feet, can cause the single **note of a flute to echo five times.**

■ The meticulously engineered and decorated Taj Mahal required **22 years of labor by 20,000 workers.** And more than 1,000 elephants were deployed to carry construction materials.

■ In 1648, Shah Jahan moved the capital of the Mughal Empire to Delhi. Despite his devotion to Mumtaz Mahal, he likely did not visit the Taj Mahal again and only **saw it from his prison at Agra Fort,** after his son Aurangzeb usurped the throne.

---

"From the time he could speak, he always called it the 'Haj Matal' and drew it at school when everyone else's favorite building was Buckingham Palace or Big Ben," his mother recalls.

Oliver's dream of visiting the Taj Mahal was realized when he was seven, on a hot April day during a trip with his parents and brother.

"A lot of times, visiting these great monuments is anticlimatic, but the Taj Mahal lived up to, and

"Did you ever build a castle in the air? Here is one, brought down to earth, and fixed for the wonder of the ages."—*Bayard Taylor, American novelist (1855)*

even exceeded, my expectations," Wapshott says. "There was a feeling that the spirit of the building was still alive, like the original intention of the building—as a symbol of love—was still there."

The love story behind the Taj: In 1628, Shah Jahan became ruler of the Mughal Empire. His favorite wife, Mumtaz Mahal (which means "chosen one of the palace"), was his loyal travel companion. In 1631, while accompanying Shah Jahan on a military campaign to expand the empire into South India, she died in Burhanpur after giving birth to her 13th child.

Grief-stricken, the emperor went into mourning and threw himself into creating a monument to their love. In 1631, construction on the Taj Mahal began. Materials from various regions of India, Central Asia, and the Middle East were brought to Agra, and thousands of workers labored more than 20 years until the structure was completed.

"One of the most magical aspects of the Taj Mahal, and one few visitors take advantage of, is the view of it from across the river," says Divay Gupta, director of programs for the Indian National Trust for Art and Cultural Heritage. At Agra Fort, for example, children will appreciate seeing the Taj from across the Yamuna River, just as Shah Jahan did during the last years of his life, after he was overthrown by his son and imprisoned there.

To enter the Taj Mahal complex, visitors must pass through security (do not take anything with you besides cash for tickets and a camera) and make their way to the entry gate, where they first glimpse the Taj Mahal. Wide paths lead to the raised platform in the middle of the garden, then to the mausoleum.

Gupta suggests taking a detour to show children the Taj from a different perspective. "Meander through the garden. It offers very interesting views of the Taj, perhaps what it looked like in the Mughal era. The present clear view and lawns were a British invention; it was otherwise in a thick, wooded area," he says.

Rebecca Sullivan, an Australian who lived with her family in Mumbai from 2009 to 2011, says that her daughters enjoyed roaming the large grounds and suggests that kids take their own photos.

"The apparent obsession with symmetry in the Taj is easily captured and observed by kids if they have a digital camera. They also can capture the iconic image of the Taj reflected in the water of the pool," she says. Rebecca's daughters were impressed by the scale of the mausoleum and by touching the marble and inlaid stones. Eight-year-old Emma says she particularly remembers, "the special boxes where they were buried together forever."

In the completely symmetrical Taj Mahal complex, the tombs are the only nonsymmetrical components. Mumtaz Mahal's resting place lies at the center of the mausoleum, and when Shah Jahan died in 1666, his tomb was placed to his wife's right. "When we saw the tomb, everyone was silent," Oliver recalls. "While it's touristy, it felt very religious as well." ∎

# Galle

## *King Solomon's Port*

Sri Lanka, once known as Ceylon (which gave the tea its name), is an exotic place of steaming jungles, hundreds of miles of untrammeled beaches, elephant treks, and phantasmagorical festivals. But a first stop for the kids should be Galle. A walk along the ramparts of its fort on the southwest coast of Sri Lanka "will capture the imagination of any child," says Sue Gregory, an adviser at the fort, which sits atop a small, rocky peninsula overlooking the Indian Ocean. "They can imagine battles being fought and lost." For more than 420 years the fort has guarded the town of Galle. Nineteenth-century politician and traveler Sir James Emerson Tennant thought the city was the biblical metropolis of "Tarshish," which King Solomon is said to have used as a port for trading gems, ivory, spices, and peacocks. Over the centuries, international traders from the Persian Gulf, South India, and Malaysia all sailed here, bartering their goods for produce. Galle came into the hands of the Portuguese in the late 16th century, after seafarers from the country were washed ashore by a storm.

• • • • • • • • • • • • • • • • • • • • • • • • • • •
### INSIDER TIP

Little ones can take surfing lessons and snorkel at Unawatuna Bay in Galle. The beach is protected by a reef, which breaks the impact of the waves from the Indian Ocean so the water is calm enough for kids to safely enjoy. If you are looking for an adventure, rent a traditional log fishing catamaran, and head out to the main waters of the Indian Ocean.
• • • • • • • • • • • • • • • • • • • • • • • • • • •

The rule was short-lived; the Dutch captured the Portuguese-built fort in 1640 and extensively restored the area, building massive walls and spacious housing that still stand.

A UNESCO World Heritage site, it is one of the best preserved sea forts built by colonials in Asia and includes within its impregnable walls of granite and coral—so strong they withstood the 2004 tsunami that devastated villages along the coastline—a city noted for masterful architecture with hallmarks of both Europe and South Asia: Nearly 500 houses, a lighthouse, a Muslim mosque, and ancient churches. Here you'll encounter food carts, three-wheelers, and families socializing on streets once used by 17th-century colonists. Stop for a taste of Sri Lanka's local cuisine at Serendipity Arts Café, which also offers tours led by local author Juliet Coombe. "Nibble on traditional string hoppers sweetened with palm sugar," suggests Galle native Jeremy Gopalan, "as you watch schoolchildren in their immaculately pressed uniforms play alongside idle cows, all communally taking refuge from the blistering tropical sun."

To explore the fort with your children, start by walking through the ramparts to the high bastion walls, where panoramic views reveal some of the most vibrant city gems—the old Dutch and English churches, the governor's house, and the Portuguese Zwart Bastion (Black Fort). Tread along the ramparts during the afternoon sunset as the surf crashes into the rocks below. At the Jetwing Lighthouse Galle, at the edge of the fort, locals gather to fly kites as the sun sets. Let the kids roam around the grassy patches where

Galle children often play cricket, Sri Lanka's longtime passion. The 85-foot lighthouse, rimmed with croton bushes, offers idyllic views of the ocean, once home to the sprawling harbor port.

Three miles southeast of the fort you can swim or snorkel safely at Unawatuna, a crescent-shaped beach. The kids will get more out of the visit if you read them some of the stories from the epic of Ramayana, warrior tales based on the Hindu god Rama (*The Ramayana for Children* by Bulbul Sharma has eye-popping illustrations that will get their attention). The Unawatuna area is thought to have inspired the descriptions of beach paradise in the saga: "[A] seashore dotted with thousands of trees, coconuts, and palms dominating, strings of houses and hermitages along the coastline, human beings and superior beings such Gandharvas, Siddhas, and ascetics, living in them and countless bejewelled celestial nymphs thronging the shore, the coast intermittently visited by heavenly beings, Gods and demons." ∎

## BOOKS FOR PARENTS
■ *Delightfully Imperfect: A Year in Sri Lanka at the Galle Face Hotel* by Paul Harris (2006) This work chronicles a journalist's experience living at a legendary Sri Lankan landmark, for one year. His time at the oldest hotel in the world east of Suez reveals a noteworthy perspective on the conflict and politics that have burdened the tropical island.

## Know Before You Go

### BOOKS FOR PARENTS & KIDS
■ *Around the Fort in 80 Lives: Galle Fort, Sri Lanka* by Juliet Coombe (2008) Based on a new concept of travel writing, author Juliet Coombe chronicles the lives of individuals living in merchant cities such as Galle and documents the city's fascinating history and

culture for future generations, including interviews and charming stories of Galle residents who live among the ancient Galle Fort in the seaside town.

■ *Sri Lanka, 5th (Footprint Travel Guides)* by Sara Chare (2011) This travel guide offers itineraries for families who want to experience an adventure off the beaten path.

# Trans-Siberian Express

*The Epic Rail Journey*

**H**ave your kids think about the coldest they've ever been. Really cold. That's what Siberia has an abundance of. In fact, on February 6, 1933, it registered the world's lowest temperature outside of Antarctica: minus 70°F. Siberia is all extremes, an epic place that offers the curious an epic trip—aboard the Trans-Siberian railway. So, once the kids consider cold, challenge them: How big is big? Then go to the map. Astonish them by tracing the route's great arc. It's plenty big. It covers 5,700 miles from Moscow to Vladivostok on the Pacific (with connections to China through Mongolia and Manchuria). It's a trip equal to round-trip between New York and San Francisco. So vast is Siberia that an obelisk on the route marks where Europe and Asia meet. The trip takes a week. You cruise across the taiga then roll into Irkutsk on Lake Baikal, the world's deepest lake (398 miles long, 50 miles at its widest) with 20 percent of the globe's

fresh water. This 20-million-year-old freshwater lake is the planet's oldest and supports more than 1,500 types of animals, some found nowhere else on Earth.

By the time Tsar Alexander III began construction of the railway in 1891, buzz about the colossal project had reached a frenzy. Jules Verne likened it to "a girdle round the Earth," and news reports referred to it as "the spinal cord of the Russian giant."

"The sheer scale of it is mind-boggling," agrees Adrian Bridge, who took the train from Moscow to Irkutsk with connections to Beijing—a variation called

the Trans-Mongolian—with his wife and two teenagers. "There's an immense sense of covering a vast amount of ground and moving between different worlds." The real fun is finding adventure in unexpected ways. Highlights for his son included bargaining for a Russian hat, sleeping in a yurt, and trying his hand at archery in Mongolia. "It's magical to experience the rhythm of the train on the tracks, especially at night," says Tim Todd, manager of T.E.I. Tours and Travel. He's taken the Trans-Sib, as it is nicknamed, many times and especially loves passing "fairy-tale villages with bright wooden houses, vast 'oceans' of trees," and the "*babushkas* [older women or grandmothers] selling homemade snacks on the platforms."

Tom Flanigan of Chicago journeyed to Novosibirsk on the Baikal train number 9/10 with his wife and two daughters, ages five and seven: "They loved eating in a dining car and seeing the world going by. They've seen it in old movies and it's something hardly anybody does anymore in the United States."

Flanigan says his pretrip worries about cabin fever were ill founded. "The train stops every four or five hours in remote towns, where you can stretch your legs and go into the station. The kids didn't have a cooped-up feeling."

It offers an extraordinary opportunity for families to simply be together, says Mark Smith, who chronicles his Trans-Siberian trips on the website The Man in Seat Sixty-One (*www.seat61.com*). "In a world that has come to regard journey time as 'lost' or 'wasted' hours . . . being together as a family on a train, with our own cabin or sleeper, away from distractions such as TV, phone calls, doorbells, or computers, is actually quality time with your kids." ■

**BOOKS FOR PARENTS**............
■ *In Siberia* by Colin Thubron **(2000)** An atmospheric description of a journey through Siberia, where "white cranes dance on the permafrost" and "mammoths sleep under glaciers," is more than a mere travelogue. It richly outlines the history, geology, and haunting beauty of a region few know about, and paints a compelling portrait of the locals along the way.

Know Before You Go

■ *Russia Off Track: Trans-Siberian Railway* by Jarret Schecter **(2010)** A window-eyed view of a trip across Russia, this book is filled with pictures that the author took while on his train adventure in 2009. The photographs arrestingly capture 5,778 miles of scenery from the Pacific to Moscow.

**MOVIES**..............
■ *Trans-Siberian Rail Journeys: An Astonishing Look at the Seven-Day Train Trip from Moscow to Beijing* **(1997)** This DVD gives viewers an in-depth look at what you can expect from this once-in-a-lifetime rail trip. It features stories ranging from day-to-day life to historical information on how this railway was constructed.

PAPUA
NEW GUINEA

*Great Barrier Reef*

*AUSTRALIA*

NEW
ZEALAND

Pacific
Ocean

□ *Uluru*

*Southern Alps* □
*Milford Sound* □

□ *Tasmania*

*Easter Island* □

Indian
Ocean

*ANTARCTICA*

SOUTH
AMERICA

*South Pole* □

Atlantic Ocean

**Map Key**

□ Selected point of interest

Scale varies in this projection.

# Oceania &
# Antarctica

......................................

# Great Barrier Reef

## *The Glory of Looking Down*

"**W**e spend so much time encouraging our kids to look *up*," says Ben Alcock, father of two. "We point out the stars in the night sky, the peaks of faraway mountains, even the distant horizon. These are all part of expanding their minds and developing their sense of place in an enormous world. A trip to the Great Barrier Reef does that, too, by forcing them to look *down*. Down into an unexpected place that wobbles and sparkles through crystal waters. There really is another universe under there."

The Great Barrier Reef—a marine park about the size of California that parallels the Queensland coast of Australia for 1,250 miles from Bundaberg past Cape York—is composed of more than 2,900 different reef systems. The only living organism visible from space and named by some as one of the seven wonders of the natural world, the reef is among the most biologically diverse places on the planet. It is the largest structure built by living organisms—when corals die, the limestone skeletons pile up and form the reef's bedrock.

Over hundreds of thousands of years, this process created the reef as we know it today. It is home to some 400 different types of coral, more than

"Then I sailed for Australia, New Holland as it was called, and I explored this magnificent land and glorious reefs on the east coast for two thousand miles, and took over the country in the king's name."
—*Captain James Cook* (Endeavour Journals, *1773*)

in the discipline (see *www.divingcairns.com.au*).

Younger children can still get up close and personal with Nemo and friends by snorkeling. "It can be challenging for kids the first time," advises Sarah Pye, mother and creator of *kidswelcome.com .au*. "Take a trip to Green Island before tackling the Great Barrier Reef. Here, beginner snorkelers can learn the ropes in calm, shallow waters."

Then, head for the outer reef. Many day trips offer instruction and guided tours. "Check whether a tour operator has child-size masks and mouthpieces, and if not, perhaps look at renting or buying equipment before you go," suggests Pye. "There is nothing more off-putting than a poor-fitting mask that leaks or hurts kids' mouths."

Once in the water, have your kids count the different colors they see in the fish, and watch for larger sea creatures like the dugong (sea cow) and

---

# GET INVOLVED

•••••••••••••••••••••••••••••

■ The **WORLD WILDLIFE FUND (WWF)— AUSTRALIA** is part of a global network in more than 100 countries. With thousands of active projects in the Oceania region alone, WWF works to conserve local plants and animals by ending land clearing, addressing climate change, and protecting freshwater, marine, and land environments. For more, visit *www.wwf.org.au.*

---

1,500 species of tropical fish, 20 types of reptiles, and 5,000 species of mollusks—and because kids can swim right next to dolphins, rays, unicornfish, and other marine life, a trip here is better than any science class field jaunt to the local aquarium.

Visit between April and November, when temperatures are cooler than in Australia's scorching summer months. Begin your Great Barrier Reef visit in Cairns, where most international flights arrive. A wealth of family-friendly tour operators take visitors out to neighboring islands for single- or multiday reef tours, and there is a wide range of accommodations suitable for families.

One of the best ways to experience this World Heritage site is to get right in the water. "The colors really are mind-blowing," says Alcock, who visits the Great Barrier Reef frequently. "One minute the sea is dark like midnight, the next you're floating across an indescribable turquoise. And if you jump in, it can feel like you are swimming in liquid light."

Advanced swimmers can take scuba diving lessons, and kids 12 and up can earn a junior license

---

## FAST FACTS

■ The **Great Barrier Reef** is home to the world's largest oyster, weighing approximately 6.6 pounds.

■ The world's longest **earthworm,** stretching up to 13 feet, resides in the southern region of Victoria.

■ Stretching over 1,600 miles, the Great Barrier Reef is the **biggest living structure on Earth.**

■ The reef's impressive coral gardens bring together more than 300 different kinds of hard corals—**the largest collection in the world.**

■ The reef zone is a breeding area for **humpback whales,** whose babies drink up to 130 gallons of milk a day.

green sea turtle. "We couldn't keep our five-year-old novice swimmer out of the water," says Alcock of his son Spencer. "He said he felt like he was flying."

Don't want to get wet? Many tour operators have glass-bottom boats so visitors can still see the best of the reef without diving into the water.

"Even without being in the ocean, your kids' attention will be drawn downward, through the bottom of the boat, as the reef reveals itself dramatically from the impossibly deep-blue depths as you slide across the surface," explains Alcock. "Clearly visible corals of peculiar shapes cluster together sheltering schools of comically colored fish that dash and gather busily with their own kind."

The Great Barrier Reef isn't just about the ocean, though. Daintree Rainforest, part of the Wet Tropics of Queensland World Heritage site, borders the reef on land in northern Queensland. Comprising some 295,000 acres, "the area provides a huge range of exciting kid-friendly adventures like cruising on the Daintree River and seeking crocodiles in the wild," says Alcock. "Stunning, gorgeous, and unforgettable."

Visit the Daintree Discovery Center *(www.daintree-rec.com.au),* an eco-friendly education center that offers access to a canopy tower, where

kids can view the rain forest from 75 feet up in the trees. Learn how the Eastern Kuku Yalanji Aboriginal people use the forest's plants, and see dozens of species of wildlife, including flying foxes, blue Ulysses butterflies, cassowaries, bandicoots, and wild tree frogs. Dozens of tour operators leave from Cairns or Port Douglas.

Also ashore is the Australia Venom Zoo, where "boys, in particular, will love watching venom extractions," says Pye. "And the Australian Butterfly Sanctuary houses more than 1,500 butterflies."

"The Great Barrier Reef is a place of stories," summarizes Alcock. "The reef itself tells us of both the potential of tiny things, and the fragility of enormous natural ecosystems. Rest assured, your children will leave this place with their own tales to tell." ∎

---

**ACTIVITIES FOR KIDS**....................
■ **Virtual World Great Barrier Reef: Experience the Underwater Eden Online** Scroll over sea creatures for facts and photos at *www.nationalgeographic.com.*

■ **Science Kids** Enjoy the amazing world of nature with online experiments, brainteasers, games, project ideas, fun facts, and more. Plus, see video footage of the

## Know Before You Go

thriving life underwater at *www.sciencekids.co.nz.*

**BOOKS FOR PARENTS**....................
■ *In a Sunburned Country* by Bill Bryson (2001) Humorist, naturalist, and historian Bryson gives his take on Australia. Think quirky anecdotes and laugh-out-loud

moments against the backdrop of sunbaked deserts, winding coastlines, and the woolly outback.

**MOVIES FOR FAMILIES**...............
■ *Finding Nemo* (2003) With an Oscar for best animated film, this delightful Pixar production vividly brings to life the journey of Marlin, a tiny clown fish braving the dangers of the Great Barrier Reef to find his son, Nemo.

# Uluru & the Aborigines

## *Ancient Dreamtime*

**M**ore than 10,000 years ago, creator-beings—people, plants, and animals—traveled the land and, through a process of creation and destruction, built the world as we know it today. This time of creation—*alcheringa*, or dreamtime—is the foundation of Australian Aboriginal society, and kids visiting down under can delve into the art, history, and culture of this ancient people.

The heart of it all is Uluru—formerly known as Ayers Rock—one of the most recognizable icons of Australia. It is sacred to the Anangu, the Aborigines who live in the area. According to legend, two ancestral tribes were invited to feast in the area, but were distracted by the Sleepy Lizard Woman at a water hole. The hosts were very upset when their guests were tardy, causing a great battle between the tribes

and much bloodshed. The earth rose up in grief, and thus, Uluru was formed. Today, we know it as a huge red sandstone monolith located in the middle of the country in Uluru–Kata Tjuta National Park, which both the government and the local tribe own.

To explore the area, take older kids on the 6.5-mile Base Walk that circumnavigates Uluru and passes by overhangs, caves, and water holes. "There are caves to be discovered around the rock with very old Aboriginal drawings in them that kids can find and learn from," says Australian photographer R. Ian Lloyd. There are also "unusual animals to be seen such as wallabies and dingoes."

Younger kids will enjoy a shorter 0.6-mile trail, where they can see a water hole and traditional rock art.

The Anangu also lead guided walks of the area. Learn about bush foods (like *kaliny-kalinypa* nectar and the *tjanmata,* or bush onion) and listen to stories told in the rock art, which date back tens of thousands of years. Kids might even get a kick out of wearing fly-protection nets—a must for any visitor to Uluru. Pack a picnic and watch Uluru change colors—brilliant red, orange, and indigo—during sunrise and sunset.

Taking a painting workshop is a must-do in Uluru. At the session (which can be booked through local resorts), "you meet up with native artists and, under their tutelage, make a traditional Aboriginal dot painting," says father and author Roff Smith, who often leads tours in the area. The four-hour workshop is "quite fun, and of all the various Aboriginal experiences I have had, this was by far the best."

Because of its remoteness, plan to spend a couple days in the area. Most visitors arrive in Alice Springs, some 270 miles northeast of Uluru. Take a day trip from there, or spend the night at Ayers Rock Resort in Yulara, which—only 20 minutes from Uluru—offers a wide range of accommodation (from camping to large apartments) and activities (like camel trekking) for families.

## FAST FACTS

■ Believed to be the world's oldest civilization, **Aboriginal** people have lived and thrived in Australia for more than 50,000 years.

■ Australia's mainland is the **largest island** and the world's **smallest, flattest continent.**

■ Because it is so remote, Australia has a **unique ecosystem,** with many animals that live there and nowhere else in the world, including the platypus and kangaroo.

■ Although Australia is rich in natural resources, more than one-third of the country is **desert.**

■ **Uluru,** the sacred natural formation that emerges like an enormous whale's back from the red desert, is one of the largest rocks in the world.

■ Australia is one of the most **ethnically diverse** nations. Nearly a quarter of the people who live there were born in other countries.

At night, attend the resort's starlight dinner, which takes guests far away from the tour buses and crowds. After an exquisite meal (which includes local fare like barramundi, kangaroo, and emu), "all the lights are doused and you get a really fine look at the desert stars," explains Smith. "Some astronomers give talks about the southern skies and the Aboriginal myths surrounding the

# OBJECTS OF WONDER

The **didgeridoo** is a wooden wind instrument native to northern Australia. Though traditionally played as an accompaniment to dancing and singing, today its drone enlivens music the world over. Purchase a "didge" as a souvenir and try out this one-of-a-kind windpipe.

constellations." Several telescopes are available for guests, too.

The Aboriginal experience extends to the nearby Kata Tjuta, or, colloquially, the Olgas, a collection of 36 rock formations—some 500 million years old—that represent the creator-beings like Malu, a kangaroo man; Mulumura, a lizard woman; and Liru, a venomous snake man. When visiting either section of the park, keep an eye out for its real-life residents like the dingo, red kangaroo, and hopping mouse.

Beware: Many kids may find the heat (which often soars above 100°F) and physical activities in Uluru to be strenuous. They might prefer Kakadu National Park—located about three hours east of Darwin at the top of the Northern Territory.

# CONNECTIONS

**Australian Broadcasting Corporation (ABC)**
*www.abc.net.au*
ABC's Red Centre Way podtour guides you through some of the spectacular desert country in Australia. Download the full one-hour tour, or select a specific landmark.

**Uluru–Kata Tjuta National Park**
*www.environment.gov.au/parks/uluru*
The park is a World Heritage property listed for both its natural and cultural values. Its Anangu heritage is seen as an integral part of the landscape.

**Tourism Australia**
*www.australia.com*
"There's nothing like Australia," according to Tourism Australia, and its website offers more than 25,000 experiences to prove it. Peruse the site's interactive photo map for inspirational ideas.

## BUY WORTHY

The **boomerang** is a 10,000-year-old weapon, percussive musical instrument, and recreational toy—it's the quintessential Australian tool. When thrown correctly, the boomerang follows an elliptical path spiraling back to its point of origin. It's in good Aussie spirit to try your hand at it.

"If I was going to give kids an unforgettable Australian experience, I'd go to Kakadu, just before the rains, when the billabongs (lakes) are full of wildlife and birds, and loads and loads of crocodiles," says Smith.

Kakadu is one of the few World Heritage sites listed for both its cultural and natural importance. It is home to dozens of species of frogs, fish, and mammals, like the black wallaroo (unique to Kakadu), sugar glider, kangaroo, and wallaby. Many vulnerable and endangered species also live here, including the emu, masked owl, golden bandicoot, speartooth shark, and pig-nosed turtle.

In September and October, thousands of magpie geese land to feed in the Mamukala Wetlands. Take an Aborigine-guided tour along the Yellow Water billabong and try to spot the "big five"—five species of kingfisher, the smallest of which is less than an inch tall.

Kakadu has some of the most accessible rock art in the country. Visit Ubirr and Nourlangie to see what the Bininj/Mungguy people believe the spirit people made. In Ubirr, look for the stories painted by Kurangali, the Rainbow Serpent, one of the most powerful spirits in Aboriginal mythology. ∎

# Tasmania

*Riding the Waves*

You stare slack-jawed at your plate. You've just polished off a dozen rivetingly tangy Bruny Island oysters bathed in syrupy soy sauce and wasabi at Fish Frenzy. The dockside restaurant comes by its seafood locally. It's in Hobart, Tasmania, Australia's southernmost state, a wild, sparsely populated island beloved of nature and adventure lovers. Hobart began life as a penal colony, and in the early 1800s it was the center of the whale and seal slaughter in the Southern Ocean.

This meal is the start of a day of adventure that will take your family on a wild aquatic experience in the waters around Tasmania's Bruny Island. Take a two-hour drive and hop a ferry from Kettering to the island, motoring past eucalyptus stands and rustic cottages along the coastline.

"This is shack country," a tour guide says. "What we call holiday homes." Some hardly look like shacks. "Well, you can have *million-dollar* shacks," he replies.

> ## GET INVOLVED
>
> **■ TRAVELING TASMANIA IN NATURAL BALANCE:** The Parks and Wildlife Service of Tasmania invites eco-friendly families to join its Green Guardians program *(www.parks.tas.gov.au)*. Visitors help with hands-on conservation projects.

Park at Adventure Bay, where British explorer Captain James Cook last provisioned before heading to Hawaii—and his death—in 1779. Then, take off on a Bruny Island Cruises *(www.brunycruises.com.au)* boat with sunny skies and a steady swell, if you are lucky. Owner Rob Pennicott is at the wheel of a self-designed monster of an open-sided boat. A former fisherman, he reflects the nature-loving ethic of Tasmanians. He talks about his Bruny Island home, where he and his two kids harvest oysters and crayfish from a backyard river. "Bruny is special. Think about it—634 inhabitants on a place the size of Singapore," Pennicott muses. "We have one of the most beautiful places in the world. And we know it." The captain resolutely wears shorts and a fleece while everyone else is bundled up in layers of cold-weather, waterproof gear and gloves.

"I'm getting optimistic," he says when asked about the endangered right whales, so named because whalers considered them the *right* whales to hunt, and did so with abandon. "We're seeing more southern rights in these waters than we did five years ago. They come up from Antarctica and hang around. You see more seals, too, and not as many caught in fishing nets."

He points to carpets of forest in the distance. "Roughly 60 miles of Bruny Island coastline is national parkland—and it's the only place in the world where you'll find white wallabies—about 400."

Soon the boat passes Penguin Island, Captain William Bligh's last landfall before facing the mutiny that finished him. ("We like him,"

---

## FAST FACTS

- Heart-shaped **Tasmania** is Australia's only island state.

- Tasmania has a population of about **500,000 people**—almost half live in greater Hobart.

- The colloquial expression for the state is **"Tassie"** (pronounced TAZ-zie).

- The **Huon pine,** one of the oldest native trees in the world, flourishes in the island's remote ancient forests.

- Tasmania has the world's largest areas of **dolerite rock;** the distinctive shapes and steep faces provide evidence of past glaciation.

---

# NEST

■ **Maxy's by the Sea**
*Sunset Bay, Bruny Island*
A three-bedroom retreat on the Sunset Bay waterfront is ideally situated to explore Bruny Island's natural bounty.
*www.brunyisland.com/accommodation/maxys.php*

■ **Captain Cook Caravan Park**
*Adventure Bay, Bruny Island*
Captain Cook's cabins, villas, and campgrounds are set across the road from Adventure Bay Beach, one of the island's most popular swimming areas, and home to a range of activities, including Bruny Island Cruises and Ol'Kid Fishing Charters.
*www.capcookolkid.com.au*

■ **Salamanca Inn**
*Hobart*
Within a short stroll of this inn, all of Hobart's famous landmarks are conveniently located on the doorstep of the iconic Salamanca Place. Contemporary family suites provide the comforts of home amid a charming historical ambience.
*www.salamancainn.com.au*

■ **Somerset on the Pier**
*Hobart*
Spacious family residences feature loft-style bedrooms and offer a welcome alternative to a hotel. Somerset is located on the Hobart waterfront, overlooking historic Sullivan Cove and just a short walk from bustling Salamanca Place.
*www2.somerset.com/en/australia/hobart*

■ **Hatcher's Manor**
*Richmond*
Located 20 minutes from Hobart, this place is set on a 100-acre working farm and orchard. It provides plenty of room for children to run, feed the chickens, and pet the horses, while being elegant enough for parents to relax.
*www.hatchersmanor.com.au*

says Pennicott. "He introduced grapevines to Tasmania.") He points out immense patches of brown algae, the world's fastest photosynthesizing plant—it converts carbon dioxide into more benign compounds.

Pennicott pulls within yards of gaping caves that riddle the 160-million-year-old Jurassic dolerite walls. A few albatrosses ride the gyres (wind currents) above. "We've had days when you'll see as many as a thousand of them," he says.

He gestures to a peregrine falcon nest and observes, "Some nests have been carbon-dated to be 1,000 years old. The peregrine is the fastest bird in the world. It can hit its prey at up to 200 miles per hour."

The boat reaches Breathing Rock, where air is sucked in at the tide line and explodes in a foamy broth that rains down seawater. Pennicott stabs the air toward a white-bellied sea eagle nest—"it's only the 52nd found in Tasmania."

Churning through roughening seas, you near Friar Rocks, where the Tasman Sea and the great Southern Ocean meet. You cruise past smelly fur seals as a stew of colliding tidal currents arc the boat from side to side. A bruised sky develops as a front advances after a 1,500-mile landless run from Antarctica. You and your kids are at the tip of Tasmania, seemingly at the end of the world.

The chop causes the boat to yaw. Just 20 yards away is a boil of marshmallowy sea that would likely make tinder of Pennicott's craft.

You watch, then Pennicott turns tail toward the dock. During an otherwise straight haul back, he can't resist plowing full throttle through what looks like an impossibly narrow gap between two rock towers. The squall eventually catches up, driving rain sideways, clouding the air. Eventually, as the boat reaches the bay, the spray resolves to offer your family the memory of a perfect rainbow. ■

---

**BOOKS FOR PARENTS**.................
■ *When We Eat: A Seasonal Guide to Tasmania's Fine Food and Drink* by Liz McLeod and Bernard Lloyd (2004) This recipe book will take your family on a food journey through Australia's island state.

■ *A Guide to Tasting Tasmania* by Graeme Phillips (2011) Take along this informed guide to the best of Tasmania's seafood and wine; it highlights notable restaurants,

## Know Before You Go

cafés, and watering holes. Visit *www.tastingtasmania.com*.

**ACTIVITIES FOR KIDS**.....................
■ **Creature Feature** The words "Tasmanian devil" are likely to evoke images of the whirling, maniacal, and ravenous cartoon character—Taz—and that isn't too far from reality. Tasmanian devils,

found only in the wild of this Australian island state, are a feisty and fascinating breed to behold. See *www.kids.nationalgeographic.com/kids/animals/creaturefeature*.

■ **Global Bros.** Brothers Stefan and Tyler are traveling the world. Join their Aussie adventure through photos, blog posts, and video clips, including details of an unforgettable "Terrific Tassie" tour. Visit *www.kidsblogs.nationalgeographic.com*.

# Milford Sound

## *Call of the Wild*

**F**iordland . . . is one of the most astounding pieces of land anywhere on God's earth," wrote *The Hitchhiker's Guide to the Galaxy* author Douglas Adams, "and one's first impulse, standing on a cliff top surveying it all, is simply to burst into spontaneous applause."

Part of Fiordland National Park and the South West New Zealand (Te Wahipounamu) World Heritage area, Milford Sound is a should-not-miss part of any family's New Zealand itinerary.

According to Maori legend, Milford Sound (or Piopiotahi) was carved by the god Tu-te-raki-whanoa with his adze, a tool for planing wood. Milford's distinct landscape is most recognizable by its snowcapped peaks, which stretch some 5,000 feet into the sky—Mitre Peak is the tallest at 5,551 feet.

"Milford Sound is a rare snapshot of the way the world was before people transformed the landscapes of just about everywhere else on this planet," says mountaineer and father of four Peter Hillary. "It is a different place because it is a glimpse of the past—before people. Imagine a world without people." Today, Milford Sound's tranquillity allows children to experience the call of a spectacularly wild part of the planet.

Older kids—ages 10 to 13—will enjoy getting up close and personal with Fiordland's flora and fauna by hiking the Milford Track, a moderate 33.5-mile backpacking trail that begins at the tip of Lake Te Anau and ends at Milford Sound. Often called the "finest walk in the world," the Milford Track winds through spectacular vistas, cascading waterfalls, and lush rain forests.

## FAST FACTS

■ As late as the 1700s the **Maori canoes,** propelled by up to 100 warriors, were among the largest boats in the world. The 100-foot open-prowed watercraft dominated the South Seas.

■ When the Maori arrived some 1,000 years ago, they met unusual fauna such as the world's largest bird **(the giant moa)** and the world's greatest aerial predator **(the giant Haast's eagle).**

"Fiordland is a place that is still relatively unexplored due to its remote and wild nature," says writer and New Zealand resident Carrie Miller. "There's a lot of magic in that, especially for kids who feel as though they missed out on the age of exploration."

Sightings of rare birds, like the flightless weka and the bellbird—a green bird whose song is like "small bells most exquisitely tuned," according to Captain James Cook—are frequent. Hike the trail independently (there are huts along the route to stay in each night), or sign up with a local guide group (Ultimate Hikes New Zealand, *www.ultimatehikes.co.nz*, is the most well known). Only 90 hikers are permitted on the trail each day in peak season (October to April), ensuring the region remains as remote as when Captain John Grono became the first European to explore it in the 19th century.

Younger kids will enjoy shorter hikes like the Piopiotahi Milford Foreshore Walk—beginning just

### BUY WORTHY
Maori **handcrafted gifts** reflect the culture's distinctive designs, which are rooted in its rich tradition. Pick up an intricate bone carving or a jade figurine shaped like ancient symbols of Pacific heritage. From whales, dolphins, and turtles to the swirling koru design, kids (and parents) will relish these mementos.

near the entrance to Milford Sound—which winds through beech forest and offers stunning views of Mitre Peak.

Many companies offer floatplane or helicopter tours, but by far the best way to grasp Milford Sound's enormity is to get right into the middle of it on the water.

"Milford Sound looks like no other place on Earth," observes Miller. "It's straight out of a fairy-tale kingdom, with towering peaks like mossy teeth, dark green ocean hiding strange sea creatures, and gnarled trees that always remind me of broccoli."

### BOOKS FOR KIDS
■ *New Zealand ABCs* by Holly Schroeder (2006) This colorful book captures the attention of little ones to introduce the culture, ecology, and history of the islands.

■ *Land of the Long White Cloud: Maori Myths, Tales and Legends* by Kiri Te Kanawa (1997) Read 19 stories rooted in Maori culture and suffused with the wonder of the exotic land.

### BOOKS FOR PARENTS
■ *A Portrait of New Zealand* by Warren Jacobs (2007) A compilation of more than 200 scenic

## Know Before You Go

photographs—with text by award-winning journalist and writer Jill Worrall—offers spectacular views of the North and South Islands.

### MOVIES
■ *The Lord of the Rings* (2001-2003) Follow a hobbit named Frodo as he quests to destroy a magical ring in the movie versions of J. R. R. Tolkien's Rings saga, which were filmed in New Zealand.

■ *Avatar* (2009) Nominated for nine Academy Awards, including

best picture and best director, this epic film captures nature's paradise, thanks to filming in Wellington, New Zealand, and out-of-this-world special effects.

### MUSIC
■ **Soul Paua** This group offers a mix of Polynesian rock, jazz, blues, folk, and traditional music, with lyrics in the *te reo* Maori language and English.

■ **Rui & Ranea** The Maori Aperahama twins deliver a celebration of contemporary music performed completely in the Maori language.

Small ships depart from the town of Milford throughout the day and cruise along the ten-mile length of the sound. Only from the water can you grasp the enormity of the peaks. Have kids keep a checklist of all the wildlife they see. Fur seals and Fiordland crested penguins can be spotted basking on boulders, and bottlenose dolphins frequently frolic in the sound.

Milford's underwater ecosystem offers more opportunity to grasp the beauty of New Zealand's diverse wildlife. Heavy rainfall in Milford Sound—averaging over 20 feet each year—creates a permanent dark freshwater layer over the seawater, filtering out sunlight. This condition combined with the sound's calm waters means the underwater environment mimics that of the deep sea. Black and red coral, sponges, tubeworms, 11-armed sea stars, sea cucumbers, and brachiopods frequent the sound, making Milford a haven for divers.

But this vibrant marine life isn't reserved for divers alone. To see some of it without getting wet, visit the Milford Deep Underwater Observatory, a small floating education center in the sound. The highlight is a 26-foot-deep underwater circular chamber offering a 360-degree view of the sound, allowing visitors of all ages to see up close the life that lives beneath the water.

Often overlooked when exploring Fiordland is the route to Milford Sound itself. State Highway 94—Milford Road—is one of the highest and most scenic routes in New Zealand, peaking at 3,084 feet above sea level. The 144-mile route from Te Anau is the only access road to Milford Sound. Watch for flocks of keas—the world's only alpine parrot—that gather to graze for berries and insects near the road. ∎

# CONNECTIONS

### i-SITE
*www.i-site.org.nz*
This online visitor network is a gateway to the 90 bricks-and-mortar, staffed i-site tourist information centers across New Zealand. It offers access to local travel experts—available via phone and e-mail—who can make specific travel recommendations for your family.

### 100% Pure New Zealand
*www.newzealand.com*
The official website of the New Zealand Tourism Board is the ultimate planning guide, with background information, an extensive map collection, and trip-building tools.

### Kids Friendly Travel
*www.kidsfriendlytravel.com*
This site is an online aggregate of regional family attractions. The website's founder, Gaye Miller, is a mother of four and author of the New Zealand tour book *Where Shall We Take the Kids? A New Zealand Guide to Family-Friendly Destinations and Activities.*

### Department of Conservation
*www.doc.govt.nz/parks-and-recreation/*
*tracks-and-walks/great-walks*
Visit here for ideas about premier walking tracks and trails to explore in the region.

### Fiordland National Park
*www.fiordland.org.nz*
This online guide to the park that encompasses more than 2.9 million acres of mountain, lake, fiord, and rain forest environment, virtually undisturbed by human activity.

### Te Anau Glowworm Caves
*www.fiordland.org.nz*
Enter the luminescent Te Anau Glowworm Caves and set off on a magical journey. The enchanting lights and sculptured rock are only accessible via guided tour.

# Southern A🌲ps

## *Into the Big Sky*

**N**ew Zealand's Southern Alps encompass some of the most stunning landscapes in the world, with wildly raw and jaw-dropping vistas of turquoise lakes, glaciers, and snow-crowned mountains. And the best way for a child to experience it is from the air. You can access slopes to hike and ski by helicopter, but the real thrill ride is in an unpowered plane—a glider.

"Omarama is one of the best places to glide on the planet," says glider pilot Carrie Miller. About 45 minutes from Mount Cook and two hours from Queenstown, the town of Omarama and its airfield perch on the spine of the mountain range.

Omarama means "place of light," but pilots call it "place of flight." What makes it unique is that it's one of the few spots in the world where you can find all four types of lift—thermals, ridge lift, convergences, and wave—often in the same day.

"Pilots regularly set records for speed, height, and distance," says Miller. "Gliding is the closest thing to being a bird I can imagine. You're harnessing the Earth's energy to get you from place to place. It's quiet, it's powerful, and it's a way to see the world unfolding beneath you that you would never see otherwise.

"It offers incredible views," Miller continues. "I saw the Tasman Sea from my flight around Aoraki ['the cloud piercer' in Maori], also known as Mount Cook, and pilots tell me that they often get to see both oceans when they cross the South Island. And for kids, it's a fantastic introduction to wind, the weather, aviation, and navigation. It is also more environmentally sustainable than power-flying or helicoptering."

• • • • • • • • • • • • • • • • • • • • • • • • • • • •

## INSIDER TIP

Don't let a fear of flying deter you from seeing this awe-inspiring mountain range. Explore via land, water, or any combination thereof. For a more laid-back experience, try rafting the Kawarau River (Class II–III/beginner) through the picturesque Gibbston Valley (aka the "Valley of the Vines"). A paddle through *The Lord of the Rings'* "Pillars of the Kings" will enthrall the kids.

• • • • • • • • • • • • • • • • • • • • • • • • • • • •

# CONNECTIONS

**Te Ara Encyclopedia of New Zealand**
*www.teara.govt.nz*
This online database serves as a guide to New Zealand's peoples, natural environment, history, culture, economy, and society. Peruse the current events blog, Signposts.

**Kidz Go New Zealand**
*www.kidzgo.co.nz/
queenstown-and-southern-lakes*
A family travel guide to the heart of the Southern Alps—Queenstown, Wanaka, and Fiordland—this site features kid-centric options only, such as casual eateries, rainy-day activities, and convenient accommodations.

**New Zealand History Online**
*www.nzhistory.net.nz*
New Zealand History looks at New Zealand through the lenses of three broad categories: culture and society, politics and government, and war and society. A media library delivers information in print, photograph, audio, video, and interactive formats to engage audiences young and old.

**Department of Conservation (DOC)**
*www.doc.govt.nz*
This site has information about the protection of the country's natural and historic heritage, where you can enjoy public conservation areas, and how you can get involved in preservation.

"Omarama is considered to be the best mountain soaring site in the world," adds Gavin Wills, former head guide at Mount Cook and founder of Glide Omarama *(www.glideomarama.com)*. "This means a child's introductory flight can last several hours and climb higher than 20,000 feet."

Wills adds that the best age to start kids gliding is when they are big enough to be safely strapped in the cockpit—usually about nine or ten. They can begin to control the glider as soon as they can reach the rudder pedals (the youngest pilot to solo was 12).

Many kids will be a bit nervous at the prospect of flying with no engine. "But all aircraft fly without engines," explains Wills. "It's the wind over the wings that keeps all airplanes aloft. The engine supplies power to gain altitude, while a glider uses updrafts that occur naturally to gain height. So children should sit back, relax, and take in the landscape below to the horizon and the cloudscapes all around. Notice the changes in the glider's attitude, feel the sensations of flight."

While in the area, families should also take to the air on a helicopter tour to see the Franz Josef or Fox Glaciers, the two largest in Westland Tai Poutini National Park, which has more than 140 ice floes. New Zealand is one of two places on Earth (Chile is the other) where glaciers are so close to the ocean. Consequently, they grow and advance ten times faster than those in the Swiss Alps. "The glaciers are great ribbons of ice, marching down to the sea," says Miller. After a ten-minute ride, the helicopter sets you down on a centuries-old frozen landscape that few people ever see. ∎

# Papua New Guinea

*Land of the Jungle*

C hildren are fascinated by the idea of a place lost to the mists of time—like the dinosaur-infested tropical island in Steven Spielberg's *Jurassic Park*.

To show your kids a real-life version of such a spot (sans dinosaurs, of course), take your family to Papua New Guinea, where you can meet members of remote tribes and talk to former headhunters, and where you may encounter a 60-year-old tribal chieftain who once ate his enemies.

Papua New Guinea, with some of the highest peaks in the Pacific, at almost 15,000 feet, forms the eastern half of New Guinea, the world's second largest island (after Greenland). Some 800 languages are spoken here, including English-Creole (Tok Pisin), a mix of English, German, Portuguese, and Melanesian that was developed by slave traders to converse with the natives they wanted to capture. "Jesus Christ Mixmaster" means helicopter,

for example, and "plunk plunk" refers to a piano.

For millennia the sea isolated the island from Southeast Asia, and its creatures evolved in isolation—birds of paradise, cassowaries (large flightless birds), butterflies, and marsupials. The world's first known farmers started tilling this soil some 9,000 years ago, growing coffee, tea, and sweet potatoes. The number

## GET INVOLVED

........................................

■ **THE CHILDREN OF PAPUA NEW GUINEA:** Children make up almost half of Papua New Guinea's largely rural population. For these remote residents, the inaccessibility of basic health, educational, and other services is near crippling. UNICEF and partners work to protect basic human rights and promote healthy, happy, and harmonious childhoods for all. See *www.unicef.org/png*.

of pigs a family has indicates its wealth. "If you want a good, hardworking wife," one guide explains, "it will cost a lot of pigs—40 or 50."

"Papua New Guinea is a fantastic place to take kids," says photographer Chris Rainier, father of a five-year-old son and author of *Where Masks Still Dance: New Guinea*. "Visit there for the annual 'sing-sing'—the huge gathering in August during which tribes from across the country show off their exotic masks and costumes. They are painted and decorated to the hilt with birds of paradise feathers, flowers, and the ochre mud and green leaves of the island forest. Thousands of people gather in the Central Highlands to strut their stuff and exhibit their costumes. These are people of the forest, the children of former headhunters who still live closely connected to the ancient ways of the region. This event is a wonderful way for kids to get a sense of how closely humans were connected to nature. All humankind once lived simply—hunting and fishing, with a keen relationship with the forest to maintain survival, shelter, and food."

A good introduction to Papua New Guinea is the Western Highlands. A guide is a must. The area is immense, green, and choked with palm trees, dotted with thatched longhouses, and blazed with fields of sweet potatoes. Visit the colorful Mount Hagen

## FAST FACTS

■ Melanesian peoples **first settled the islands** that make up Papua New Guinea over 40,000 years ago

■ **Tok Pisin** and **Pidgin Motu (Hiri Motu)** are the most widely used languages along with English.

■ Papua New Guinea's **colorful culture** is spread across more than 600 islands divided into 4 major regions and 20 provinces.

■ Papua New Guinea has **over 20,000 square miles of coral reef.** Kimbe Bay alone has more than 413 species of hard coral, more than half of the world's known species.

■ Isolation caused by the **mountainous terrain** is so great that some tribal groups, until recently, were unaware of the nearby neighbors mere miles away.

■ Papua New Guinea is home to one of the largest areas of intact **rain forest** (120,000 square miles) outside of the Amazon.

## BUY WORTHY

**Le Riche Colours'** limited-edition prints, hand-painted cards, and tribal stickers are among the souvenir options that allow you to pack Papua's vibrant colors in your suitcase. The gallery is in the port town of Kimbe or online at *www.picturetrail.com/leriche*.

market. Here you'll find lime green mandarins that are mango sweet; live chickens that resolutely sit on a table waiting to be bought, dozy and indifferent to their fate; lumpy bananas; and new and sweet potatoes, cucumbers, and coconuts.

After visiting there, have your guide take you to a village. In one such village, you first enter a glade crowded with curious young kids and then come to a small clearing where there is a semicircle of locals. If ever there is a time to teach your children the nature of commerce, it is at a moment like this. The villagers create—and sell—wonderful masks, bowls, and brightly colored bags. Commerce is emotional and basic. Do you love it?

If yes, then buy, the natives urge. Next, however, comes the haggling. Keep it simple. Offer half of the asking price and see what happens. Take care, though; it is rude to push the seller to a point at which he or she is uncomfortable.

Next, you come into the village proper. Makeshift museums, the dilapidated huts sometimes contain a stone axe, miniature mud men, wooden arm bands, a human-hair "helmet," a kudo drum, a penis gourd, a ceremonial loin cloth, and a poison crusher (a stone pestle and mortar used to create the poison with which the islanders killed their enemies). Wood shields, javelin spears, bows, and arrows also on display are all artifacts of a world away from Western culture.

Move on to a spirit stone house, a 20-foot-around circular thatched home with a roof of kunai grass that displays artifacts: Chiseled, sacred stone bowls and faces meet you at the small entrance. In the past, when a villager committed a crime, says your guide, "the stones came up and demanded an answer. People confessed their crimes and they offered a pig in

atonement. It was slaughtered and the blood put in a rock bowl and offered to the gods. The pig's jaw was taken and put in the spirit house."

Peer into a small nearby hut and see pig jaws all around. This is the sort of bizarre scene that will delight some children and scare others.

"And if you get a chance," says Rainier, "arrange to take a walk in the forest with the hunters. You can see how they track prey and depend on their knowledge of intricate parts of the flora to find food. It's a rare opportunity for kids to experience a culture that still, for the most part, relies on their relationship to their immediate environment for survival." ∎

**BOOKS FOR PARENTS**...............
∎ *The Last Men: Journey Among the Tribes of New Guinea* by Iago Corazza **(2010)** A photojournalist's voyage into pockets of prehistory reveals a glimpse of cultures untouched by time.

**BOOKS FOR KIDS**...........................
∎ *The Turtle and the Island: A Folk Tale from Papua New Guinea* by Barbara Ker Wilson **(1991)** The myth of how the island of New

Know Before You Go

Guinea was founded by a giant sea turtle who brought the first man and woman to stay on the sandpile.

**VIDEOS FOR PARENTS**...................
∎ *Lost Mummies of Papua New Guinea* **(2010)** The National Geographic Channel takes an in-depth look at the macabre art of mum-

mification. See *www.natgeotv .com/uk/lost-mummies-of-papua-new-guinea.*

**MUSIC**.............................................
∎ *Bosavi: Rainforest Music from Papua New Guinea* **(2001)** A three-CD anthology from Smithsonian Folkways Recordings includes cross-generational sounds in a musical portrait of life in a rain forest community. Visit *www .folkways.si.edu.*

# Easter Island

*Where Magic Surrounds You*

I t is slightly after 9 p.m. on an autumn night 2,000 miles off the coast of Chile, on Easter Island, one of the most remote places on the planet. Six immense statues stand shoulder to shoulder on a stone *ahu* (altar). These *moai*, as they are called, have their backs to a surging ocean. Above is a full moon. Eerily, a moonbeam arcs through a wreath of clouds, spilling dabs of light on the giant stone sentinels. A misty rain falls. The sounds of the scattering hooves of wild horses pierce the darkness.

The behemoths, created by a culture that thrived here thousands of years ago, have an intimidating size and grandeur that stagger kids' imaginations and spark the thought: How could humans have possibly created them? That is just the start of what children can discover on a trip here.

"This is where kids can find out about one of the last chapters of man's conquest of Earth," says archaeologist Edmundo Edwards, who, for more than 30 years with his fellow archaeologists Claudio Christino and Patricia Vargas, has attempted to untangle the island's mysteries and

## GET INVOLVED

.........................................

■ **EASTER ISLAND WELCOMES VISITORS** from around the world, but it recognizes the need to encourage responsible tourism. As an island, it faces the necessity for a dedicated recycling and composting program. One simple way you can help is to always carry reusable bags when you travel. Likewise, take any plastic bags you use off the island. For more information on the pressures being exerted on the island, contact the Easter Island Foundation (*www.islandheritage.org*).

helped his fellows preserve and study the statues.

"We have no magic bunnies on Easter Island, but magic surrounds us," observes Edwards. "Here kids can learn about the past feats of Polynesians who navigated without instruments across the Pacific Ocean, guided only by the stars, currents, and wave patterns. They managed to settle in and adapt to environments from small coral atolls to places where snow falls on high peaks. The Polynesians settled on Easter Island last because it was more remote and difficult to find."

The island, Edwards continues, was populated by a group of Polynesians in two boats under the command of Chief Hotu Matua about 1,000 years ago. "Today, Easter Island is the most isolated inhabited place on Earth," he observes. "Our closest neighbor is Pitcairn Island, 1,300 miles to the west, where the mutineers of the H.M.S. *Bounty* found home in 1790."

"We've heard theories that Easter Island was settled from outer space," adds Christino, "that it represents the last vestige of the lost continent of Atlantis, that the final remains of Genghis Khan's armies arrived here with elephants, which supposedly raised the statues." Now, that's lore that no child visitor can resist. "But it is all bunk."

Families will find traces of the true origin of the stone sentinels at Rano Raraku, a spooky, volcanic hump of mounded green, its slopes dotted with 397 statues—some prostrate, heads tilted to the sky, others tumbled, sundered, or facedown. This is the quarry where all the moai were born, most never to find a home beyond this graveyard. One unfinished work is 67 feet high and would have weighed 230 tons and taken 1,000 workers to move had it not been doomed by the unworkable physics of its sheer size.

Made of the compressed silicon and cinder of volcanic tuff, the statues are believed to have been hacked from the rock by legions of submissive

# CONNECTIONS

**Easter Island Statue Project (EISP)**
*www.eisp.org*
EISP is the longest collaborative and evolving artifact inventory to be conducted within the context of the Easter Island archaeological survey. A digitized inventory is accessible through the project's official website, along with a range of related research articles.

**"The End of Easter Island"**
*http://video.nationalgeographic.com*
A short video by the National Geographic Society shows the early islanders' exhaustion of natural resources as a timeless lesson for us all.

**Secrets of Easter Island**
*www.pbs.org/wgbh/nova/easter*
At this PBS interactive website, test your skills against ancient technology with the "Move a Megalith" challenge.

laborers terrified by the death threats of high priests, who claimed to have the *mana*—power—to animate the statues to walk to distant altars. Christino and his confederates believe these stone figures were levered off the ground, teetered onto their backs, and settled on huge sleds with wheels. They were then hauled to and erected on the altars elsewhere on the island. At Ahu Tongariki, on the coast, for example, 15 elements-eroded heads, backs to the sea, loom atop one such altar that took 500 years to build—the largest ceremonial monument in Polynesia.

For all of the allure of the island's statues of brooding mystery, though, there are less celebrated Easter Island attractions for families.

"There are more than 4,000 wild horses on the island," notes Edwards. "It's also exciting to trek to the island's highest point, on the outer slope of the Terevaka Volcano, where you get a 360-degree view—it gives you a feel for how far we are from the rest of the world. Or, at Anakena Beach, you can snorkel surrounded by tropical fish and corals."

Hook up with the locals in Hanga Roa, the capital, a 1960s-flavored, frontier town of 3,300. "In town, kids will enjoy meeting other friendly children their age," says Edwards. "The children here want to exchange ideas and thoughts, and let you know about their lives, show you how to dance their traditional dances, and sing their songs. Kids should understand that even in the furthest inhabited place on Earth, they are not alone.

"My children love boating around the bird islands and fishing for tuna and wahoo on the way," continues Edwards. "They explore hidden caves, where the ancient people would seek refuge during times of war, but, most of all, they love hearing stories about the stone giants who, it is rumored, once roamed the island; the ghosts and spirits of nature who supposedly protected men from harm; and those people who are said to have flown with a magic cape to the faraway heavens." ■

## FAST FACTS

■ **Easter Island** was named by Dutch explorers in 1722, who landed there on Easter Sunday.

■ Research suggests there may have been a forest of up to **16 million palm trees** on Easter Island, most likely of a species similar to a **Chilean palm** that can grow up to 65 feet.

■ In 1960, a tsunami hit Easter Island, destroying the **Ahu Tongariki** altar and carrying 15 multiton *moai* 700 yards inland; the site has since been restored.

■ The largest **moai** is known as **Paro;** it weighs 82 tons and measures 32.2 feet tall.

■ Petroglyphs are carved into rocks across the island; common iconography includes **birdmen, sea turtles, and images of Makemake,** the chief god of the Tangata Manu (birdman cult).

---

**BOOKS FOR PARENTS**.................
■ *Among Stone Giants* by Jo Anne Van Tilburg (2003) The author relates the story of the pivotal expedition of English ethnographer Katherine Routledge and her early 20th-century attempt to uncover the origins of the island's mysterious giant statues.

**BOOKS FOR KIDS**............................
■ *The Day the Stones Walked* by T. A. Baron (2007) This book is an imaginative tale of the creation of the *moai* masterpieces.

## Know Before You Go

**MOVIES**................................
■ *Digging for the Truth: Giants of Easter Island* (2008) Host Josh Bernstein delves into the world of ancient Pacific Islanders to revive the lost art of Polynesian navigation, re-create techniques of enigmatic masons, and participate in daring native rituals.

■ *Easter Island Underworld* (2010) Ride along as a team of National Geographic Society scientists and explorers embarks on a groundbreaking expedition—the first ever attempt to map the vast underground cave system of Easter Island.

**PODCAST**..............................
■ *Easter Island* by the Bradshaw **Foundation** This audio work, available on iTunes, thoroughly explores humankind's artistic legacy through the lenses of the disciplines of archaeology and anthropology.

# Antarctica
## *Place of Extremes*

**T**here's no question that a trip to Antarctica will change a child's life," says naturalist Tom Ritchie, who has been leading trips to the region for Lindblad Expeditions since 1977. "But it is a very serious trip and a real investment. Younger kids will have fun, but it is especially good for those ten and up, when children start to get serious about life and learning. Antarctica is different than anything anyone has ever experienced. Everything is so exotic and so diverse. It is totally unique. So you want kids who are mature enough to get something out of the experience—and what a place it is to take an impressionable child."

Quite simply, there is nowhere on Earth like Antarctica. No, not even the Arctic, where you find Eskimos and polar bears. In Antarctica, there are seals but no land mammals and no native peoples.

There's no litter, either. It is a place of extremes. At the South Pole, the mean annual temperature is minus 58°F, and, below 60° south latitude, the sun sets in March and rises in October, giving the area one long day and one long night annually.

Nearly twice the size of Australia, Antarctica is considered a desert; each year it gets only eight inches of precipitation along the coast and less inland. About 98 percent of the continent is covered by ice, which at its thickest is almost three miles deep. The area accounts for 90 percent of all the world's ice and 70 percent of all fresh water.

It is also undeniably a rarity of magnificent, eye-arresting snowscapes, plentiful aquatic life, strangely contorted ice, and monster blue bergs. The great white continent is truly singular—and it takes a trek to get here.

"If Antarctica were music, it would be Mozart. Art, and it would be Michelangelo. Literature, and it would be Shakespeare. And yet it is something even greater; the only place on Earth that is still as it should be. May we never tame it."—*Andrew Denton, television producer and host*

First, you fly from Buenos Aires to Ushuaia on Argentina's side of Tierra del Fuego. From there, the ten-day trip takes you across the Drake Passage—with its sometimes fierce storms—down the western coast of the Antarctic Peninsula and past the Antarctic Circle. You'll see Half Moon Island, with its rocky cliffs and chinstrap penguin rookery; Deception Island and its flooded volcanic crater; ice-cliffed Paradise Harbor, home to gentoo penguins and a place where minke and humpback whales congregate and orcas terrorize seals and pick off penguins; and jagged-peaked Lemaire Channel.

"Sometimes we cruise through ice that seems like steep mountains rising thousands of feet straight into the air," says Ritchie. "It's like navigating the rugged, jagged tops of the Alps or Rockies. It's a dreamscape."

A typical day involves Zodiac cruises around icebergs, kayaking, at least one landing on a pebbly beach, and the option of hard or easy hiking. "We have fun on shore, but it is hard fun," says Ritchie. "But remember, it's mild. We go November to March, during Antarctica's summer. Temperatures can get up to 40°F. When people hike, they often take off their parkas."

A highlight is a visit to a penguin colony, some of which may have as many as 100,000 nesting pairs. "I tell people to sit down and observe," reports Ritchie. "Pretty soon penguins gather around you. They might peck at your boot or pull on your backpack."

As otherworldly as Antarctica is, children quickly grasp the special gift a trip here offers. "They learn despite themselves

## FAST FACTS

■ Antarctica **wasn't always cold.** Fossils show this now isolated continent was once host to plants and animals.

■ No one owns Antarctica. The Antarctic Treaty allows its 45 members to use the land, but only for **peaceful purposes.**

■ It is the fifth largest continent, but without its ice caps, it would be the **world's smallest.**

■ In September, Antarctica is **much bigger** than in March, due to sea ice.

■ Winds of up to **218 miles an hour** have been recorded in Antarctica.

here, because if they experience it, they'll remember it," says Ritchie. "They love finding things. Wreckage from old ships. Ancient bones from the early 20th-century whaling days. Pieces of seal carcass. They slide down snowy ridges, have snowball fights, or make snow penguins. They see the remains of a stone hut from 1903 where shipwrecked men survived for two years eating penguin and raw seal."

Another thing kids see is the effect of climate change. Ritchie has been coming here for more than 35 years, witnessing, for example, the disappearance of the permanent ice around James Ross Island. "Coming here really gives children a different perspective on the world," he concludes. "They can't help but be affected. And think of the bragging rights a child has when he comes home from Antarctica." ■

# The Travel Dozen

*12 things to consider when planning, packing, and preparing for travel with kids*

**Y**ou hear it so often: My kids are too young to travel; they'll get nothing from it. Not true. Children are born to travel. Get them going young and they develop a muscle memory for it. I remember leaving the Congo when I was four; I can still see, viscerally, the airplane porthole infused with flickering runway lights as we took off. The earlier you introduce kids to the rhythms of traveling, the easier it becomes, says former Peace Corps country director for Kazakhstan John Sasser, a father of three. "You reap what you sow. A camping trip across Europe when our children were 8, 10, and 12 opened their eyes to the world. We later followed them to places like Armenia, Mongolia, and Sikkim. Travel teaches children to cooperate, to be organized, to be on time, and to take inevitable setbacks in stride."

Advance preparation for a trip with kids is critical—it helps prevent meltdowns, reduce stress, and instill the confidence that inspires exploration. This 12-point checklist will help. Also factor in destination, budget, children's ages, and mode of travel. Wherever you go, whatever you do, enjoy the ride and let your child's interests be your compass.

**1. PASSPORTS:** All children, no matter how young, must have a passport to travel internationally (it takes up to six weeks to secure). Kids must apply in person with both parents (an absent parent must provide a notarized consent form). For up-to-date application requirements: *http://travel.state.gov/passport.*

**2. MEDICAL:** A few months before traveling abroad, review destination-appropriate vaccination guidelines at *wwwnc.cdc.gov/Travel* and get any shots you need at a pediatrician's office or clinic. Up-to-date immunizations are essential, says infection preventionist Roberta Smith of Children's Hospital Colorado, a top children's facility. "Many countries have diseases not found in the United States—polio, for instance. Typhoid and yellow fever vaccinations aren't routine in America. Make sure you and your kids are covered and that you travel with

your immunization records." If headed to malaria-infected countries, bring a mosquito net to cover your child's bed.

**3. INSURANCE:** Ask your health insurance provider if your policy applies overseas and covers emergency expenses such as medical evacuation. If not, buy supplemental travel insurance to handle kids' illness or injury. Bring at least $500 in local currency since local health professionals will expect cash for services rendered.

**4. SCHOOL:** As kids get older, schools will increasingly determine when and how long you can travel. Private schools tend to be more flexible, while public schools are stricter. If your child will miss class to travel, alert teachers early, says Gennifre Hartman, executive director and founder of the Traveling School (*www.TravelingSchool.com*), a Bozeman, Montana–based nonprofit dedicated to encouraging academic exploration among teen girls. "Families should work with a school to ensure a child will be up to speed academically when you return. Be prepared to demonstrate that your child was actively learning while abroad. Have your child keep a portfolio, including a travel journal, photographs, essays, and interviews—something imaginative and informative to show the myriad ways the world is a powerful classroom."

**5. AIR TRAVEL:** Check airline websites for information about discount tickets, government-approved child restraint systems (CRS), "lap child" requirements, early boarding options, baggage fees, and carry-on restrictions for strollers, car seats, and other equipment. Regulations can differ between domestic and international airlines. For up-to-date information on U.S. airport security screening procedures for babies and children, visit *www.tsa.gov/travelers/airtravel/children/index.shtm.*

**6. CHILDCARE:** Hiring part-time, on-the-ground help? Demand the same high standards you expect at home. Get recommendations from other parents and work in advance with your hotel; hotels usually have trustworthy, screened care providers. And make sure anyone watching your child has first-aid training. "Choking is the most prevalent medical emergency for children, so first-aid certification is even more important than CPR training," says Rebecca Van't Hof, president of American Child Care *(www.americanchildcare. com)*, a Chicago-based hotel babysitting and on-site children's provider. "Make sure a caregiver is trained to handle a choking child and, ideally, is fluent in English. Clearly communicate special needs or instructions, particularly important for infants or toddlers."

**7. FIRST AID:** Bring a prepackaged or homemade first-aid kit on car trips, and pack essentials in airplane carry-on: bandages, antibiotic ointment, hand sanitizer, tweezers, and child-safe, over-the-counter pain, allergy, diarrhea, and motion sickness medications (some are elusive or expensive in remote or international locations).

**8. BABY GEAR:** Bring necessities like diapers, pull-ups, wipes, baby food, and formula. After Virginia mom Rachel Heiss and her then six-week-old son Eli were stranded at an airport for 12 hours without diapers or formula, she has since carried a backpack filled with all the must-haves. "I never leave home without a changing pad," she says. "No matter where we are, I know I have a clean, sanitary surface to change the baby."

**9. DIVERSIONS:** Have kids create travel backpacks filled with personal favorites (iPod, iPad, game players, smart phone, chargers, and headphones), plus low-tech staples (drawing pad, crayons, LEGO bricks, magazines, and playing cards) that work when the power doesn't. Add a small flashlight or clip-on reading light and extra batteries, plus personal items like a brush, lip balm, and toothbrush.

**10. SNACKS:** Bring nonperishables in zip-top plastic bags, bento boxes, or other snap-lid containers. Laurie Jewett of Plum Island, Massachusetts, involves Michael, five, and Lily, six, in making healthy snack choices to ensure they'll eat what she brings. "Having the kids participate helps avoid surprises that could provoke a meltdown," she says. For car and plane trips, Jewett suggests freezing kid-favorite yogurt tubes and fresh grapes, blueberries, and strawberries the night before for a cool treat without bulky ice packs.

**11. STEWARDSHIP:** When planning an itinerary and packing your child's carry-on and clothing, look for ways to conserve local resources, reduce waste, celebrate and respect local culture and traditions, and leave no trace. Bring reusable containers to store restaurant leftovers; pack comfortable, yet culturally appropriate clothing for your child; teach kids a few courtesy words in the local language and the basics of local etiquette; and look for lodging that embraces composting, recycling, energy-saving appliances and heating/cooling systems—and features locally grown produce.

**12. PRESERVING THE MEMORIES:** Encourage kids to share their travel experiences. "As young children, my sister and I were encouraged to keep a journal of our travels," says Caroline Lamar of Maryville, Tennessee. "I'm continuing that with my three daughters. It helps them capture memories of a trip on their own terms. And not only encourages writing, always a bonus, but also helps them remember details they might otherwise forget. A journal is a great place for them to store travel keepsakes such as postcards, dried and pressed flowers, sketches, tickets from climbing to the top of a lighthouse." Lamar also suggests giving the kids a durable digital camera. "Children capture entirely different perspectives missed by the adult eye. And since they are digital photos, who cares if they take 25 pictures of rocks or moss on a tree?"

# SPECIAL THANKS & ACKNOWLEDGMENTS

This book is dedicated to Adam, Chase, and MacKenzie, my little treasures, who I want to witness all the globe has to offer—and who have made coming home so wonderful.

And I give thanks to the folks who have supported me:

To Melina, without whom I wouldn't have my youngest children and the wisdom to be the dad I am.

To my mom and dad, who are no longer with me but gave me the gift of travel and the genes to pursue it.

To my second parents, Carl and Suzy, who mean more to me than I can say.

To Sully. You know why.

To Elisa Gibson, a ray of sunshine who can design gold out of clay.

To Barbara Noe and Caroline Hickey, new colleagues who suffered through all the deadlines.

And to my inestimable staff at *Traveler* for their great patience and support. And thank you for understanding what it meant when my door was closed.

To my terrific agent, Cynthia Cannell, who allowed me to bend her ear, dealt elegantly with fits and starts, and endured my always out-of-townness.

And I offer a HUGE shout-out to the grandparents, parents, and parents-to-be who helped me put this book together: Maryellen Kennedy Duckett, mom of the century, and her husband, Randall Duckett, who helped wrangle much of this book into shape; Joe Yogertz; Jeannette Kimmell (a total ace who I hope finds great happiness with her new husband); Jayne (Ask Me About Italy) Wise; Karen Carmichael (who worked through Thanksgiving and made cool facts her business); Mr. Brazil, Stefan Caifa; Katie Knorofsky (who tracked down the great John Heaton); Susan Hackett (a musical presence who brought home Cuba); Ingrid Alhgren (who discovered Costa Rica before me); Christine Wei; Emily Haile (thanks for the Warriors); Stephanie Yoder; Stephanie Robichaux; Meghan Miner (one of the most curious interns I know); Elena Chiraboga; Nick Rowlands; and Matthew Long.

Happy travels.

# ILLUSTRATIONS CREDITS

# INDEX

Published by the National Geographic Society
1145 17th Street N.W., Washington, D.C. 20036

Library of Congress Cataloging-in-Publication Data

100 places that can change your child's life : from your backyard to the ends of the earth / Keith Bellows, editor.
   p. cm.
Includes index.
ISBN 978-1-4262-0859-1 (pbk. : alk. paper)
1. Voyages and travel--Juvenile literature. 2. Children--Travel--Juvenile literature. I. Bellows, Keith.
G570.A17 2012
910.2'02--dc23

2012014500

ISBN 978-1-4262-1596-4 (special sale edition)

The information in this book has been carefully checked and to the best of our knowledge is accurate. However, details are subject to change, and the National Geographic Society cannot be responsible for such changes, or for errors or omissions. Assessments of sites, hotels, and restaurants are based on the author's subjective opinions, which do not necessarily reflect the publisher's opinion. The publisher cannot be responsible for any consequences arising from the use of this book.

The National Geographic Society is one of the world's largest nonprofit scientific and educational organizations. Founded in 1888 to "increase and diffuse geographic knowledge," the Society's mission is to inspire people to care about the planet. It reaches more than 400 million people worldwide each month through its official journal, *National Geographic*, and other magazines; National Geographic Channel; television documentaries; music; radio; films; books; DVDs; maps; exhibitions; live events; school publishing programs; interactive media; and merchandise. National Geographic has funded more than 10,000 scientific research, conservation and exploration projects and supports an education program promoting geographic literacy.

For more information, visit www.nationalgeographic.com

National Geographic Society
1145 17th Street N.W.
Washington, D.C. 20036-4688 U.S.A.

For information about special discounts for bulk purchases, please contact
National Geographic Books Special Sales: ngspecsales@ngs.org

For rights or permissions inquiries, please contact National Geographic Books
Subsidiary Rights: ngbookrights@ngs.org

Cover and interior design: Elisa Gibson

Back cover photo: Rebecca Hale/NGS

Printed in the United States of America

15/CW-CML/1